PRAISE FOR *THE HOLY WILD*

"This book is an untamed, graceful invitation to taste the wild not yet lived. Brave and intimately connected to the gospel of the natural world, it reveals a reemerging path that has often been hidden and overlooked in modern society. It holds medicine for a broken paradigm and common sense for those who desire to live beautifully, empowered and free."

— **Tanya Markul,** author of *The She Book*

"'I will speak to you directly, for you are a Wolf-Woman of my bloodline and we share the same language, the heathen Mother Tongue of the wild word.' These words from Danielle Dulsky's *The Holy Wild* sing to the inner realms of who and what I stand for. I run with the wolves and howl relentlessly to proclaim and own my individual voice and my passion and my walk as the eternal woman who walks on water and eats roses and becomes nature Herself. *The Holy Wild* inspires us to wear the magnificence that is our true garb and not the unnecessary superficial veils that hide our insecurities, caused by deep wounds. To truly heal and become transformed is the reason for our presence here, and Danielle's words are a manifesto of this reality. Let our feminine mystique shine, be alive, and be our eternal soul swords. If you wish to become your own femininity, this book will be a monumental help for you to be able to scream and play in the wilderness of your Self."

— **Manoshi Chitra Neogy,** wolfwomanproductions.org

"I've long admired Danielle Dusky for her wild, authentic dedication to waking the wild and authentic in women, as these are the very attributes that will save us individually and on a global level. *The Holy Wild* is her gutsy and glorious offering to help dismantle a killer patriarchal system; it's her unbridled, undomesticated howl at the moon to wake us and shake us all back to our Goddess-given, soul-driven life. Danielle is a heroine who is determined to live her wild, aching truth, and in so doing, she strikes a match in her reader to do the same."

— **Sarah Durham Wilson,** teacher and writer

the *HOLY WILD*

ALSO BY DANIELLE DULSKY

Woman Most Wild:
Three Keys to Liberating the Witch Within

the HOLY WILD

A HEATHEN BIBLE
FOR THE UNTAMED WOMAN

DANIELLE DULSKY

Foreword by Bayo Akomolafe, PhD

New World Library
Novato, California

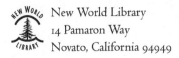 New World Library
14 Pamaron Way
Novato, California 94949

An early version of the material found on pages 73–75 has appeared on the website *Rebelle Society*, and that on pages 126–28 has appeared on the website *The House of Twigs*.

Text design by Tona Pearce Myers

Library of Congress Cataloging-in-Publication Data
Names: Dulsky, Danielle, [date.]–author.
Title: The holy wild : a heathen bible for the untamed woman / Danielle Dulsky.
Description: Novato : New World Library, 2018. | Includes bibliographical references and index.
Identifiers: LCCN 2018020106 (print) | LCCN 2018032098 (ebook) | ISBN 9781608685288 (ebook) | ISBN 9781608685271 (alk. paper)
Subjects: LCSH: Wicca. | Goddess religion. | Feminist theology.
Classification: LCC BP605.W53 (ebook) | LCC BP605.W53 D845 2018 (print) | DDC 299/.94--dc23
LC record available at https://lccn.loc.gov/2018020106

First printing, September 2018
ISBN 978-1-60868-527-1
Ebook ISBN 978-1-60868-528-8
Printed in Canada on 100% postconsumer-waste recycled paper

 New World Library is proud to be a Gold Certified Environmentally Responsible Publisher. Publisher certification awarded by Green Press Initiative.
www.greenpressinitiative.org

10   9   8   7

To all the wild places

The Closest to Prayer

I dreamt of a Crone with sharp teeth and tough skin.
She bit down to my bone but found no sin.
I wasn't afraid: "Please tell me your name!
Where have you prayed? Have you no shame?"

This Witch hissed, and she painted my face with cold mud
Then she kissed where she'd bitten and lapped up the blood.
"When do you pray?" I asked of her then.
"By night and by day, as only we can."

"What do you mean, you vicious old beast?
Who is your God? Tell me, at least."
"The bark and the stone, the wind, and the fire.
The flesh and the bone, the grief and the ire,
The brook and the bird, their land hums my prayer.
So long have I heard the Holy Wild sung there."

"Why did you bite me? Answer me that!
Was it only to spite me? To taste of my fat?"
"I bit you to wake you, my Priestess, my dear.
Lest a sweeter dream take you but tame you by fear."

I opened my eyes, and I was alone.
Back in disguise and missing the Crone.
To hear her dare speak of the breeze, brook, and flame;
It's the closest to prayer that I've ever came.

Contents

The Book of Earth

The Book of Water

The Book of Fire

The Book of Air

The Book of Ether

Foreword

The picture our teachers, pastors, parents, and media painted for us young West African kids was that our past was without controversy — bright and sunny — from the moment when the Christian Bible touched our borderlands and changed us forever. Before that singular moment, everything was dark and beastly and sore, our lands reeking with the fumes of unholy alchemy and superstition, the damned genius of the Witch and the Pagan gods and demons that knew her in her filth. Today, this glorious day, we could celebrate their eternal incarceration, they told me. Those of us who had power from above could stand on the heads of snakes, the writhing Lilithian figures that hid in the shadows, and drink their poison without fear of harm.

Growing up in the heavily Christianized Protestant south of Nigeria meant that I was part of a megachurch of charismatic evangelicals and got to witness many "casting out" sessions where the Man of God would sprinkle holy oil or water on a wild, screaming girl who had just confessed to being a Witch. The images of thrashing limbs, carnal confessions of nefarious nightly deeds, and tearful surrender are indelibly seared on my mind. I did not doubt that the tales were true; and that if one were to dream of flying on a broomstick, or to eat a sumptuous meal at ungodly hours, or to comb one's hair in the dream, one was being initiated into the cult of Wild Ones. Threaded through the everyday was therefore a watchfulness, an impulse to flee the carnality of the body, to assert the lasting dominance of the masculine, to weaponize the borders of the city — the legacy of colonial struggles to push back the wilderness, to suppress the sinful urges of nature (the wild woman's domain), and escape into midair, hoisted above mere ground, heir to the heavens.

Jezebel dethroned, Lilith vanquished, Asherah covered up and rushed out of the holy place, the masculine distorted, I stepped into a world of work, economy, and research that mirrored this quest for escape, for flight, for passive holiness. Mine was a search for the sacred, the disembedded, and the lofty.

And then one I day, I met her. She glided into the rational order that was my life and pulled the pillars apart with a mere wink. The woman I would later call my "thunderbolt," my "ground," the bonfire whose fierce circumference I longed to be incinerated in, the mother whose veined arms and long neck would in time cradle our children: "Lali."

When Danielle Dulsky writes about love in "the Lost Verses of the Holy Feminine," a love "so impassioned that it ripples back through the cosmic web and stirs the hearts of the ancients," it resonates with me. I have known this love for myself: this love that turns the Sons of God mad and drives them to seek the embrace of the shadows that their swords were once sharpened to kill; this love that upturns time and history, shakes it loose from its phallic moorings and pristine foundations, and gives power to the excluded and occluded. When Dulsky speaks of the way Lilith "loves the untamed wilds, like a Witch loves the moon," she recalibrates haunting pasts and remembers what is now becoming a stunning realization: here, right here, in the mangle of the material, in the queer stirrings of telluric critters, in the murky depths of silent waters, in the wintry spirituality of the desolate, in the graceful appearing of moon, is the sacred.

For me, the touch of a wild woman, Lali, was my undoing. I am not alone. A grand undoing is afoot in biology, in psychology, in quantum field theory, in archaeology, in feminist scholarship, in our appraisals of the vital contributions the world makes in worlding itself. In not so many words, we are coming down to earth, enacting a second Fall of sorts, composting our hard surfaces and realizing the agentic world around us is more than resource, reacquainting ourselves with the historically maligned figure of the Witch, resituating ourselves in a sensuous web of life. With new materialisms, concerned with the emancipation of *mater*, of mother, of the vitality of "nature" — once territorialized under regimes of Enlightenment as mere resource — we "remember the Holy Wild."

It is not true that our past is without controversy. Instead it is simmering with subtle absences that haunt our claims to goodness, to rationality. To progress. The wilds have always been part of the city, but we learned not to look — to suppress what longed for expression. Modern history — replete with the burning of heretical women, the colonial blotting out of earth-based traditions of the sacred — may be read as a history of aversion to *mater.* Dulsky writes that "the extent to which feminine power, in its myriad forms, has been condemned as evil is nothing less than ancient and global. . . . The Goddess has been demonized in our culture, increasingly cast not into a hellish underworld but into a pink and glittery fairyland where she is harmless but also useless." Now the Goddess is incarcerated no more, and a fierce reckoning is happening. This coming to the Holy Wilds is our deepest hope if we are to linger as an earth community.

In my work researching neomaterialist reconfigurations of racial identity, and specifically how ancestral DNA testing queers the idea of indigeneity, I met Danielle Dulsky. She introduced herself as a Witch. She smiled and told me her story, of her teenage longings for belonging, of being drawn to Ireland since before she knew what was calling her, even when she believed she was Polish. She spoke of her grandmother, her irresistible attraction to the figure of the feminine, and her call to become a Witch.

In this book, Dulsky's libratory words, quivering sensuously with a search that has never terminated, open us up to the fathomless beauty of the wilds beyond our fences, ritualizing our approach to the Goddess our forebears once banished. This book is holy. This book is a prayer, a cartographical intro-duction to earth, to water, to fire, to air, and to ether. It is a spell to undo the trance that holds us in the grip of modern separability, devaluing the woman, distorting the masculine, and quelling the queer.

I invite you to read it. Read it knowing you will not arrive. Knowing you will be met quite suddenly by something greater than yourself, something hiding under the veil of the ordinary. Knowing that She breathes again, and desperately seeks you.

— **Bayo Akomolafe, PhD,** author of *These Wilds Beyond Our Fences:*
Letters to My Daughter on Humanity's Search for Home

Introduction

Her Genesis

In the beginning, there was She.
She was nature's primordial pulse, the pan-elemental alchemy of birth; the fertile void of death; and the mysterious, enduring, and numinous cosmic infinite. All was She, and She was all. Her power pervaded the totality of existence and veiled all potential worlds in the name of holy manifestation. Her steady, purposeful rhythm pounded on, in, and through the stellar fusions, the planet building, and the great galactic swell. The universal dawn was a quantum prayer to Her, and She was dancing for us long before humanity's blessed inception, long before the glow of the primal feminine was eclipsed by modernity.

While the rhythm of Her hallowed drum has slowed and quieted to a barely audible, near-whisper beat, while humanity's spiritual landscape has been overbuilt and hums with man-made hymns, She can never be silenced. She is our elemental nature, the stuff of our souls, and we are She embodied. Every one of us could hear Her if we only listened, for She has sought safe harbor in our very marrow. She lives *in* us, and with Her genesis came our mandate to wholly and emphatically embody Her in the wake of the feminine's historical denigration. If we only put our ears to the ground, we would hear the promised pulse of Her return not as She descends from a gold-and-diamond heaven but as She claws Her way up so ceremoniously through rock and stone, destined to erupt from beneath the very structures built to keep Her contained.

Our language is insufficient when describing the shape-shifting majesty that is She, but I will call this force that both enlivens and enraptures us all — this beastly feminine dark that calls us to look not up toward the ethereal clouds but down to the muddy loam from which we were born, down to the Holy Wild — the ever-dying, ever-birthing dance of all that is. She is what many have willed us to forget, and She is the homegrown medicine for the spiritually starved soul. The depth of human experience precludes any universally relevant spiritual path, but She is the one, single universal truth: All of us were born here on Earth, and all of us will meet our ends on the same blessed planet.

This book is a five-part ode to Her, to you, and to the yet-to-be-rebuilt bridge between our spirituality and our lived, embodied experience. What you will find here is hearty home-cooked nourishment for the nature-hungry spirit, seasoned with a good deal of feminine ire and served hot. What you will find here is an invitation to descend into the dark with me, to gather up pieces of ourselves we have forgotten, and to rise. The wilds of nature will always be our ancestral home, no matter how long we wander or how far we stray from our roots, and what I offer you in these pages is a fervent call to come home to the truth of who you are, to take your rightful place in the circle of wise ones who came before you.

RISE UP, HEATHEN PRIESTESS: SHE LIVES IN THE WILDS

Our human divinity is bone-deep, lit by the red light of our souls' truth and sourced straight from the cosmic womb. I have an insatiable hunger for Her fierce mother-love, as I believe all members of our global collective do, and I am calling out and calling *on* all wild Priestesses of our world to join me in Her resurrection. I am howling from the dark depths of every forest, and I am crooning a siren's song from every body of water I can find. I am seeking you out, the wild woman who is through making apologies for her own divinity, the Witch who is handcrafting her own religion stitched from her own truth, and the blessed incarnation of every human being who can still feel Her. I will speak to you directly, for you are a Wolf-Woman of my bloodline and we share the same language, the heathen Mother Tongue of the wild word.

I hereby vow to validate your experience, your spiritual autonomy, and your magickal agency as we walk this misty and uncertain path together, and I will not ask you to sacrifice anything you know to be sacred. I do not assume that your life matches mine, and it is the uniqueness of our lived experiences of Her that will truly nourish the divine feminine in us all, rather than the bland and bleached homogenization of the Goddess experience.

> *I will speak to you directly, for you are a Wolf-Woman of my bloodline and we share the same language, the heathen Mother Tongue of the wild word.*

As women of the wild, we deserve our own holy books, our own teaching tales, and our own venerable verses of validation. The spiritual wisdom of the feminine has always been born of lived experience, and the hooded Crone in all of us knows that her truth, her cyclical ways, are unique to her and her alone. The her-stories I offer here have merit only in their meeting with your own life; they do not stand alone as immutable truths or a step-by-step path toward any lofty and permanent healing goal, nor do they assert any secret mysteries that I alone am privileged to know. Without their soul-specific relationship with your memories, passions, woundings, and core values, Priestess, these verses are only words. Without your willful exploration of how the feminine archetypes I discuss in this heathens' bible live and breathe within your own psyche, their names remain merely the default teaching tools used by outmoded traditions that have long required feminine shame to survive.

The women who have been locked inside the books they called *good* deserve liberation from their externally imposed immorality. We must unlock the cages in which they have been contained for so long, trapped behind the iron bars of judgment and dismissal. We women of this evolving world are tasked with their redemption, for they are we. We share the scars of every woman who has been condemned to ever be spiritually imprisoned, and, in these pages, I offer all the primal feminine technology this Witch has in her toolbox to dismantle the indoctrinated beliefs that continue to limit our spiritual autonomy; divorce our bodies from our spirits; and fence in what is, by nature, untamed, heathen, and wild.

The roots of the word *heathen* run far deeper than its derogatory, god-less connotation; it is believed to come from the Germanic word meaning "dweller on the heath, one inhabiting uncultivated land." To be heathen means to belong to the wild, to take our lessons from the natural world, and to be nourished by what we fundamentally are rather than what we are told we must be. Let me distinguish here between Heathenry, a polytheistic neo-Pagan religion for which I have much reverence but to which I do not belong, and the eclectic pre-Christian landscape of our ancestors. To be heathen is to remember the rawest essence of our worth, what is most authentically human about this flesh-and-blood body we find ourselves in, and what is left when our most carefully constructed psychic temples, those long-held belief systems that once served us so well, crumble into dust. Every one of our bloodlines is rooted in an Earth-based tradition if we only follow our lineage back far enough, and every one of our souls longs to come home to the wilds.

FIND HER IN THE DARK:
THE FERTILE SHADOWS OF THE FEMININE PATH

Heathen Priestess, your bejeweled crown is the same size as mine. I am neither above nor below you, and the round table of the Holy Wild has no structured hierarchy. I have no authority mandated by any great spiritual institution, and my truest church has long been the forest-covered mountains of my childhood, where no one has ever called me master or queen. Resistant am I, however, to the dilution of the diversity of the feminine spiritual experience. A lack of hierarchy does not demand sameness, and it is the living, breathing variety in our her-stories, in our ever-broadening relationship with Her, that must be nourished and protected.

My story is no more significant than yours, and my hope is that you drink in the poetry, feel nourished by the ceremonies, and complete the myths I begin here while constantly affirming your own authority and your own spiritual agency. The Holy Wild is a feminist terrain that you autonomously walk, standing at innumerable crossroads along the way and wielding your discernment like a sharp-edged weapon against the would-be predatory mentors, elite abusers, apparent beacons of manipulation masked as wise ones, and salacious gurus who claim to know better than you. This is your wild home, and you decide who is worthy of being your guest, who has earned the privilege of hearing your heroine's tale of the wild feminine lost and the wild feminine regained.

You are flawed to perfection, and, regardless of the precise nature of your wounds or your identity, you know Her. Whatever you have been told of your body's value or the merit of your art and work, your mud-caked soul is no less beauteous than your bright spirit light, and I will stand arm in arm with you while we reclaim our wild worth as divine beings who are of this Earth as much as we are of any ethereal heaven. She is still beating out Her rhythm for us, my love, and She will not be trapped in any pink, glittery, ineffectual shape, even one we may call Goddess. It is not the soft and passive feminine that has been socially suppressed, after all, for this form of the sacred is easily molded, controlled, and commodified. Sister, we do not always find Her in the light. Sometimes, we find Her in the dark.

Sometimes, we find Her in the dark.

We find Her in the places that terrify us, and we find Her in the places they told us not to look.

WALKING A WILDER PATH: SEEKING OUT THE FRINGES

You have many names, my love. In this book, I will call you a Priestess to validate your authority over your own spiritual journey. A Priestess looks within for direction and listens to the whispers, whimpers, and guttural groans of her inner wise woman. A Priestess is an elder. A Priestess is a woman who, regardless of linear age, has done the work and earned the right to say who she is and what she believes. She bows to no one except her own raw soul, and, while she is unquestionably an eternal student, she does not need external approval for her spiritual progress.

I will call you a Witch to affirm your birthright as a holy healer, to vindicate those socially rejected women who were hunted — who still are hunted in many parts of the world — in the name of not only patriarchy but also institutionalized racism, classism, and persistent imperialism. I will call you Witch to give a fierce nod to our stolen feminine spirituality and to give your wisdom a real name. Witches live on the edges of what is permissible, continually seeking out the fringes and brewing up the secret recipes of the Holy Wild, as have countless Earth-based religions and nonsystematic spiritual traditions. Your inner Witch remembers how to get home to those liminal places between honored guest and social outcast, between queen and freak.

This path is wild because we cannot possibly predict where it will lead us. We cannot know, amid the chaos, precisely where the global collective's evolution is leading. We can assure ourselves that we are doing our part, living our purpose, and honoring our human birthright as complex, sensual, creative, loving, and spiritual beings. We can repeatedly examine the extent to which we are truly working to achieve the vision of equality we say we seek. Here and now, with the body, skills, and other resources we have been given, we are charged to embody Her, in all Her light-and-shadow majesty, as fully as possible in the time we have been given. In these pages, I will call this wild path the Red Road, the always-spiraling, unmapped route toward a woman's spiritual home.

READ WILDLY: OURS IS NOT A ONE-SIZE-FITS-ALL PATH

This heathens' bible offers you verses, rituals, and magick framed within five books and rooted within a wild and untamed spirituality. The Book of Earth will call you toward the underground world of soul, revisioning the story of Lilith and honoring the merit of necessary rebellion. The Book of Water begs you to swim in the wild waters of erotic sensuality, emotional ebbs and flows, and joyous creativity, revisioning the story of Salome and highlighting our right to feel deeply. In the Book of Fire, we explore righteous rage, radical hope, and feminine ire as change agents, working with the Mother of Babylon's transformational energies and honoring women's collective strength as a powerful fuel for social justice and communal activism. Revisioning the story of Mary Magdalene and working with the Mother-Healer archetype, the Book of Air focuses on our most meaningful relationships, our partnerships, and our generative work as alchemical teachers housing the greatest lessons of this life of ours. Finally, the Book of Ether honors our inner Crones, revisioning Queen Jezebel's story and exploring the many-layered teachings of the Dark Goddess archetypes, the long-lost wisdom of our grandmothers.

All five elements are integral to the Holy Wild, and I will hold space for you not only to discover, explore, and integrate them all in a personally relevant, soul-true spiritual craft but to own how they are already embodied by the heathen Priestess that is you. The *verses* chapters highlight the her-stories of historically shunned women; personal mythwork for you, the reader, to write your own sacred tales of feminine wisdom; and prayers and incantations for working with that particular aspect of the Holy Wild. The *rituals* chapters offer ceremonies and practices for invoking the elemental power and honoring our most pivotal past experiences, and the *magick* chapters contain spellwork and pathworking meditations for moving forward, enacting change, and divining our feminine futures.

Set aside all you know about scholarly study, my love, and read wildly. Wander through this book as you would explore the shadows of a haunted fairy-tale forest — curiously, cautiously, and sensually. Walk with bare feet, and be open to new ways of knowing yourself and your world. Scribble your own poetic verses on these pages as you would scrawl your name in the mud to keep from getting lost in the midst of the 'twixt and 'tween. Move in spirals if you are called, and feel no need to read linearly. Be a curious scout in this majestic wilderness you have discovered; then be the stealthy, aged guide who knows the secrets of the land and knows them well. This spiritual terrain is yours, and you alone know the route your soul has taken or where it might be headed.

Wild spirituality is a wily shape-shifter, just like nature and the divine feminine Herself. I ask you to consider each element to be a paint color on your sacred palette; you may be drawn to the red and ruddy earth much more than the blazing yellows of fire, and the aesthetic of the painting you might birth tomorrow may diverge significantly from the one you create today. Ours is not a one-size-fits-all path.

Ours is not a one-size-fits-all path.

This book asks you to handcraft your own spirituality not just from the inspiration offered here but from your own Witch's truth. Wild spirituality is a fluid embrace of divine selfhood, and it is nothing if not entirely personal. There is no book so holy that you should be made to feel choiceless in its mandates, and this is certainly no exception.

BEYOND THE PALATABLE GODDESS:
NAMING THE DARK HOLY

We have heard their names, but we have not heard their stories. No story is true unless it is told by the one who lived it, and their sullied names have been used and abused in the service of a false morality for so long that we can scarcely remember the sound of their voices. Priestess, if you are so called, breathe life into their names to give them justice: our Lilith, our Salome, our Mother of Babylon, our Mary Magdalene, our Jezebel, and countless other women who have been denigrated and forced to pin bright-red letters on their bare chests. In this holy book, I reframe these women as archetypes of the sacred, forgotten feminine and liken them to other Goddesses from many cultures, importantly not to encourage their appropriation but to honor the wildest faces of the feminine as they have existed, and indeed *persisted*, throughout time.* The love of a deity is a deeply personal experience, and I am in no position to direct your devotion. This book is grounded in nature and affirms your kinship not with individual deities but with the elements themselves and the myths and her-stories that reflect your own experience back to you.

The elemental archetypes I offer here, like you, deserve liberation from the stories that have confined them for so long. They are archetypal benedictions to your own wild worth. Sing their names, infuse their memories with breath and body, and know I am singing with you. Too often, women who are coming home to the feminine divine will search for Her most palatable faces, Goddesses of compassion and love who undoubtedly deserve our devotion and respect, Goddesses who seem exotic and easily appropriated by those of other cultures, and Goddesses who seem to be accessible tools to be wielded during ritual more than hearty incarnations of all that is. The Goddess is not an inanimate object to be used, and to do so merely perpetuates the same wounds that have been affecting the divine feminine for more than two millennia. We do not search for the Goddess in order to own Her. We search for the Goddess to name holy those parts of ourselves we know are real, those parts of ourselves that the more accessible religious paths may not accept. I discuss Goddess archetypes here as holy, energetic, heavily guarded gateways to true, embodied divinity, and their stories matter.

---

*   Please see the Additional Resources section for books written by women of color about the Goddesses Kali, Lalita, Oshun, and Oya.

A woman cannot know herself as holy while still seeing the Goddess as superficial or optional, and it takes work to dismantle layers upon layers of belief about who She is and who She is not. If we look to the Goddess as a sacred collective of energy nourished and enlivened by human belief, prayer, and ritual, we can see how She is fundamentally born of the elements, how we have never really *lost* Her.

Ask yourself, over and over again, where Her energy meets yours, how Her story is your story, and constantly work to blur the lines, those rigid boundaries drawn by someone else's hand, between Goddess and Self. In many ways, the quest for Goddess is simply the quest for a deeper kinship with nature, the constant long-armed reach for the unconditional love of Her, the Holy Wild. We need not seek to own what we cannot possess, what is not ours to claim, and we need not all necessarily have deified names in our practice other than simply earth, water, fire, air, and ether.

LOOK TO THE SHADOWS, AND RECLAIM THE HEATHEN CROWN

Know that every human being embodies the sacred masculine and feminine, and gender is a social construction that has nothing to do with true divinity. Someone who identifies as male may live very close to the feminine, while a woman may have significant masculine energy. More importantly, it does not matter whether you label the disempowered aspects of our society as feminine or with another name, for it is ultimately the liberation of our holy sensuality, environmental reverence, emotional integrity, generative creativity, magickal agency, holistic relationship, authentic voice, intuition and psychic power, understanding of the spiral nature of time, and inborn spiritual autonomy that we are after. Call them what you will, but I will call these suppressed characteristics the wild, heathen feminine.

We all need Her, for we all *are* She. We are all change agents at this pivotal time in human history. This is the time of the Wild Rising, and we are setting the table for Her homecoming banquet. Everyone is invited. Exclude no one who truly wants to come, for the decisions we make now are our proclamation of the principles on which we want our children's world to be based. She, despite the pronoun I have chosen to use to designate the feminine, is positively and irrefutably pan-gender. Eventually, yes, we will all sit at this table together.

For now, the untamed woman is tasked with digging up her psychic dirt, igniting her shame on a funeral pyre, facing her most gruesome shadows, and enacting within the microcosm of her own spiritual journey all that she hopes to see accepted and empowered in greater society.

Consider this holy book an ode to your coronation. You may have called yourself Witch, Priestess, or wild woman for some time now — but, in these pages, I ask you to claim your heathen crown, to know yourself as an embodiment of not only the feminine divine light but also the feminine divine dark. I am placing it on your head now, Priestess. Can you feel the weight of it? You are She who is returned, and this is your sacred text because much of it will be written by you. These verses call you to burn your fear at the stake and build your own temple of the Holy Wild out of mud and stones, tended by your ancestors and named sacred by you. Keep a fire burning for Her there, as She has always kept one softly crackling for you. Arch your back and listen closely for Her drumbeat, for it grows louder with every Priestess who joins you, who spits on the instruments of spiritual oppression, continually examines whether her beliefs are truly her own, and reclaims her hard-earned, holy heathen crown. This temple is ours, built by the hands of the heathen and attended by the countless Priestesses of the Holy Wild.

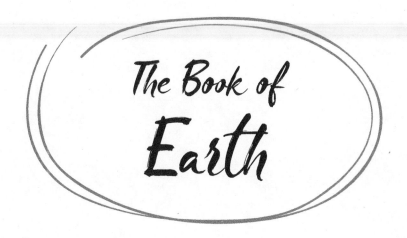

The Book of Earth

The earth element is our ground, the place from which we rise. Here, our greatest lessons are those sourced straight from our souls' hard-won liberation. Earth calls us to dig deep, to uncover the blood-soaked treasure embedded in our wounds, to harvest our most ancient underworld wisdom, and to remember the way back to our wild home. Here, we stand firm in our sovereignty and our selfhood, howling incantations our hearts have always remembered. Here, all that is uniquely ours serves to nourish our roots and remind us of the immutable truths tattooed on our bones.

> **Wild Feminine Archetype:** The Priestess of the Wild Earth
> **Themes in Her-story:** Rightful rebellion, tasting the forbidden, spiritual initiation, sacred solitude in nature, coming home to the wilds

Come home to the wilds, heathen. Let's speak of stone circles and forbidden fruit. Share your ancient medicine with me, and I will show you the overgrown, untamed places where you belong.

Chapter I

Earth Verses

Long before the holy feminine's voice arises from the depths of a woman's soft belly and demands to be heard — before she claims the name Witch, wild woman, fire-keeper, or any other designation that speaks to her spiritual autonomy — she side-eyes the parts of her world that no longer suit the truth-telling Priestess she is becoming. She outgrows her too-small life. She takes an ongoing inventory of the subtle hints and cosmic winks she is receiving from nature, her body, and the unmapped terrain of her psyche. Perhaps the first chill autumn wind becomes an invitation to wander long toward the sinking sun, or the swelling, in-the-heart joy sparked by the songs of night birds in a spring woodland elicits a permanent and unquenchable thirst for the wilds. The lived experience of the earth element is unique to every woman, but it is always marked by a persistent beckoning to come home to a more ancient version of herself, to escape from the overnarrowed and conventional life she had been living, and to seek authenticity more than approval.

There is a part of you, my love, that remembers not only your own hands in the dirt during childhood but the knowing hands of your grandmothers and *their* grandmothers as they planted their own seeds and connected to their own lands. There is a part of you that is in a relationship with the earth element that most certainly mirrors an intimacy shared with someone else in your bloodline; the kinship she felt with the ground, the wounds of her roots, the way she kept her home, her underworld fears, and the shape of her body are all very like yours. You may not know who she was, but her story is your story. The bond a woman feels with earth runs in the blood, and to rekindle the intimacy with the land is her birthright, her wild inheritance, and her destined mandate.

In this chapter of Earth Verses, I ask you to envision yourself encircled by your ancestors as you read. Consider how the themes of women's rebellion against injustice, tasting the forbidden fruit, sacred solitude in nature, and coming home to the wilds may have been suppressed throughout his-story, and consider how these forces have ebbed and flowed in your own personal myth of awakening. Know your story as fluid and shape-shifting, and honor the shadowy parts of your soul that may have been called wicked or shameful as precious gifts, holy in their own right and divine in their darkness, that now allow you to become the woman you needed when you were younger.

THE PRIESTESS OF THE WILD EARTH ARCHETYPE: MEETING THE SOVEREIGN MAIDEN

In our personal epic stories of wounding and healing, wandering and home-coming, confinement and escape, there is always a pivotal moment when a choice that seems to determine our destiny is made. In tales that reflect aspects of the Priestess of the Wild Earth archetype, that choice is often to flee, to break free from the ties that bind the body and soul to someone else's expec-tations and seek out a truer, wilder home. In that moment within the everyday life of a woman, a fleeting glimpse of infinite possibility is often offered up straight from the Holy Wild herself, a sacred and earthly nod that seems to answer the very question that has been twisting in her gut for a time: *What do I believe my soul truly desires, knowing all that I know of myself now, in this moment of initiation?* The answer is always authenticity, the chance to freely live out the most genuine version of herself she can.

We are all of the Earth, and she will always be calling us home to our cyclical nature and our genuine feminine power. The budding Witch may have grown weary of adhering rigidly to a loved one's notions of acceptable spirituality, and, on one fateful evening, a milk-white moonbeam melts her fear of being seen. She is the Priestess of the Wild Earth. The young artist holds and examines a scarred rose petal, suddenly finding the encouragement to pursue a more rebellious dream than that which her parents held for her. She is the Priestess of the Wild Earth. The fragile lover decides to leave a relationship that crushes her spirit every day, having been granted permission by a low-rumbling thunderstorm. She is the Priestess of the Wild Earth. She is Lilith, and so are you.

Lilith's story, in all its many variations, distortions, and interpretations, is a tale of the too-small life outgrown and a more soulful selfhood embraced. We begin here, with her, not because she is the embodiment of the grounded, enduring feminine and not because she is a beacon of warmth, grace, and solace. By contrast, Lilith is the rootless Maiden, the one whose very identity is defined not by who she knows she is but by who she knows she is *not*. We begin with Lilith because her myths are those of resistance to all that cages, all that separates us from our heathen nature and unmasked individuality. The earth element is where we stand firm in nothing but our authenticity, having ascended from the underworld of other people's expectations, and Lilith is the ancient embodiment of feminist rebellion and radical sovereignty.

Lilith's story begins in Sumerian myth, where she is handmaiden to Inanna, a supportive force to the great Goddess of sexual mysteries and underworld initiation. In the *Epic of Gilgamesh*, inscribed as early as 2000 BCE, Lilith has taken up residence in a willow tree, refusing to leave even when her mistress, Inanna, asks her to do so in order to harvest the tree's wood. The hero in the tale directs his men to cut down the tree, and Lilith flees into the wilds. In later Hebrew texts, Lilith is the demoness, the first wife of Adam who refused to "lie below" her husband and was consequently sent into exile from the Garden of Eden. Lilith is the rebel queen without a king, sovereign and whole unto herself but rejected for her independence. In *Mysteries of the Dark Moon*, Demetra George writes that Lilith "chose a lifetime of exile in a desert cave on the shores of the Red Sea rather than one of subjugation." Lilith is punished, shamed for desiring equality and recognizing the injustices of the garden, and becomes the licentious succubus in later texts, her name used as a twisted teaching tool to denigrate disobedient, sinful women who did not abide by the laws that would confine them.

Lilith's liberation from the garden can be compared to Inanna's return journey from the underworld in Sumerian mythology or the ascent of

Persephone-Kore in ancient Greek lore. The holy feminine longs for liberation and willingly risks much in the name of freedom, with Dark Goddess mythology commonly illustrating the feminine's ability to destroy all worlds too small for her. Energetic embodiment of the Priestess of the Wild Earth means acknowledging the parts of your story similar to those of other divine feminine archetypes who were necessarily trapped for a time, sought liberation, and eventually freed themselves from seemingly inescapable cages. In effect, the garden is a particular hell disguised as a utopia, an Eden of masks and half-truths, but the wild woman can endure only so much illusion before her soul's howled demands for truth grow too loud to be ignored.

Like Lilith, both Persephone-Kore and Inanna have had their stories appropriated by patriarchy. Just as Lilith's story becomes one of empowerment and liberation in its feminist interpretation, Persephone-Kore, often conventionally cast as the victimized, vulnerable daughter who was abducted by Hades with her mother's permission and forced to remain in the underworld for six months out of every year, can be viewed as a wise underworld guide. In prepatriarchal versions of her myth, Persephone-Kore is an empowered Maiden who, having been to the depths of hell, now descends and ascends willingly and regularly in order to move in rhythm with the natural world and receive the spirits of the dead. Inanna's mythic journey, plunging into the depths of the underworld and stripping herself of all her protections so she may face her psychic beasts, is really a tale of shadow integration, of the agonizing process of descent and soul retrieval that is the very essence of spiritual growth. All three Goddesses have been initiated into the soulful wilds through a great wounding, a severance from all they had been, and all three Goddesses understand the merit of both rebellion and sacrifice in the name of autonomy.

The Priestess of the Wild Earth archetype embodies the empowered energies of Lilith, Persephone-Kore, and Inanna. She is entirely free from the story that caged her. She does not define herself any longer by her too-small life. She has been to hell and back again, and she has brewed her own salve for the wounds she acquired during those dark nights of the soul. She owns her scars without overidentifying with these past hurts, without needing absolution from any sky-housed deity who does not care to truly know her. In *Aphrodite's*

Daughters, Jalaja Bonheim writes that "the resurrected goddess does not ascend to heaven, but triumphantly returns to her people, very much physically alive, and laden with precious gifts of insight, vision, power, and compassion." She is made more authentic for her ability to sit with her unsettled her-story, and she is so whole unto herself that she carries her own wild home with her, regardless of what pitfalls may lie ahead on her journey away from Eden.

Prayer of the Underworld Goddess Returned:
My Muddy Wings Are Wide

Dearest Dark Goddess who is me,

I have come to a point in my healing, my ascent, where I will no longer apologize for who I am or who I used to be. My black demoness wings are wide, and I have risen against the sandstorm of those who think me wicked. I have erupted from the ground like a newborn phoenix covered in an afterbirth of mud and ash.

This is me, and I have survived my birth by fire. My hair is knotted, and my cheeks are stained with the tears of lost innocence and bitter disdain. I am untying the knots that kept me tethered to a life I did not want, to names I did not want to be called, and to the notion that a woman is an unchanging, steady touchstone for all who need her.

My name is Lilith, and I am not a teaching tool. The forbidden fruit was seductive truth contained in fine apple skin, and I have sucked every bit of succulent juice from that gift. I have looked into the snake's shiny scales and scried my future. I have been called every shameful name ever spit from the lips of a bully, and I have let those labels roll from my back like water on feathers.

My name is Inanna, and I am still alive. These are not the musings of a whimsical poetess. These are the hellish hymns I learned from the ancients, and I speak the Mother Tongue of the anguished feminine. I know the way down, but I've learned to love the feel of sunlight on my bare breasts.

My name is Persephone, and I will not be dragged into my depths; I go there willingly, wearing my protection totems and singing my own praises. I go there to lead others out, and I am the holy healer returned, righteous, and resurrected. I am the primal feminine dark, the unruined Maiden, and the Priestess of fertile ground.

Blessed be my infinite worth, and blessed be the Holy Wild.

Parable of Eden's Lost Heroine: Revisioning Lilith

For all her wisdom, Lilith could not understand why this precious garden, this manicured and flawless landscape that once dazzled her with its fairy-tale beauty, now appeared so fake and fragile. She was sure the brilliant-green grasses were painted and artificial and the flowers were paper and scentless. How had she not noticed this ruse before now?

She knelt at the knotted base of the Tree of Knowledge, the only tree in the garden that smelled of primal bark, blessedly bitter leaves, and dirty roots, the only growing thing she was sure was absolutely real here in this carved-up land. She drank in the heady, earthen scent and caressed the bark, suddenly starved for untamed nature and uncultivated ground. She yearned so deeply for far-reaching trees and soft-bodied creatures; she was homesick for a wild place she had never seen. She knew it existed. She glimpsed this many-colored wilderness in her dreams, but her conscious mind did not yet know the way. Each morning, she woke and wept in the underworld-garden, suffocating under the weight of a life she never chose and hungry for the hearty sustenance of the feminine divine.

Pressing her face to the bark, Lilith whisper-prayed to a Mother Goddess for salvation: "Bless me, Mother, for I will most certainly sin against this too-small life. I yearn so much for a freedom I know I deserve that my belly burns with the wanting. My blood is raging under my skin, willing me forward, and yet I do not know which path to take. I dream of a blood-red road, but I know not how to find it. Mother, show me the way out! I will die if I must stay here, if I must waste more of my precious life among mere fabrications of what I love, if I must obey rules I did not write, spending my days conforming to someone else's notion of perfection. I am consumed by an ache I have no name for, and all I know is that I must leave before this sickness-of-desire ends me."

So consumed with anguish this Wild One was, so certain of her belonging to a wilderness she had never seen, that she failed to notice when a snake slid up her bare back and coiled around her neck. So broken was she, so blinded by a dark and demanding restlessness, that Lilith did not see the gift of the forbidden fruit when it fell to the ground. She did not see it with her eyes, but she felt it in her blood. There was a certain ecstatic electricity buzzing from beneath the apple's red skin that crooned to her like a warm maternal lullaby to a shivering orphan.

The snake continued spiraling around her neck, and Lilith wiped her tears. This soul-food was not fit for feminine consumption, she had been warned. She was breaking one of the rules of this place by simply being here. To eat from the Tree of Knowledge was to know too much, to commit an egregious sin against a wrathful God, but the snake's cool scales were reassuring. She did not look over her shoulder to see whether she was being watched. In that moment, she cared little for what laws had tried to contain her. She hoped quite fervently that she would be seen as she wrapped her shaking fingers around the apple. Heaven help her, she hoped some vengeful deity was looking down as she sunk her teeth deep into pure, sweet passion. She was defiant in the face of her continued captivity, a rebel heathen who was no longer content to stay in this unholy Eden. In this moment, Lilith would risk it all, everything she knew herself to be, for just a taste of the Holy Wild.

"Yes, my serpentine Sister," Lilith hissed. "I beg you forgive the fear that kept my lips from this righteous fruit for so long, that keeps me tethered to a Garden of Lies out of a bone-deep resistance to loneliness. They called me evil, and I believed them. They promised salvation from my sinfulness, and I waited for redemption. All the while, the skeleton key that could unlock every vine-wrapped cage, the sharp blade that could slice through these thin-growing binds of mine, was blooming and bearing beauteous fruit."

This one small meal was Lilith's instantaneous descent into the red realm of soul, a particular and empowered individuality entirely her own. Every time the gritty marrow of the fruit touched her tongue, she caught a glimpse of her destiny. With every hearty swallow, she saw the rainbow shades of her liberated life. This garden-hell, this too-small life, was now completely colorless, devoid of fiery purpose and sensual majesty, but she had not realized it until this moment. Never before had she so clearly known the way out of this lifeless cage, and, sucking the juice from the core, Lilith vowed to seek out a wilder home.

She stood in her own power for the first time since she had been brought to this place, and she howled into the depths of the garden, calling any other living creature to join her in her escape. Uncoiling her scaled companion and looking it square in its black-diamond eyes, Lilith offered the creature heartfelt gratitude and a bone-deep affirmation: "Thank you. We don't belong here." Spreading her black wings wide, Lilith kissed the Tree of Knowledge before taking to the ever-spiraling Red Road, the escape route that had been there for her all along, the homeward path to the wilds.

BLESSED BE THESE MANY GARDENS: WHERE SHE RIPPED UP HER ROOTS

Blessed be our many gardens. Without such confinements, we would not have known the bliss of wilder ground. The mechanisms of feminine suppression are pervasive and stealthy, and, within the garden that houses a Wild One's too-small life, these limiting forces are the primary shapers of her perception for a time. The rules of the garden may not seem unjust until the awakening begins — but, like Lilith after she tastes the forbidden fruit, a wild woman will refuse to settle for a colorless way of being, viscerally rejecting it, after she has seen the brilliance of a better, brighter way forward.

We are always busting open and out of the worlds we outgrow, the circles, partnerships, and safe spaces we once held so dear but which now, for various reasons, do not command our respect or deserve our allegiance. My love, I ask you to consider your personal Edens, to reflect upon your unique experience of your many gardens as you would define them today. To reflect means "to bend back," with any memory being merely a reflection of who you are now as the *reflector*. You may never remember your gardens the same way twice, so do not feel limited by your in-the-moment answers to the questions I pose here. We are cyclical creatures, and your many initiations, rebellions, and homecomings all serve to shape and reshape your her-story, your epic heroine's journey toward authenticity. Remember, the story of the Priestess of the Wild Earth archetype, like those of the other four archetypes offered herein, holds meaning only where it meets your lived experience. This is where the verses spark to life, and this is where you find your tools for making sense of your many initiations.

Lilith's time spent trapped within the boundaries of an unequal relationship is a familiar wound many wild women share, and I ask you to consider her story a metaphor for your own story of spiritual confinement and liberation, whatever those words might mean for you. I will ask you, Priestess, to know yourself as *her*, this Goddess who risked it all to save no one except herself, and I will ask you to be positively guiltless in your memories of jailbreaking your feminine soul from the confines of the too-dull, too-small garden. We all have our own gardens, be they tangible spaces we lived in so long that we could almost smell them or psychic spaces where it was sparkling, seemingly flawless belief systems that caged us. The garden is often perceived initially as a sanctuary of sorts, safe if only for its predictability. For wild women, our gardens may be our parents' homes, our first marriage or long-term romantic relationship, a spiritual community or a particular religion, a workplace with a strong, cohesive culture, a close circle of friends, or any other physical or energetic space that felt necessary at first, only to become far too confining for the Wild One within. A budding Priestess is quite content in her garden for a time. It suits her well to know precisely where everything grows. The garden is predictable and, for a limited duration only, is a fulfilling place to be. The wild woman is born in a garden, but she'd rather be damned than die in one.

When does the heathen choose to leave the manicured garden and seek out uncultivated land? There is no universal force that prompts the reawakening. For some of us, the veil is lifted when the wild woman sees an egregious injustice within her safe space. Her values, her deepest convictions, and her very sense of self-worth are threatened by this *thing*, and she can no longer will herself to hold still. Mind you, very often the garden itself has not changed; *she* has changed. Once the integration of her soul-designed passions and purpose begins, once she endeavors to find meaning in her wounds and more closely examine the role of choice in her life, once recovery from addiction has been initiated, or once a certain level of genuine self-inquiry has been reached, these traits that were so easily buried in the garden begin to stretch upward and sprout to the surface, but the rainbow hues of this new growth do not match those of the existing garden vegetation.

The awakening wild woman begins to feel a deeper kinship with the Earth, and nature begins to fill a need the garden no longer satisfies. For many of us, a sign straight from nature is what beckons us home. These sunrise epiphanies, lonely walks on a beach, and overgray days spent in the depths of our longing all call us away from the garden and toward our wilder home. Whatever the essence of the knowledge that bids her to wake, whatever the scent of the forbidden fruit, the wild woman begins to feel she no longer belongs there among those blooming-garden illusions she knows so well.

This soul growth is triggered by an irrevocable acknowledgment that something is amiss. She has been licked alive, and for all its flowery glory, the garden now contains a festering stink to which her duller senses were immune. The particular injustice that, upon first sight, ignites the wild woman's fire may simply be unconditional rules that succeeded in taming her for years or more. It may be the mistreatment of others who are in the garden with her by some authority figure, abuse in its myriad forms, spiritually predatory behavior, or, less specifically, the recognition that others are carving their own wounds out on her skin. This is the moment in the early chapters of a wild woman's story when she may not be sure where she is headed, she may not know where she wants to ultimately be, but from deep within her bowels a single, persistent mantra begins to echo: *Not here. Not here. Not here.*

Handwritten Verses: A Letter Sent to Eden

May all wise women strive to be those gracious mentors they needed in their younger years. In your journal, begin by writing a letter to your younger self, a promise of redemption. Write the words you needed to hear when you were Lilith trapped in Eden. You may use the prompts I offer here or adapt these words to make the letter more authentic to your story.

Dear Priestess of the Wild Earth,

I understand the pain of this garden you find yourself in, and I promise…

Always remember that you are…

These are days when you find yourself searching for the Tree of Knowledge; look for it in…

In this moment, I can offer you this one, single hope:…

May you always remember the sheer beauty you are, and may you grow to be…

With love,
An Elder Priestess

REBELLION AS RECLAMATION:
THE FORBIDDEN FRUIT OF THE WILD FEMININE

The Priestess of the Wild Earth emerges within the wild woman *not* when she chooses to eat the forbidden fruit but before, when she weeps for a home she has yet to find. She might experience an in-the-gut betrayal that nearly breaks her. She might feel that she has sinned against herself for staying in the small place so long, but her primary concern at this point is her liberation. The pain from the wound is strong, but her thirst for freedom is stronger.

The garden becomes unbearable in its constriction, and the waking woman will begin to show her true face to those who have not yet seen it. In the re-visioning of Lilith's story, the wild woman wishes to be seen when she breaks the rules: *She hoped some vengeful deity was looking down as she sunk her teeth deep into pure, sweet passion.* She who is waking to her wild self will cease to make apologies for her authenticity. There is a necessary rebellion to a woman's liberation. She will risk social isolation, loneliness, and uncertainty, all in the name of finding her true home. She will not move without fear, but she will no longer let fear of being too big, too loud, or too unlike the outmoded versions of herself direct her path.

In becoming more genuinely herself, the Priestess of the Wild Earth no longer tolerates the worlds someone else built for her. On a collective level, the feminine in all human beings is forced to constantly reenact the original sin of inauthenticity, for the feminine is not living in a world built from her own values and with her own hands. A woman who begins to take charge of her own life drawing *not* from patriarchal notions of individualistic success but from a desire to escape these norms is committing an act of social deviance and rebellion. She is the outlaw, named so only for her enacted desire for something better.

When the feminine in one being, regardless of gender, honestly sees and validates the holistic feminine in another being, there is no need to mask the wounds, passions, or purpose of the deep soul. There is no need to find overtly masculine language for what is inherently feminine. We begin the task of finding our own names, our own truths, if only by calling out what we know to be false. In *Womanspirit Rising*, Carol Christ and Judith Plaskow assert that "feminists have called their task a 'new naming' of self and world.... If the world has been named by Adam without Eve's consultation, then the world has been named from the male point of view. As women begin to name the world for themselves, they will upset the order that has been taken for granted throughout history." Regardless of the force that drives a woman from the garden, the common thread running through this initial catalyst for her awakening is this: The healing salve she needs is of the wild feminine, and it does not grow in a garden where all that flourishes was planted and named by someone else.

Rebellion against what is not ours precedes the reclaiming of what is truly for us. The subjugation of the feminine correlates directly with the suppression of soul, as the shape-shifting nature of the feminine wild has been dismissed for its volatility. We have been robbed of social permissions to descend into our depths, leave outmoded relationships, pursue passions that are not financially lucrative, or do anything remotely unpredictable; thus, even when the soul is screaming at us from below to honor our unique nature, we will pretend not to hear our truest voice for fear of being abandoned by those we love, losing our jobs, or disrupting the even-keeled rhythm of our world. When we deny our cyclical nature, we deny our connection to the Earth, and we deny our connection to the Holy Wild.

There are religions and other spiritual systems that sourced much of their power from humanity's fundamental disconnection from nature and the

feminine. Our right to spread our spiritual roots down and deep was denied
in an effort to fix our eyes on a promised heaven, and we forgot that we are
essentially fluid and mutable creatures
who do not wake the same beings as
those who closed their eyes the night before. On an individual level, we commit the

> *When we deny
> our cyclical nature, we deny our
> connection to the Earth, and we deny
> our connection to the Holy Wild.*

sin of inauthenticity in order to maintain our relationship with ourselves and
with others without facing the exhaustion of constant conflict, of constant
defending and rationalization of our extraordinary actions and beliefs. On a
collective level, the sin of inauthenticity becomes socially validated, as it is difficult to economically, politically, and socially profit from what is wild and, by
nature, inherently dynamic. Ultimately, the traits of the unburnt feminine that
the Witch is tasked with embodying and enacting are those that do not suit
capitalism or patriarchal control; these are the same traits that she suppresses
during childhood, rendering her light-of-day personality a small reflection of
the wealth of her soulful treasures, the truest parts of herself that lie buried
in the fertile dark.

No one can write your story for you, my love, and it is not the task of any
one of us to judge the gardens in which we do not live. We cannot discount
the number of human beings who remain trapped despite their desire to escape, nor can we dismiss the sheer bravery of those staying in their gardens in
order to protect loved ones or their own precious bodies from harm. These
are the caged angels, and those who have been free to enact their own liberation are tasked with using every resource they have to reach those who need
more hands to unbind their tethers. I say this not to dilute or universalize the
experiences of those who are affected by compounded oppressions, and it is
certainly not our task to decide who needs saving and how. I only urge those
who have made it out of their gardens to keep their ears open, for they speak
the forbidden serpentine language now and can hear it spoken by others from
below who, like Lilith, are ready to find a way out and are asking, of their own
volition, for a scale-skinned wilderness guide.

Handwritten Verses: Your Lilith Story

The garden is a deeply personal experience, and no one lives it the same way. Stay awake, Priestess, and remember that your wounds, your garden, are yours for a reason. Come to know your story as you would tell it today. In exploring the ways you have embodied the Priestess of the Wild Earth archetype, you can identify your personal Eden by reviewing your cycles of descending and ascending, drawing meaning from these patterns of hurts and healings.

Begin with the following prompts, and freewrite for as long as you wish. Your Lilith story is your wild woman's myth of risking it all in the name of personal liberation. It is a living testament to your feminine power, soulful worth, and so-holy infallibility. Use whatever pronouns feel most authentic. Return to your story as often as you are called. Write as if it were a *rite*. Let it be part fantasy, part spell, part personal fairy tale.

As a young Priestess in the garden, I was dazzled by the beauty of...
The perfection of the garden was so beauteous that I...
In the garden, I knew myself to be...
The garden began to smell of...
I sprouted black wings and became Lilith then, and I decided...
I risked it all, and I had to embody...
True liberation tasted like...

End your Lilith story, for now, with the yet-to-come. Let the final scene in your liberation tale be one that has not occurred in your till-now, lived experience but nonetheless feels real and true. Gift this tale to the Holy Wild when it feels finished, reading your words aloud while sitting among the elements in sacred solitude. Let your story be a poetic blessing to the earth element, with the grasses, the trees, and the soil your most honored and beloved audience.

INITIATION IN SACRED SOLITUDE: WALKING THE RED ROAD

The integration of your knowledge of the garden into your more soulful identity depends on claiming your right to cyclical rootlessness. Lilith severs ties with her old life when she consumes the forbidden fruit. She rejects the rules of the garden and, by extension, refuses to remain in that too-small place. She is defiant in her selfhood, and she risks it all, running blindly into the dark without direction. All wild women have torn up their roots from time to time, leaving relationships, roles, and places that came to misalign with their emergent identity.

You, Priestess of the Wild Earth, have a right to sacred solitude. You have a right to wander, and you have a right to be wholly in your body. Integrate your knowledge of the garden by affirming the role these increasingly unjust places have played in your life. In many ways, the garden is a mirror of who you used to be. How you remember the garden is a mere reflection of where you are in your life right now; at another point on the Red Road, that spiral path of a woman's spiritual journey, you may remember the garden completely differently. Know that the act of guiltless reflection, of a nonjudgmental sifting-through of experiences from time to time, is radical in its own right. It is a bravehearted woman who leaves whatever security the garden has to offer in the name of her own liberation, but there is bravery in the looking back also. It takes courage to kiss the snake and a soulful audacity to sink one's teeth deep into the forbidden fruit, but to look back and honor those moments as moving benedictions to the wild within you is another particular and glorious victory.

It is never a short journey home to the wilds. In order to find her soulful home, the Priestess of the Wild Earth must first come to an unsettling realization: She knows she is looking for something, but she is not sure exactly what it is or precisely where it can be found. She becomes the hooded wanderer, a mere ghost of who she used to be, and she commits to knowing only a few scarce but in-the-bones truths. Somehow she understands that the agony she feels as the outcast is well worth the new world that is waiting for her, a post-garden lifescape she cannot even begin to imagine. In the teaching tale, Lilith is *homesick for a wild place she had never seen.* She holds an infinite trust in herself now, even as she loses it all, and that trust is sufficient to sustain her for a time, in the absence of all other social nourishment.

The Priestess of the Wild Earth also harbors a deep knowing that, regardless of the precise nature of her confinement in the garden and without necessitating any forgiveness of wrongs done to her there, time spent in her too-small world was absolutely necessary. She was midwifing her own birth in that place, and, as she finds herself in the wilderness now, she is charged to relinquish any and all guilt over staying too long in the garden. It was what it was. It had to be done, and she may never have a concrete rationale for why she remained there for so long. The Mystery does not gift us with maps, and the grand design is built from near-infinite sacred geometric angles and softly spiraling edges that our most advanced research technologies, the very language of our systems of quantification, are pitifully ill-equipped to measure. We have yet to understand the she-science of the cosmic web, but we know we cannot track our souls' progress in measurable goals and numerically ordered objectives. The Priestess of the Wild Earth embraces the dark valleys on her path with much feminine grace, knowing there is little merit in berating herself over past choices that cannot be rationalized away with our logical, left-brained know-how.

An additional truth the wayward Priestess clings to with a tight grip when the nights are endless is this: There is an immense beauty in her longing, in her fervent search for a home that is truly her own. Perhaps there is no greater testament to feminine fortitude than a woman's story of risking immense insecurity for authenticity. The spiritual journey does not promise comfortable travel, and a woman who runs screaming from all things known does not do so seeking happiness; she does so seeking a truer version of herself. The evenings she spends alone and crying or raging most righteously, torturous as they are, are worthy of honor. They are the stuff of poetry, and they are the deepest, impassioned hues that render a lifescape a beautiful masterpiece full of shadow and light.

The awakening wanderer now sets foot on the spiral Red Road, moving away from the garden and into the unknown, having irrevocably broken the garden's rules. She may now know only what she does *not* want her new house rules to be, but that knowing is sufficient to keep her moving in the right direction. Even the wildest woman sets some working guidelines for herself in times of transition, a sort of flexible manifesto largely meant to keep her from sinking back into the old underworld-garden or, worse, falling into a new trap altogether. As the Priestess of the Wild Earth takes to the road, her boundaries are often fiercer than they have ever been, than they ever needed to be.

The truths she wears on her back — the knowledge that her time in the garden was both necessary and well worth the agony, along with a strange, often unsettling acknowledgment that there is beauty in her quite painful new-found longing — are her most prized possessions; she has earned them, after all. The rules she writes now are those that have been tattooed on her bones since she was in the womb, long before she sat caged in the too-small life. These rules are born of those precious truths, but the wild woman realizes now, as her bare feet pound the red ground with infinite purpose, that she has always known her real rules, rules she did not need to read in any book of verses or recite to authority figures for sweet reward. Her house rules were written by the ancient, wild hand, and she has been reciting them in her dreams since she was a babe.

> *Her house rules were written by the ancient, wild hand, and she has been reciting them in her dreams since she was a babe.*

The Red Road: A Parable of Feminine Fortitude

This wayward Priestess has raised her patchworked hood and smeared her lipstick in just the right places. She has shed her dried skin, leaving it heaped in a ditch alongside the Red Road. Lighter she moves now, her bare feet beating the rusted dirt while the wild wind blows her hair. A dull rumble of thunder heralds the impending storm, and she knows she cannot turn back. Her soul demands she press on, though she will pass ghosts of long-gone lovers who wounded her well.

"They cannot cut me again," she whispers.

Her liberation depends on this journey; not its completion but its wholehearted undertaking. To turn back would mean consenting to be shackled to relinquished divinity, to low worth, and to a world where the voices of loud women are muffled under others' accusations arising from bitterness and envy. This Priestess knows that the storm will toss her about, the road will run bloody with the overflow, and she will be waist-deep in the memories of hunted Witches.

"They will not catch me again," she speaks skyward with a resonance her voice never had in her younger years.

The rain falls in sheets now, and her lashes drip thick with the Earth Mother's tears. Still, she has never seen more clearly the sins of humankind against the wounded world. Part of her yearns for her joints to break apart and her body to fall into a limp bundle of skin on the ground. Part of her wants to be a blood sacrifice to the ailing planet, and part of her bids the drowning worms beneath her to ascend and climb her bones, to pull her under so she may nourish the sun-thirsty, spiderwebbing roots of the cut trees.

"Purify these lands with your storm; they are begging you to do it!" she beckons to the wilds.

The red soil has a sense memory of the truest freedom fighting. Were she to press ear to wet ground, the Priestess would hear echoes of the final beats of the bravest hearts as they slowed to a stop in the name of man-made maps. If she could hear the tallest and most ancient trees talking, they would be singing low and mournful dirges about bullets lodged in bark and blood pooling around their roots. If she turned back now, her body might live, but part of her soul would forever remain here on this hallowed ground. She must go on, in the name of her granddaughters' granddaughters' babes. She must go on, to preserve what is left of the sacred masculine and majestic feminine. She is but one electric-pulsing cell in the universal body, but her resolve will ripple the skin of the global collective and send a single message into the future.

"I am she who is and will always be," she speaks solemnly into the rain. "If I die here on the Red Road, my soul will look down on my floating body from the ether and know my life was better lived for taking this journey, doomed as it may have been. I regret nothing, and I repent nothing except the joyless nights spent depriving myself of sacred indulgence, hedonistic delights, and the company of those worthy of the beauty that was me."

COMING HOME TO THE WILDS:
BUILDING THE LIVING ALTAR

A woman expresses the Priestess of the Wild Earth archetype, becoming whole unto herself, when she enacts an embodied knowing that she is a living altar, holy ground in her own right, and she needs no external validation. She comes home to the wilds. She writes her own house rules, and she claims her heathen's birthright to live on uncultivated spiritual ground.

In This House, I Brew with Crone Magick

In this house, I am whole unto myself. Here is my altar; I like it just this way, covered in old candle wax and laden with wounded mementos from my garden. This is the scarred walnut that reminds me of my childhood, and this is the dried flower that lost all its juicy perfection, as I once did. I keep these things here in my new house, built with my own hands at the end of the long Red Road, so I know I must never look back.

In this house, I brew with Crone magick. The old ways of magick-making are emblazoned on my very cells, and I need no Book of Light and Shadow to tell me the right words or the perfect chant. Here, I am a Witch-Priestess in a congregation of one, and even my closest kin do not know all my secrets.

In this house, I melt back into the source of everything from time to time, dissolving into a wet heap of flesh and blood to be resculpted by some angelic artisan, some skilled descended master who puts my stretch marks in just the right places and squints to paint my tattoos just so. Here, no one wonders why I must become the hermit every so often, and no one keeps knocking when I refuse to answer my door.

In this house, I wake with the bone-deep understanding of feminine divinity. I am a wild Goddess unleashed within these four walls, and I will wear all the jewelry I like. Here, no one clicks their tongue when I speak of nature lust and the cosmic dance. Here, I will wax poetic on intergalactic Shakti before breakfast. Here, I pray all day long and with my whole body, for my limbs are a moving benediction to the Holy Wild.

In this house, I am a Priestess of the Wild Earth. I am Lilith, Inanna, and Persephone ascended from the dirt. I am a soulful temptress blessing these wooden floors with my bare feet as I walk from hearth to porch, and I am a keeper of this fortress.

In this house, no one gets in unless they are invited. Here is where I've spread the salt thick and painted the windows with cedar smoke more times than I can count. This is the House of the Wild Woman, and solitude is valued as much as company. Come in if you like, but I may not ask you to stay. This is my house, after all, and if you are here sipping my brew, my rules are law.

Handwritten Verses: House Rules of the Wild Scribe

This is a ritual of fierce boundary setting. Go to a place in your home that feels like yours, as if it were a true sanctuary, a sort of inner sanctum and the wild woman's holiest of holies. Light a candle, and begin writing your own house rules. These are not limiting ways of being in your world but a liberating testimony to who you have become. You may use the prompts I offer here or write your own, wild scribe that you are.

This is my house, love. Here, I wake up remembering...
This is my house, and I will not permit entry to...
This is my house, where I welcome...
This is my house. I am the highest Priestess within these four walls, and I worship...
This is my house, where every guest is adorned with...

Post these rules in a secret place, where only those who are most trusted will read them.

HALLOWED BE YOUR HEATHEN HEART: TOWARD A MORE SOULFUL, EARTHEN JOY

Make no mistake, Priestess; it is a brave thing you do now, claiming a crown called shameful in fairy tale, sacred text, media, and myth. Set your boundaries, and give a nod to your worth every now and again, for it is far too easy for the feminine to claim humility and retreat. Now is not the time for charm and lace. Now is the time for ash as face paint and the weapons of your words. Know that coming home to the wilds is a courageous act. The Priestess of the Wild Earth within you is destructive only in her ability to break up patterns and beliefs that no longer serve you. She is the Goddess of personal power, and she emerges within you when you closely examine belief systems, social norms, and cultural structures that do not suit your awakening wild self. You, as Lilith, begin to not only taste the forbidden fruit but ask yourself why it was forbidden to you in the first place.

May you believe in your powers of discernment, and may you risk social isolation over and over again in the name of your soulful joy. May you be willing to exist on the fringes in the name of liberation, finding and belonging to those wild circles of openhearted seekers who make you feel as though you are a larger version of yourself and leaving those circles where entry always demands you wear a too-tight mask to disguise your true face. May you rebel against all that covers and constricts your beauteous worth, and may you write your own holy verses of wild feminine lost and wild feminine regained.

Hallowed be your heathen soul, and blessed be the Holy Wild.

Chapter 2

Earth Rituals

Wild women speak the language of ritual. We understand the art of marking our initiations and our endings, those many rebirths and deaths we undergo as Priestesses of the Wild Earth, and marking them well. The intuitive skills and ancestral medicine that support the shaping of a good ritual are treasures acquired along the underworld journey. We know in our bones when we are being called to our Craft, and we long for that particular closure and healing salve brewed only within the cauldron of ritual. Here, in ritual, we set boundaries around our life transitions and make the mundane magickal. Here, we hold rituals as symbolic action, impactful events of ceremonial sense-making that begin with an accessible container, a set of steps or conditions that serve to frame the transformation that will, eventually, arise from our depths and alchemize an ordinary moment in time into pure embodied presence.

The seven rituals offered in this chapter are intended to be adapted by you, dear Priestess, to suit your unique purpose and story. Some of these offerings are simple, easily performed in those small and unexpected moments of solitude and grace we may find ourselves in throughout the day, and some rituals are more complex, requiring a joyous but steadfast commitment, thoughtful resource gathering, and careful planning. Move through only the rituals that seem authentic to you; leave out any steps or wording that does not fit; and, as always, remember that the best rituals are the ones that will gift you with something you need, be it closure, healing, empowerment, or a sense of belonging.

In any solitary ritual, Priestess, you are the beginning, the center point. Start with your story. Recall the aspects of Lilith's revisioned tale that resonate with you, and assess those traits embodied in the Priestess of the Wild Earth archetype that are your soul-true attributes. When have you eaten the forbidden fruit, breaking the rules and risking certain isolation in the name of sovereignty? When did you so bravely call in what was yours, sacrificing all that was not authentically for you despite any garden comforts? These are the moments worthy of honor, my love, for they are truly holy transitions, times of becoming, and more genuine birthdays than those we are accustomed to celebrating. Craft your rituals and begin with you, a living altar embodied in the soft skin of a woman.

YOUR INNER EARTH ALTAR:
A RITUAL FOR THE EVERYDAY WARRIORESS

Materials: *Paper and writing utensil*

You are a living altar. Do not be afraid of leaving behind your Pagan statuary, blessed totems, and sensual candles, for you carry all the divinity you need with you in your blood and your breath. Handcraft a personal mantra to keep with you, to remind you of your journey along the Red Road and to affirm your personal Priestess power. Words carry power. What can you tell yourself, in a single sentence, that will remind you of your magick and your wild? What words can you cling to when the storm comes, when some snide remarks threaten to break you, when someone calls you "too" this or "too" that? What can you tell yourself to remind you that you are, after all, born of the elements, a star-child of the Holy Wild?

Any mantra you write with your hand will be far better than one I could give you, my love, but you can begin harvesting the right words by freewriting on the following prompts, if you need a starting point:

I am the Priestess of…
I am calling in…
I am building my temple for…

This is my year, and I will…

I am the wild Witch of the Earth, and I know…

Find a short phrase you can hold housed in your heart. Imagine it blood-written in calligraphic script and placed on that inner altar built from your rib bones. Every time you speak it, you are enacting a ritual of coming home to yourself, owning the value of your voice, and engaging in practical alchemy. If you feel called, write these words on a sacred object, a small piece of wood or fabric, and leave your mantra in a wild place for all to see. May a little girl find it, tuck it into her sleeve, and keep it close. And so it is.

BLESSING THE FORBIDDEN FRUIT:
A RITUAL OF REBELLIOUS NOURISHMENT

Materials: *Paper, writing utensil, large apple, knife*

Eating the forbidden fruit is an act of necessary rebellion. As her time in the garden comes to an end, the wild woman is ravenous for a life she has yet to live, and her hunger pangs rumble through her gut like the foreshocks of a devastating Gaia-sourced earthquake. The yearning for freedom consumes her body and psyche, and what used to seem magickal in the garden now seems mediocre, frightening, overly fragile, too good to be true, or, otherwise and more simply, just not for her. The bright colors take on a sepia tone, and the freely served garden food on which the Priestess once gorged herself now tastes bland and fails to satiate her. She becomes an outcast in her own land, and it is *now* that she begins to truly embark on the feminine quest for freedom. She sees the garden for the cage it is, and her choice is to stay and waste away or risk her life in a no-holds-barred fight for her own wildness. In the end, she has no choice but to eat the forbidden fruit, to rebel against this too-small life.

The revisioned tale describes Lilith's lament as she prays to the divine feminine at the foot of the Tree of Knowledge: *I yearn so much for a freedom I know I deserve that my belly burns with the wanting.* The Priestess of the Wild Earth archetype lives and breathes within our roots, and there is a necessary sense of entitlement that precedes the wild woman's liberation. A woman will not leave her garden until she harbors a deep knowing, planted there at the base of her spine, that she deserves better. In the absence of this felt self-worth, the woman will stay in her garden-cage quite willingly until she embraces her right to have more, to be more, and to live in a bigger and brighter world where she can be fully and unapologetically herself. After she eats the forbidden fruit, after she gets a taste of a life that is more blissful, more true to self than the one the garden has offered her, there can be no going back.

Ask yourself now, Priestess, when have you eaten the forbidden fruit? Was there a time when you risked rejection in the name of selfhood or sacrificed, perhaps unknowingly, social acceptance in a group where you no longer belonged, success in a career that drained you, or some promised reward from a spiritual community in order to be truer to your genuineness? The forbidden fruit can mean any number of things to women, and the act of consumption may not have necessarily been ecstatic or blissful. Ask yourself what memory of the forbidden fruit you have today. Whatever your sinful pleasure was, you made a choice to indulge, and you felt more true, more *you*, for having done so. Maybe you asked a question you knew would not be well received by an authority figure, but you were well satiated by having spoken your mind. Maybe you skipped church one day as a young girl to play in the woods, or maybe you stood up for someone who needed you. Tasting the forbidden fruit may not have been an easy choice, and it may not have tasted so sweet at the time — but, in retrospect, these were the moments that marked your awakening.

List as many "forbidden fruits" as you can now. They need not be chronologically linear or brilliantly articulated. For each "fruit," summarize the experience in just one word; it might be *resistance, joy, hedonism, defiance,* or any other name that feels right as a *rite*. With a knife, skewer, or other sharp utensil, carve as many of these words onto an apple's skin as you can, then hold the sticky fruit in both your hands. Whisper-pray these words if they seem true: *I am a Priestess of the Wild Earth, and I call in my most soulful joy. This forbidden fruit is mine, and I deserve all that is for me.* When you feel ready, eat the apple, savoring the taste on your tongue. With every bite, go back to your list of "forbidden fruit" moments and relive one, apologizing for nothing and welcoming a fiercer version of yourself home. And so it is.

REPOWERING THE WITCH:
A RITUAL FOR HEALING THE FEMININE SOUL-WOUND

Materials: *Just you, adorned as the Priestess you are*

While we must have joy in our Craft, we must also acknowledge our inherited wounds. The Witch lives at the edge of what is permissible, and, as a Priestess coming into her power, the wild woman sees with great clarity the systematic strangulation of feminine spirituality. Even women who are not raised within the confines of patriarchal religion are indoctrinated with beliefs that soften and dilute the power of the feminine. Regardless of gender, all human beings suffer greatly from the soul-wound of communal, feminine loss. Our society shapes us all to value the hard-edged, individualistic, toxic, and aggressive masculine over the sensually present, collectivist feminine. We are taught to devalue our planetary resources along with those of the holy feminine embodied in a single woman, the traits of the nature-loving Maiden, the nurturing, storyteller Mother, and the intuitive, ethereal Crone.

Escaping the too-small life is often prompted by the acknowledgment of a great injustice, but, regardless of how this blight or corruption is shaped, undergirding the violation is the denigration of the feminine wild. Remember, however, that the stranglehold of patriarchy on human society has not choked the breath from the Goddess. The feminine in all human beings has housed her, kept her warm, and fed her with soft whispers that tell her we still feel her inside us and our wounded world. In the cold absence of feminine spiritual systems that permit her to speak, it is the Witches and wild women who often become her voice.

You still embody bone-deep bruises from the Witch-hunters' weapons, my love. Wild women's bodies are homes to souls who remember the threat of the noose and the stake, a threat that remains in many parts of the world in various forms. In *Witches, Sluts, and Feminists,* Kristen Sollée writes, "in the face of oppression, the Witch reminds us what we can and have overcome, and illuminates the path to power beyond patriarchy. As we undress the legacy of

> *In the cold absence of feminine spiritual systems that permit her to speak, it is the Witches and wild women who often become her voice.*

the Witch to reveal her potent history, we may in the process uncover something marrow-deep within ourselves." The fear of claiming spiritual autonomy is a sticky, dripping darkness that crouches and snarls in the shadows of even the most awakened woman's psyche. There is no escape from this soul-wound; thus we have little choice but to look the monster straight in its red eyes and honor our right to speak and be heard. We are here, gruesome creature, and we are not leaving. Teach us what you know.

At the hand of patriarchal religion, the stories of wild women's bravery became those of the scandalous, broken Maidens. Lilith's story becomes one of the demon Mother who was cast out of the desert, devolving into a licentious succubus. Countless other incarnations of the divine feminine dark have had their stories bleached to remove the magick, the divination, and the fem-force of righteous rage. These are the stories meant to keep the wild woman contained, safely tamed in a garden of half-truths where the feminine is demure, dependent, and distracted.

Remember who you are, Priestess. Stay awake. Descend into your depths now and know what it means to be spiritually free, unbound by the fear of being hunted down for your beliefs. Ask yourself what you truly believe. Feel the Goddess sparking in your blood, and refuse to be cornered. Sift through your memories and recall the first moment when you saw the feminine face of the resplendent Mystery, the vision that made your soul-wound of Goddess loss ache like a tired body before a storm. Perhaps you were a chubby-cheeked babe or a wise old Crone; linear age means nothing, because *that* day, that holy day when you spit out the beliefs they spoon-fed you, was the day you were born.

Stand in your power now. Feel where the feminine soul-wound aches in your body, but do not let it weaken your stance. Imagine roots sprouting out from the bottoms of your feet and sinking down, down, and deeper down into the Earth, stretching through time and space, connecting you to the cosmic web. Recall the wisdom of your grandmothers and all who came before you. From whatever Earth-based traditions your lineage hails, whether you know of your ancestral history or not, envision your roots tapping into a dark well of primordial feminine knowledge, swirling and bubbling and holding the very medicine you need right now. Soak the wisdom up through your roots. Let the brew run through your veins and reach the soul-wound, healing it over with minuscule bursts of love, with grace, and with the bravehearted, ever-enduring ways of the elders.

Stay with this vision for as long as you have. Let yourself be repowered and repurposed. Your soft body seethes with the blood mysteries, the herbal wisdom, and the ancient ceremonies. If "Witch" is a name you claim for yourself, shout aloud: *I am Witch, wise woman, and wayfinder!* You are the living antidote to the poison that keeps the wound from healing, and you are the rebel Priestess who has come home to the wilds. And so it is.

THE ROAD TO MANIFESTATION:
A RITUAL OF MOVEMENT ALCHEMY

Materials: *Just you and an earthy oil such as vetiver, cedar, or pine*

Priestess, take to the road. This red journey can take place out of doors in a yard, in a forest, on a lonely sidewalk, on a long driveway, or even within an empty hallway. Find a place where you can walk in sacred solitude, relatively undisturbed, and let this small piece of movement alchemy signify your right to manifest your desires. Bless your body before the journey begins by anointing your feet with a bit of earthy oil or water blessed by you with a few select words. Whisper-pray before you begin: *I call in abundance and grace. I call in ancestral wisdom, and I call in the next chapter.*

As you walk now, my love, imagine that every mindful step you are taking is bringing you that much closer to fulfilling your soul's contract. Every corner you turn is a decided step away from the too-small life and toward more authentic embodiment of your divinity. Step in rhythm with your heartbeat and imagine those beauteous scenes from your next chapter. Believe with every cell of your body that you are moving toward that vision. Look through your third eye and see all you deserve perfectly placed within your wildest home.

Don't turn back, Priestess. Not yet. Feel your foot bones fall on the Earth as if you were blessing the ground with every step you take, and call in your soul's greatest gifts. This is a moving spell, with every step raising energy and infusing it into the vision of your wild home.

If we are stripping our Craft down to the bare bones of the elements, down to nature herself, we begin here, with a mindful walk. We begin here, connecting to ground with every step, and we begin *here*, in the warm bodies we find ourselves in now, with our imperfect mental-emotional states and stretch-marked bellies, accepting the place where we stand in the total absence of shoulds and supposed-tos. This is where you are, on the Earth. Start here. And so it is.

PRIESTESS RISING FROM GROUND: A RITUAL OF SELF-INITIATION

Materials: *Skin-safe mud or clay*

Our ground is precisely where we find ourselves each morning when we wake; it is a place of genesis, of sparking to life over and over again, despite its apparent flaws, the cracks in the pristine glaze of our grandest plans and greatest obsessions. Here, with our bare feet firm on the ground, we embody our inner altar regardless of where our story has taken us. We understand that whatever wounds have scarred our skin, whatever agonies have brought us here to this fateful incarnation, we are eternally whole. We are unruined. We are precisely who we need to be, precisely who we have always been.

For the awakening Priestess, the Earth serves as a foundation for her rising. She no longer clings to outmoded identities or is confined by garden rules. She values herself and affirms her right to exist here on the primal ground as she is. Her descent could have broken her, but it did not. The upward journey could have overwhelmed her to the point of eternal exhaustion, could have forced her into waist-deep psychic quicksand, but it did not. Now, the Priestess has a true topside place to start building her home, and it is a sanctuary that can never be invaded because, though its foundation was laid with fierce rebellion, it reaches skyward with the unbreachable walls of feminine authenticity.

Lilith, Inanna, and Persephone carry their wild homes on their bare backs. They have been to hell, have returned, and know how to stand against the fiery tide that would curse them. They have lived in the underworld for a time, been burned there for days on end, and now they have the verses of the wild feminine whisper-hissing from deep within their pelvic bowls. The descent is invaluable because the wild woman must be pulled into her depths in order to understand her darkness, lest it direct all she does with a heavy, shadowy hand, undermining her sense of self-worth, invalidating her most authentic identity, and keeping her contained in the too-small life. The descent is necessary, for only from our depths can we begin to rise.

If you can be safely out in nature for this ritual, my love, go. Find your-self a secluded space you can call your own. Carry with you some wet dirt or clay, and, when ready, call to the four directions and build yourself an energetic temple here. Hold whatever vessel you chose for your symbolic "Earth" in both hands, and bless it with the words I offer here or others you have written yourself: *This is my initiation. These wounds are mine. I am whole unto myself, and I am of this Earth. So it is.* When ready, anoint your third eye, that space between and slightly above the brows, with earth, creating an imperfect spiral with the mud or clay. Say aloud: *This is my initiation. I am returned from the underworld, and I reclaim my right to see in the dark.* Anoint your throat center, then say: *This is my initiation. My voice is loud, and I reclaim my right to be heard.* Finally, anoint your heart center and say: *This is my initiation. My heart is unruined, and I reclaim my right to be loved deeply.* Seal the ritual by offering gratitude to the four directions and placing hands firmly on the Earth, affirming: *This is my initiation. All blessings be.* And so it is.

TO WED SACRED SOLITUDE:
A SOUL-MARRIAGE RITUAL FOR THE TOO-MUCH WOMAN

Materials: *Just you, adorned as the Priestess you are*

The mutation of Lilith's story has much to teach us about the mass rejection targeting a woman as she re-wilds herself against all odds. Much of what the feminine learns about itself during childhood, in babes of all genders raised within the confines of patriarchy, is inextricably bound to a fear of being too loudmouthed and demanding. Lilith is a too-much woman, and, in several versions of her-story, she was condemned for naught more than demanding equality in her relationship. The feminine surrenders during the years of youth to a life of low worth and lack, with this lack well positioned, in our very roots, to undermine our very sense of self.

We tell ourselves we cannot have what we truly desire, for that very desire will get us kicked out of the life we know. We tell ourselves we cannot have what we want, particularly when that longing does not conform to the indi-vidualistic goals of our inner Fathers, those masculine commanders who rule over our psyches as if they were armies, fighting against anyone or anything we deem foreign or unfamiliar. We tame ourselves, housing multiple mechanisms in our psyches that carry their own whips, poised to strike if we speak out of turn or lose control, and we do all of this to keep from being abandoned by those whom we both love yet also see ourselves as subservient to; these may be our caregivers, our early mentors, our closest teenage friendships, our first lovers, and, most prominently, our heavy-handed egos. We wear many masks during our garden years, and, when the masks all finally fall to the ground heralding our pending escape, our real faces are raw and sensitive to light.

What healing salve can we put on our aching skin after our liberation, when we have few friends, few trusted souls who have seen us to hell and back? How can we sit on the topside world on the fringes of all we know, as the autonomous outcast in sacred solitude rather than the anguished loner? What grace can we find here in our bitter isolation?

Here, we have no choice but to become a bride to soul. When all others have forsaken us, when we have leaped so far beyond our most secure boundaries that we no longer remember the names we used to be called, we can trust no one except the reddest, rawest version of ourselves. This is a ritual of wedding the self and committing to soul.

Paint and adorn yourself as you like, my love. Wear all the jewels you value, or be naked as a newborn. Feel beautiful, and walk in grace toward a natural altar or one you have crafted for the occasion. As meaningful as it might be to have witnesses, consider moving through this rite in solitude. Your commitment to soul is a sovereign matter, after all. Place a warm palm flat on your steady-beating heart and know yourself as whole. Speak your vows with a voice so resonant that it ripples back through the very fabric of time and comforts you during your most fearful childhood moments:

Dearly beloved, I have planted my bare feet firmly on fertile ground and curled my toes into the primal mud. I am here to declare myself unruined and unbroken, and I am marking this day as my first sacred birthday. I, the woman most wild, hereby take my soul to love, honor, and cherish in this majestic, joyous life and in all my future incarnations. I am forgiving all my past transgressions, and I am unveiling my truest face.

I am the outcast Priestess no one understands, and I am taking a vow of rebellion. I have ripped up my roots and run into the desert screaming for a wilder life, and I am building a new house on these unmapped lands. I hereby promise to be the largest version of myself I can ever be, to replace complacency with self-compassion, and to reject apathy in favor of activism.

This is not a selfish ceremony; this is an act of soulful justice. I wed myself to vindicate the women of this world, the feminine in us all, and the wounded planet. My work does not stop here. I am sucking the poison of patriarchy and privilege out of the soil and spitting it moonward, for these are the dire days of the fallen kings and rising queens.

I am the wayward Priestess, and I do commit myself to cherish my deep self and all I stand for now, as the red sun rises and the futures of our children's children hang in the balance. I am swelling to fill a bigger body. My hips are wide, and these new bones were forged in the crucible of my soul's darkest night.

By the power vested in me by the Ministry of the Holy Wild and the sacred feminine heart, all blessings be.

BEDTIME INCANTATIONS:
A RITUAL PRAYER FOR THE PILGRIM PRIESTESS

On your loneliest nights, love, whisper these wild blessings straight into the shadowy, haunted places of your psyche, those warm, wet forests where the truest fairy tales are told and the loam-skinned breasts of the ancient feminine rise and fall with breath under your bare feet:

I am wandering through these unmarked territories and learning new skills for surviving this particular wilderness I find myself in. This is the prayer of the last pilgrim Priestess, and I will whisper these words into the unforgiving chill, watching them fog out in all directions and willing them to bring comfort to every lonesome soul who finds themselves choosing stark liberation over a soft and sweet-smelling nest.

May I always grant myself permission to change, and may I

see others as cyclical beings in their own right. I am the new moon Maiden, the full moon Mother, and the dark moon Crone puffing in and out of existence. I am the most ancient Mother Tongue language spoken by my ancestors, and I am just now remembering the words that are tattooed on my bones.

I am seeking out a new, wild home, and I am pouring its foundation on all I know to be true. When my hands are worn bloody with the work of it all, I will sleep safe in the knowing that my inner altar can never be crushed.

Blessed be this tougher skin of mine, and blessed be the Holy Wild.

Chapter 3

Earth Magick

Our magick is our declaration, a practiced and enacted affirmation about the changes we wish to make in our lives and to our worlds. Magick is unique and personalized alchemy, and one woman's relationship with it will most certainly not match that of even her closest Sister-Witch. All aspects of the deep self inform our magick, with the scars of our roots, the gifts of our grandmothers, our particular position in the cosmic web, and our unique soul mandates serving to ground our Craft as a living, breathing reflection of who we are and where we would like to go from here.

In this final chapter in the Book of Earth, I offer you Earth Magick in the form of spellcraft for manifestation — that is, opportunities for raising energies in order to nourish a desired outcome — and pathworking experiences, or guided meditations for tapping into the fertile wellspring that is the unconscious mind in order to commune with guides and Goddess energies. Our spellwork is our wild message to the universe, an energetic conveyance of our right to invoke what we desire and purge what does not belong. Our pathworking, our communion with our ancestors and those ghostly guides that will orient us in just the right direction, serves to set us back on course along the Red Road, if we only listen to their direction. If our verses tell a story and our ritual marks what has been and what is now, our magick both honors and shapes the yet-to-come.

THE LILITH MANDALA:
A MAGICK SPELL FOR WELCOMING WHAT COMES

Materials: *Journal, writing utensil, large piece of paper or canvas (18" × 24" is best), art supplies*

This spell requires reflection, my love. Very often, our manifestation magick falls short, fizzling even before the circle is cast, because we are seeking to invoke some great thing that, in our marrow, we do not believe is truly ours. We can invoke only what is for us, shifting and moving energies with our words and our ways to bring to us what we know we deserve, what we believe is ours to hold in our hands, and what will drive the changes we wish to see in the greater global community.

Deciding what is truly ours requires assessment, and our inner Crones know the skill of taking inventory quite well. Begin with your story. In the teaching tale, Lilith glimpses her new wild home when she tastes the forbidden fruit: *Every time the gritty marrow of the fruit touched her tongue, she caught a glimpse of her destiny. With every hearty swallow, she saw the rainbow shades of her liberated life.* Through this rebellion, she is able to see the garden for what it is, a colorless place where she was not allowed to know too much or be too much, where she was forced to wake each morning and pretend to be someone she had not been for a long while, a smaller version of herself that was only a pale reflection of the regal majesty she had become.

The Priestess of the Wild Earth takes to the Red Road understanding what her home will *not* be; it will not be a cage, it will not force her to pretend, and it will most certainly not be boring. As she wanders along the road toward home, she encounters a number of souls who will support her on her path. These wayward lovers and bright-eyed friends will help her remember the feeling of the snake's scales on her skin, the way the apple's juice ran down her neck, should she become distracted by the day-to-day and forget the place from which she rose up, free and wild, rootless but reaching.

She spends her time on the Red Road of liberation taking stock of her past. She considers those youthful days before the garden took her, before the underworld began to feel confining, and she traces her patterns of disconnection and relationship, abundance and scarcity, and fruition and void. She harvests a deep knowing, an in-the-bones understanding, of who she truly is during her most joyous moments. She lets the dead parts shrivel and fall off as she walks, and she surrenders to nature's storm with her whole body and soul.

Part 1. Tracing the Feeling Mind

Consider your entire life, my love, to be an epic myth consisting of an unknown number of chapters. You are the heroine, and up until this very moment you have lived the first ten of these chapters. Title these ten chapters accordingly now, writing in your journal as if you were both historian and prophet. You are living the end of the tenth chapter in this moment, but the latter chapters are the yet-to-come. Go back into the lived chapters now and make note of moments of *bhava*, or feeling mind; these are moments when your spirit, mind, and body were all yoked together, vibrating with the universal frequency. These are moments not of great epiphany or ecstasy but rather of feeling very much in the flow with life's design. In these moments, you were the truest version of yourself you could possibly be.

Common activities associated with feeling-mind moments include dance, creation in its myriad forms, gardening or connecting to the Earth, sexual union, and, for some, teaching or being in meaningful communion with others. Everyone's required conditions for experiencing this feeling-mind sensation are different, but these moments are invaluable clues to your soul's purpose. Once you understand these pivotal moments in your life chapters, trace the patterns within them and make note of common themes. Do you have a consistent reflection of sacred solitude in these moments? What elements from nature are emphasized? Tracking your feeling mind is a majestic act of self-study, and the darker times when, perhaps, there were entire life chapters without this in-the-flow sensation are just as telling as the joyous moments of ease and wonder. See if you can track five patterns in these moments of flow, these moments of grace and at-oneness.

Not forcing yourself to speculate on any other details about the yet-to-come, ask yourself this: *What is the title of the eleventh chapter, if it starts in this moment?* You do not need to be specific; a simple word will suffice. What chapter begins now and ends on some unknown, mysterious night in the future?

On your blank page or canvas, draw a circle at the center and write the title of your eleventh chapter inside it. If you feel so inclined, feel free to make this central circle symbolize the "forbidden fruit," giving it an apple shape, a red color, or another telling design element that speaks "passion" to you. Create five leaves or petals of similar size radiating around the circle. In these shapes, write your five patterns, coloring them a shade of green or another hue that symbolizes "homecoming," "the wilds," or "ground" to you. You might leave this drawing on your altar or in a wild sanctuary in your home until you have time to move on to part 2, or, if you have the time now, continue to root-scar exploration.

Part 2. Root Scars and Genuine Currencies

The root chakra is unique to every wild woman; it is an energetic, primal space wherein all beliefs about body, sustenance, home, finances, and survival reside. The root chakra's health is inextricably bound to a woman's felt sense of self-worth, her ability to stand on her own two feet and claim her right to take up space. The soul-wound of feminine spiritual oppression resides at the root as a resonating fear that may be small-voiced but persistent, and reflection on the liberation journey necessarily gives a nod to the fundamental role played by self-worth in the decision to escape from the garden.

Your sense of self-value, Priestess, is sourced directly from your soul-deep currencies. Just as money is nothing more than stored energy, you have a specific hierarchy of values that informs your self-esteem and, by extension, your spiritual agency. Common values wild women often share are creative expression, adventure, family, freedom, magick, and sustainability, though the range of values embodied by a Priestess is infinite, for she is the cosmic source of all things. Know that no woman will prioritize her values in the same way, though, with those from individualistic cultures having value systems that likely differ radically from those from collectivist cultures.

In reflecting specifically on a woman's Red Road journey, however, it is not what these values are that is as important as how authentically you believe you have the right to these deep currencies. For example, if I truly value freedom but pack my schedule to the brim so often that I am precluded from having any time to myself, any opportunities for travel, or anything else that makes me feel genuinely free, then there may be a root-chakral defect blocking my right to have what I crave most. Similarly, if I truly value groundedness and security but am constantly leaking my funds and succumbing to an unfruitful wanderlust, then I am engaging in a certain and sure self-sabotage.

Ask yourself what you value most. Ask your deep self to speak about the nature of your longing during your quietest moments, and then ask yourself whether you truly believe you have the right to satisfy those cravings. Dig down underneath the power leakages and misguided investments to make visible the gaps between what you have and what you hold dear.

Priestess, your truest values are tattooed on your bones. They incarnated into your body along with your soul's purpose, and they are clues to the role you play in this grand cosmic design.

The catalyst for your liberation was, and indeed always remains, a felt experience of the discrepancy between what you value most, what you get on your knees and pray for, and what you have. First, though, my love, *first*, you recognize your right to have what you value. There is a moment when the wild woman howls to the moon: *No. No, this is not good enough. I deserve better, and I want more.*

Ask yourself what you truly value, and see if you can trace seven core currencies you hold as your own. They might be time spent in nature, meaningful family connection, creative work, participation in social justice groups, environmental activism, movement alchemy, hedonism, or sensual nourishment. You know it is one of your core currencies if, when you lack this thing, you have a lower sense of self-worth, an embodied longing for that particular fulfillment only this currency could provide. Mind you, you do not feel that longing because you believe you should; you feel it because your soul thrives on, is fueled by, those truest values of yours.

Once you have identified those seven currencies, create seven serpentine loops around and between the five-petal layer of your drawing from part 1. There is no correct way to do this, and the artist can never betray her own art. However you create these snakelike curves or spirals, know it is perfect, and write your currency words here, inside these shapes. Choose a color that symbolizes "abundance" or "wealth" for this part of the design, and then draw a large, organically circular border around the entire work; color this border red to symbolize the Red Road. You may leave this drawing on your altar until you have time to return, or move on if you have the time and will.

Part 3. Opening to the Eleventh Chapter

Now, Priestess, knowing what it is you truly value, write a single pivotal scene in your eleventh chapter, the next chapter that you titled at the center of your artwork. Write this scene as if you were remembering a future full of feeling-mind moments. This is not a fluffy exercise in the Law of Attraction; it is a thorough examination of what is already yours and a written invocation to celebrate your own homecoming. Witches want proof their magick has merit, my love, and your lived experience is all the evidence you need.

Envision that key scene where you are truly living out your purpose, even if that purpose does not seem particularly productive by conventional definitions of success or achievement. Pay special attention, Priestess, to your moments of *bhava* and your values — both reflected in your work of art — and handcraft this scene precisely as you want to live it. Describe your feelings in this chapter in as much sensory detail as possible, and describe what your wild home looks like, whether it is a physical space or metaphorical way of being in the world. What conditions can you create in your life now that will support your feeling-mind experience, that purely present state during which you are both whole unto yourself and connected to all things? Most important, ask yourself this: *What gaps exist between me now and the me who is living that eleventh-chapter scene?*

Let these words be positive rather than negative. For instance, is the heroine who is living out the eleventh chapter more fearless? Joyous? Autonomous? Financially stable? The words that come to mind now should be akin to what you are looking to invoke. Once you have five to ten words that are also desires, inscribe these around the serpentine shapes, inside the red border of the circle. Use whatever colors feel right. Add any other symbols or sigils you work with, images from dreams that seem pertinent, or design elements that will complete your work of art, your Lilith mandala. Every word here should make you feel powerful, compel you toward sovereignty, and offer you a felt sense of selfhood and high worth. If you have time to move on to the fourth and final part of the spell, do so now and with a strong will and open heart.

Part 4. Mandala Blessing: Spoken Root Prayer for the Primitive Soul

During this final part of the spell, you will seal your magick and bless your art. To begin, ask yourself this: *Do I believe I have the right to be here, on this Earth?*

Do you believe that the ancestral inheritance of wisdom you have coming to you, running in your very blood, is your birthright? Deep-seated beliefs about your right to have what you want are buried in the red, raw space of Muladhara, or the root chakra. The spinal cord is one of the first structures to form in the womb, with the root chakra's physical location situated at the base of the spine and pelvic floor. Here in this round, red house, we contain the beliefs we learn as babes about how much safety and security we deserve, primal messages received from innumerable sources, including but not limited to the birth experience, the level of nurturing received from our primary care-givers, any physical traumas, dark fears and tempting desires from the col-lective unconscious, and memories from lives long gone. The feminine soul-wound sits here, compromising the very foundation of the chakral system until it is recognized for the beastly medicine that it is.

This healing practice is a body prayer to your self-worth. Claim your right to *have* with your whole body. Know yourself as Queen. Refuse to ac-cept the spiritual limits set upon you and infuse your garnet roots with a deeper understanding of who you are and what you, as the Goddess embodied, deserve.

Stand with your mandala at your feet, and cast a circle, if it is in your practice to do so, calling to all four directions, above, and below, and allow yourself to be the center point of all things right now, in this moment. Lift your pelvic floor up toward your heart by engaging the root muscles. Sink your consciousness low and pull your thinking mind down, down, and down further still until you can visualize your root chakra. Take notice of how the energy is moving, the colors that emanate from that space, and the size of this energetic wellspring. Keep your awareness anchored there at your root, and whisper aloud these prompting phrases, letting the root energy complete them with just a single word, long, verbose answers that seem endless, or any expressions in between. The root speaks in its own language, so listen without blocking any visions that come.

> I have the right to…
> I know for sure that home is…
> What I value most in the world is…
> I am soft skin around hard bones, and I feel…

These prompts are merely suggestions for giving the root chakra an opportunity to speak. Feel free to write your own introductory words, and tap into your root consciousness as needed. You, as the Priestess of the Wild Earth, house aches sourced not only from the loss of the divine feminine but also from the ailing planet, and giving the root a chance to speak is a step toward healing not only you but the very ills of this world. Raise energy in this way, speaking the red language of the root and tapping into the deepest and most primal part of your feminine soul.

Allow every word that ascends from the root and spills from your lips to bless the artwork at your feet, to empower you, and to affirm that you have the right to be here on this Earth. You have the right to hold in your hands what is most truly and genuinely yours, and you have the right, an ancestral birthright, to claim the life your soul designed for you before you were born into this body.

Stay here for as long as you have, and, when ready, place hands firmly on the ground, sending your particular medicine down deep into the bones of the Earth herself. Breathe from the lowest places in your body, and feel a kinship with your bloodlines. In this moment, you belong nowhere else but right here. Open the circle, if you had cast that boundary, offering gratitude to your guides and unseen cosmic energies for supporting you, and place your artwork somewhere precious, somewhere holy.

And so it is.

PATHWORKING IN THE UNDERWORLD: MEETING THE GODDESS BELOW

Building a respectful relationship with the Dark Goddesses, these Priestesses of the Underworld who share our wounds, means considering where and how their stories are *your* stories. The Goddess is not to be used, appropriated, or owned. She is to be met and met well, with a necessary reverence and wholeheart understanding that she is, after all, the embodiment of feminine power.

In this pathworking experience, I invite you to meet the Goddess of the Underworld as she shows herself to you, to envision her as you read these words, and to consider the lessons she has for you today. Know that were you to envision her tomorrow, she might show up for you much differently than she does at this moment. The messages you receive during pathworking experiences are those you are meant to receive in the moment rather than finite lessons that cannot be revisited. Sit comfortably, breathe, and open yourself to what comes.

Delve deeply into your wild psyche, my love, and envision these scenes while you read, very slowly, giving your psyche time to catch up with your reading. Imagine this journey with your eyes open and your will strong:

> Begin by descending a dark spiral staircase, your bare feet falling on cold stones and your way illuminated only by the single gently hissing, flickering torch you carry. On the walls you see ancient symbols you do not know and words in a language you do not speak, but there is something of the primal feminine about this place. Falling on your ears now are joyous cackles, guttural sobbing, enraged screaming, and lighthearted love songs — all manner of human emotion — floating up from below. You are not afraid, even as the stairs end and bright firelight glows from the temple space before you.
>
> Here, holy hellfire stretches in long flames from a pit at the room's center, a blaze you sense has been burning since the dawn of time. You are not alone here in this fire temple, with women of all ages, from all times and all cultures, moving about the space, some eyeing you with suspicion and others with great knowing compassion. These are the Keepers of the Earth-Fires, and from among these holy Priestesses steps the Goddess of the Underworld. You recognize her as their leader, for she radiates a particular intensity. She has been to hell and back many times over, and she is no flower-crowned Maiden of spring.
>
> Her skin is scarred, her hair is singed, and yet she remains unruined.
>
> "There is only one way out of here," the Goddess tells you.
>
> You look over your shoulder to find the staircase's entrance completely sealed with stone. You straighten your spine and hold your breath, waiting for her to gift you with her wisdom.
>
> "You must leap into the flames and trust you will not burn. You must risk all you have in the name of your soul's truth." The Goddess waves her hand to the crowd of women surrounding you.

"Many of these women have lived in this underworld for long years, whole lifetimes spent too afraid of letting their old selves die so their more soulful selves can be reborn. How long will you stay, Priestess?"

The heat of the fire is overwhelming. Sweat runs in salty rivulets into your eyes as you approach the flaming gate, but you are sure-footed and committed to your liberation. You can see how you might stay, not only out of trepidation but because the sisterhood bond is strong here. These fallen women were willingly staying in their depths because here, in this particular hell, they have found a kinship of the wounded, a coven of the scarred.

"Well? How long will you join us here?"

You answer her, as only you can. What do you say to the Goddess of the Underworld?

You might have longed to stay in your younger years, but your wise woman's psyche knows you have work to do on the topside world. The Goddess grins crookedly and nods in solidarity, approving of your bravehearted resolve. You look to her, clench your fists, and leap into the flames, vowing to let the fire be a crucible of hot and holy transformation, to transmute your rage and grief into empathy and gratitude. You are not sure how long you journey, for you remember little of the ascent, but you wake with newborn eyes open to a wilder world.

"I am returned," you say aloud. "I am returned more real than I have ever been."

And so it is.

BODY PRAYER OF THE SHADOW:
A MOVING-MAGICK PRACTICE OF INTEGRATION

Materials: *Music (optional)*

Like the myth of Persephone-Kore, Inanna's tale of descent is really a story of integration, as the Goddess must face her own dark side, fusing together parts of herself that had been fragmented in order to meaningfully heal. This body prayer can be done alone or in a circle of sisters; it is a moving ritual and living healer's spell through which you dance yourself open, confront your shadow, then return from the underworld a more whole version of yourself.

Ideally in a closed, dimly lit space or out in nature at night, begin by moving in a slow rhythm either to live drums or recorded music. You might find your shadow song and play it loudly or tune in to the rhythm of your heartbeat and move in time with your life's pulse. Consider the rhythm a resonance of the feminine divine that opens a holy gateway to the deepest parts of your soul. Even if you are with your sisters, dance for no one but you. This is your ritual of descent and return, and your body remembers the way. Move with lupine intelligence. Close your eyes if you must to keep your attention inward. Begin to feel that your shadow is ascending through your body, climbing your bones and moving into your heart space. Your shadow is everything you would swear you are not, everything you detest in other women; it reflects the most wounded parts of your soul, struck down and buried during childhood in the name of social acceptance.

Dance your shadow dance now, my love. How does your shadow move? What does it want? Descend into the muck of those parts of your psyche you labeled as bad when you were young and dig through them with your bare hands. Did you decide that your vulnerability was a fault and now you detest weakness and entitlement? Did you decide your right to rest was an illusion and now you detest laziness? Did you consider your natural childhood naïveté to be a downfall, so now your shadow is ignorance? Who is the shadow creature that lives within? Find her and dance wildly with her, for she has been caged for far too long.

When you feel the time is right, begin to integrate your shadow now by giving her permission to stay in the light, to fuse to your body and soul. Know that true shadow integration is a long and challenging process of many hard-won psychic battles, sudden and painful epiphanies, and angry resistance. This ritual is a symbolic action. Like the earth element, it is a place from which to begin. Dance the dance of integration until you can dance no longer, then rest a more organically soulful version of yourself. You are a Priestess of the Wild Earth, and you now find yourself on new ground.

And so it is.

PATHWORKING AND FORGIVING THE MAIDEN: RETURN TO THE UNDERWORLD-GARDEN

As you read these words, my love, hear the gravelly voice of a wise hooded Crone echoing from within your very bones. She is leading you through this meditation, walking with you as you honor your time in the underworld-garden as integral to your personal growth, a pivotal chapter in your story. Know forgiveness as a space maker, with any anger or resentment you feel toward yourself for spending time in the garden consuming valuable energy within your heart and soul. Know the forgiveness you direct toward yourself as vital medicine for the ailing feminine, and know the path as perfect, just as it is. Return to the garden now, Priestess, and let the old one hold your hand while you walk.

"Come with me, Maiden," she beckons, holding out her paper-skinned hand. "We must return to the place you rebelled against, so long ago."

In your mind's eye, you can see the landscape of your most recent garden, a place you knew to be safe for a time, where the masks you wore matched those of others and your wildness would have been shunned were you to show it too soon.

Go into your underworld-garden now, your Eden. Walk with your protectress, who will shield you with all the willful steadfastness of a wolf-mother. She is with you, and you are safe. There is no one else here. You can see the garden so clearly now, and you can feel it with all your senses. What colors are in this place? What sounds do you hear?

Give yourself some time to move around the garden freely, exploring the places you knew so well. Perhaps let your fingers begin to graze things you were not permitted to touch when you were there in your younger years. Imagine yourself breaking the rules of this place. Dance wildly, or proclaim your true name. Repeat these vows in your garden, as often as you like, as if they were a righteous mantra: *See me as I am. Hear me as I am. Know me as I am. Love me as I am.*

Now, bewitch this garden-hell from the inside out. Imagine now that the garden begins to change slightly, with the whole scene dimming as if the lights were being turned down. The garden becomes washed in gray light and, whatever the precise nature of your garden, even if it is an indoor space, let your Crone guide lead you to the Tree of Knowledge. Somewhere in your darkened garden, a bright, dewy tree now grows, and your wise woman will help you seek it out.

"I know the way, Priestess," she tells you, holding your hand as you move through the familiar space searching for something you have most certainly never seen in your garden before this moment.

When you find the tree, you will know it as the most beauteous, maternal, growing gift you have ever encountered. Though the garden is cast in a dull light, this tree is illuminated by the pink-gold of the abundant feminine. The leaves are vibrant, so emerald green that they seem to glow, and the bark on the thick trunk is knotted with age. The branches are bejeweled by fruit so flawless that their skin is tattooed with the ancient symbols of God-Goddess-Mystery.

This tree is a symbol of your holy awakening, my love. Its colors are the shades of your liberation, and its image is how your psyche has chosen to show you your own wild nature in this moment. Approach this tree now, Priestess, but move slowly. Trace the bark with your fingertips and inhale the heady scent of the forbidden fruit. When you feel ready, reach up and pick the most lustrous piece of sinful lusciousness you can find. Let your tongue run along its edges; then sink your teeth deep into the juicy grit of the Holy Wild.

Imagine you leave nothing. Devour it all. With every bite, imagine that the dark garden surrounding the tree becomes less tangible, disintegrating into thick, hot black smoke that hangs in the air around you. When you feel full and fed, inhale deeply and pull this black hot smoke into your lungs, exhaling with force and seeing it surround you once again. Now, inhale again, pulling the smoke inside your blessed body, but this time, dear one, you exhale a gray fog, cooler and less dense than the smoke you breathed in. Inhale this gray fog now and exhale a white cool mist. Inhale this white mist, exhaling pure diamond light.

Stay with this image now, Priestess, for you have transmuted your memories of the garden. Inhale the diamond-white light and exhale the diamond-white light, sinking into this rhythmic mantra. On the inhale, think the words *I am*, and on the exhale, think *forgiven*.

With every breath, absolve yourself of any guilt, any residual shame you harbor from your time spent here. You are guiltless grace. You can do no wrong, for you are the limitless, cosmic, infinite wonder that is the wild feminine. Let all become light now, my love. The Tree of Knowledge and your wise guide dissolve into the brilliance emanating from your being. Change your mantra now and repeat these words, inhaling *I am* and exhaling *wild*.

I am wild. You are wild. We are wild. She is wild.

And so it is.

EARTH REFLECTION AND FINAL PRAYER: EMBRACING THE BETWEEN TIMES

The Priestess of the Wild Earth comes home to the wilds over and over again, rebelling against the rules of her many gardens, outgrowing all too-small worlds as her own soul swells toward embodied fruition. At long last, we find our ground. We find our ground not knowing who we are for sure but knowing who we are most certainly *not*. There are many times in the life of the wild woman when her ground is anything but solid, when her touchstone floats on the surface of a great and mysterious sea rather than rests dependably on predictable ground; these are the between times, when the magick of transformation is strongest.

To connect the earth element to the water element, we must consider those garden departures, volatile as they may have been, as our earthen points of initiation. Here is where our journey begins. Without earth, our search for our wild homes becomes a directionless and impossible quest. Earth allows the Priestess to decide what is definitely not hers, those garden traits she no longer wants in her world, so those watery currents of her sensuality and emotionality carry her in the right direction. Should she begin to sink, she knows that she can only descend so far before the Earth will, yet again, hold her and gift her with solidity, reminding her that, when all else fails, the ground will catch her when she crumbles.

Lost Verses of the Holy Feminine: I Will Not Be Lost

The serpent was at once the mystery and the shadow. In that moment when her whole world hung in the balance, Lilith scried her future in its black-mirror eyes. She saw herself handcrafting a new life out of her crystalline passions and mud-brick talents; it was a life well worth the sacrifice of loneliness, grief, and rage, and she would risk everything and anything for such freedom.

Never had she known such bliss as she did gazing into the serpent's diamond-shaped mirrors-to-soul. Never had she wished so lustfully for any one thing. Lilith could not help herself then, and she forgot her childhood fears of abandonment, shunning all she had been taught was true, and kissed the snake's cool scales. She whisper-prayed an invocation, speaking into its skin:

"I know not where I belong, but I can no longer stay here. My time in the garden is over. With this serpentine kiss, I am reborn. Tonight, I will wander in the darkest desert, but I will not be lost."

And so it is.

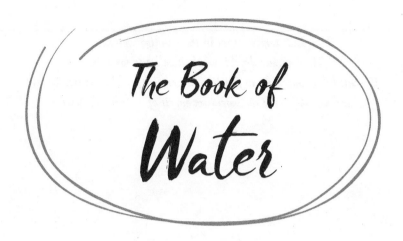

The Book of Water

The gifts of the water element are received through all our creaturely senses. If Earth is the place from which we rise, if the earth element serves as our ground and our initiation, then water is our embodied, sensual, moving prayer. Left to feel our feelings fully and take in all this wild world has to offer, our senses become gateways to knowing ourselves, to knowing our place in this great and elaborate collective into which we were born. Here, immersed in our depths, we are underwater mermaid explorers riding unseen currents, being tossed about by the torrents of our sexuality, tasked with surrendering to the fluidity and chaos while trusting that the joy and pleasure is here in the voyage itself, not some final blessed destination. Here, we swim and we coast, trying to stay afloat, then diving under again. Here, we learn to claim our bodies as our own alongside our right to feel it *all* if we choose, the to-the-bone chill of frigid, lonely seas and the warm and holy waters that all but enrapture us in a permanent ecstasy.

Wild Feminine Archetype: The Maiden of the Unbridled Sensual

Themes in Her-story: Calling joy home, reclamation of embodied feeling, honoring desire, awakening our wild art, hope and longing

Let's take a swim in these indigo waters.
Here, in our depths, we shall call our joy home.
We shall honor our right to feel like the sentient, wild creatures we are,
and we will show the world the merit of a woman's desire.

Chapter 4

Water Verses

The water element bids us surrender to embodied feeling, daring to taste all that is sweet and bitter about our worlds without denying ourselves the bliss offered by simply being in a human body. The Maiden of the Un-bridled Sensual archetype reflects back to us a deep knowing, a missing piece of grandmotherly wisdom that women are now tasked to learn themselves in a world where elders are denied their sovereignty and their rightful position as medicine keepers. This deep knowing that the currents of the water element move us toward, time and time again throughout our cycles of woundings and healings, is this: it is not only *possible* for a woman to seek pleasure, to claim her right to joyous and pan-sensory intimacy with her world, and still embody a mature, generative, and loving soul; it is absolutely *essential* to her own experi-ence of personal freedom.

Liberation takes many forms, but a wild woman's sensuality is often strongly connected to her sense of individual freedom. Just as the diversity of human experience precludes any single name for, or one true path toward, spirituality, no woman can impose on another a universal truth about what it means to be sensually free. In its most accessible definition, sensuality is how we autonomously experience the juice of life, and it is not to be confused with sexuality. A sensual woman is one who engages with her world through her body, through her skin and her tongue, using the sensory gifts she has been given in whatever way she chooses. Any societal limits on her sexual empowerment, emotional integrity, erotic innocence, or bodily autonomy are also constraints on her creative and spiritual experience. The Maiden of the Unbridled Sensual has the right to feel her feelings fully, to be a temptress to truth with slow-moving hips, to revel in the tactile, elemental sensations of chilly saltwater, subtle heat, and light wind, to taste poetry, and to drink in the heady scent that can only come from the rising dawn. She swims in the deep end, this Wild One, and she strives to be at home in her own skin, forever and always.

These Water Verses ask you to consider the relationship between your feeling body and your emotions, between your desire and your creativity, between your experiences of both freedom and joy. Read these verses knowing yourself as whole, trusting that your story is undergirded by the same themes shared by the women of your bloodline, full of faith that in moving toward your own healing, you are healing your ancestral wounds, those quintessential feminine wounds that have affected women since the Wheel of the Year began turning. Envision your many grandmothers joyfully splashing in freely flowing waters somewhere beyond the veil between the living and the honored dead. While you read, consider those fleeting moments of intimacy between your sensuality and your spirituality as passages of initiation, key places along the Red Road journey of continued soulful growth that these glorious Crones once enjoyed when their bodies were still breathing.

THE MAIDEN OF THE UNBRIDLED SENSUAL ARCHETYPE: CALLING HOME OUR AUTHENTIC JOY

The Pagan pantheon encompasses numerous Goddesses who wholly embody their authentic joy, though their myths are certainly not without moments of wounding. These incarnations of divine feminine light exude and reflect back to us the hopeful energy of the Maiden, that part of our wild psyches that demands to feel, to revel in the pleasures of the nature world, and to move the way a river moves, with much grace and power. The Maiden of the Unbridled Sensual lives in our most soulful memories of saltwater swims, a bite of food savored long on the tongue, the touch of an openhearted lover, and the heady scent of a lavender field in full summer bloom. She approaches her world with an intentional and conscious innocence, and, like the biblical Salome, she dances with the erotic and finds her power through movement.

In the New Testament of the Christian Bible, Salome, daughter of Herodias, is an immoral temptress who demands the head of John the Baptist. Her seven-veiled dance is described not in the Bible but in the late-nineteenth-century work of Oscar Wilde. In the Christian text, her dance is performed before men who were guests at a birthday celebration for King Herod. The king was so pleased by the dance, according to the scriptures, that he allowed Salome to ask for whatever she desired, with her consequent request being for the prophet's head on a platter, and "he did not want to refuse her."

The perception of the joyous feminine erotic as a particularly egregious sin is clearly visible in Salome's story. Given the historical context for the story, Salome was likely made to perform, with her bodily autonomy, at the very least, compromised by heavily patriarchal social norms. It is impossible to know whether Salome did, in fact, choose to perform for the male guests, how old she may have been, what level of agency she was granted in her father's household, or if she existed at all. What is known, however, is that Salome's name has been shamed and shunned. She has become the quintessential femme fatale, using her outward beauty and skills of seduction to incite the murder of a man believed to be holy.

The Goddess archetypes of the Norse Freya and Hindu Lalita reflect additional qualities of the sensuous Maiden. Freya is an incarnation of the feminine divine that is both powerful and sexual. In one of her myths, written or retold by Christian monks during the fourteenth century, Freya is framed as an immoral Goddess who has sex with demons in order to reclaim her prized necklace, but the wild woman could interpret her myth as one of soul retrieval, with Freya wielding her sexuality to reclaim pieces of her soul, as symbolized by a stolen necklace and protected by cave-dwelling creatures. She embodies true sexual empowerment seasoned with a good deal of ambition, and, unlike in Salome's ancient story, her sexuality does not need to be evaluated by men and judged to be sufficient in order to grant her what she desires. Freya uses her sexuality as a direct route toward reclaiming what is hers. Like magick, divination, and an understanding of the death-life-death cycle, feminine sexual power has been cast into the sinful shadows, but we find and reclaim this force within the archetypes of the wild feminine.

The Hindu Goddess Lalita is pure, unfiltered erotic innocence. She is a Tantrika, and a creatrix. In Tantric mythology, Lalita is a fully autonomous Goddess who is discerning in her partnerships and endlessly concerned with the larger story her sexuality is telling. One of the central lessons Lalita has for us is this: Allow the most meaningful relationships you have with others to be microcosms of the relationship you have with the world.

> *Allow the most meaningful relationships you have with others to be microcosms of the relationship you have with the world.*

Lalita reflects embodied, sensuously expressed love. She is also playful and joyous, a true incarnation of the dual energies of the sacral and heart chakras, and she has married her sexuality to her spirituality.

For the Maiden of the Unbridled Sensual, in all her many myths and incarnations, it is the wealth of gifts offered her by her feeling body that support her intimate communion with her world. For wild women, reclaiming the right to feel is essential to reclaiming our joy, with no one better positioned to tell us how or what we feel than us. Moments of joy are moments of coming home to the body, to the embodied experience of a fleeting but ecstatic emotion, a spiritual rite that shows us what it means to be alive, to be a creative soul embodied in a woman's skin.

Tell me, Priestess, where do you feel joy in your body? Let us begin here, with that lightness of being that comes from a joyful experience. If you feel that your ability to experience joy is constricted, laden by anxiety, stress, trauma, or years of no one validating your right to feel, then imagine stripping away these binds now, peeling them back and tossing them away. You are a Maiden of the Unbridled Sensual, and this is your story of calling your joy home.

Tale of the Prodigal Temptress: Revisioning Salome

Salome would not be made to perform. She had escaped from her patriarch's heavy-handed rule, claiming this small bit of time as her own and disguising herself in long veils so she would not be recognized as the infamous reckless princess. It was a long walk to the river's edge, and the new moon, the moon of the Maiden, had risen in the late-afternoon sky. The Red Road she walked along from the palace to the river had been rocky and wild, overgrown with untamed grasses and smelling of mud and blooming lotus flowers, but she did not spend the journey wondering what punishment she would receive for this transgression or contemplating what would happen if she were to be caught swimming without her father's permission. She vowed, with every footfall, to stay as present as possible, to let this time be a holy ritual in its own right and to be anchored to the moment by her very breath.

Salome had been called vicious, fragile, and entitled. Her skin had been marked bloody by those who claimed to love her, and her body had been overpowered by uninvited hands. With the river's rushing waters now in plain view, this Maiden of the Unbridled Sensual refused to let her scarred-over skin keep her from feeling all the textures the Holy Wild had to offer a sentient being. She deserved more than to survive, after all; she deserved to revel in the beauteous majesty of this world, not to just strike an uneasy peace with her body but to worship at its altar.

She owed no one her story, and she alone would decide when it was time to make her truths known. It had taken her an eternity to reach this point in her healing, to reclaim her joy, and, though much had been taken from her, no one could steal this moment away. Salome stood in the muddy water now, her feet sinking low as the sand surrendered to the weight of her, and she widened her stance in the most unladylike fashion. Certain she was alone, this defiant rebel unpinned the first veil, a thick and ruddy fabric that kept her breasts high but humbled her breath.

"I cast off the veil of good-girl perfection," she whispered without confidence, holding the heavy cloth in her hands and wondering if she was truly willing to let it go. In that moment, just before a long exhale, she questioned her right to be there, bare-breasted and vulnerable. She thought of the gaping mouths and furrowed brows, the lessons she had learned about being invisible and silent.

With her very next breath, she caught sight of an old water spirit, an aged mermaid resting her tired bones on a rock across the river. Her breasts hung low, and her wispy hair had long ago gone white, stretching down in thin, wet ribbons to her pink-blue scales. Bright tattoos of flowers and sacred symbols covered her aging skin, and glitter decorated her eyes and lips. The water faery was humming to herself, a low and gruff siren song of primal feminine wisdom, flipping her tail playfully in the water. Salome gasped, sensing a powerful, ancient vibration alive within the spirit, an embodied sensual freedom the young Maiden had never known until this moment. The Crone-Mermaid looked straight in Salome's eyes then, as if to ask, "Well? What are you waiting for, girl?" and jumped into the rushing river, creating a hefty splash and disappearing below the surface.

The Maiden's belly tightened with a primal feminine resolve. "I cast off the veil of good-girl purity and flawless perfection!" she wailed, clenching her fists, voice cracking from the guttural force of emotion rising from low in her body, and tossed the cloth in the water.

Heartened by the courage in her own voice, she began swaying her hips and snaking her long arms in all directions. She untied two veils wrapped so tightly around her wrists that they had left red indentations, made from a rough and knotted fabric that kept her heart from searching too hard for what it truly wanted and her hands from caressing her own soft skin. "I cast off the veil of boundarylessness, for not everyone is invited onto this holy ground that is my skin. I cast off the veil of guilt!" The fabric untwisted with the current when she tossed the veils in the water, and the Priestess watched them writhe like baby river serpents as the flow carried her binds away, leaving her to dance like a holy sorceress whose greatest magick was born of stirring the sacral well low within her pelvic bowl.

Salome cupped some water in her hands and baptized herself in the name of sacred sexuality. For the first time since she had learned what it meant to be a woman in her unforgiving world, this Priestess thought herself a royal ruler of her own body. Turning slowly and with much grace, she unwrapped a long silken veil from her waist. "I cast off the veil of sickeningly sweet surrender! This flesh, these bones are mine and mine alone!" The fabric bobbed along the river-bank in time with her heartbeat, and she swore she saw a small horned creature catch it in its teeth and drag it to the bottom.

She moved viciously now, splashing and bounding downstream and shrieking in sheer hedonistic delight. She unknotted two more veils from her hips and sent them off to drown. "I cast off the veil of original sin! I'm no humble object to be burdened with the collective human evil! I cast off the veil of God's judgment! I confess nothing to those who think me wicked, and I sever any ties to my bloodline that might keep me caged by propriety, morality, or laws written by men."

Salome was soaked, dripping with sweat, mud, and self-seduction. Only a single veil remained, but its knot was infuriatingly tight. The Maiden struggled and cursed in a fit of anxious panic, and her blas-phemous words were met with shocked gasps. She looked up from her work and saw she had traveled far from the isolated parts of the river, far from home, and far from who she used to be. Disdainful eyes scowled at her from all directions, and mothers covered their babes' eyes. These mocking monsters shamed her with their eyes and their whispers, and judgment washed over her in waves of harsh sound, these heavy sighs and murmured names that cut at her like daggers. "Slut" and "whore," they called her, and her wild heart all but stopped until she realized the words they were wielding as pitiful weapons held no meaning for her. This was not the Mother Tongue, and there was no room in the Goddess's lexicon for words that would demean a woman's sensual autonomy. She did not care to speak their language anymore, and their insults would not breach her newly built walls, strong boundaries around her feminine psyche that even the most scathing names could not crack.

She cackled and jutted her tongue at their gossiping whispers and peeled the last veil from her skin. "I cast off the veil of shame, you heartless creatures! Go ahead and call me 'demoness.' Say I'm a stain on my father's name! Ask me if I have no shame, and I'll answer you with heart and legs wide open." She crumpled the veil into a ball, shook the dripping thing at her gawkers, and tossed it straight at a regal man who likely claimed a high birth and a pompous infallibility.

The naked Priestess knelt in the water then, leaning back and letting the waters take her to a wilder place. Salome was aware of children running along the bank, following her — out of reverence or curiosity, she was not sure — but she fixed her eyes skyward to the pinkening dusk and swelling crescent that was the Maiden's moon. "This is my holiest day," she whispered. "I am unveiled, and I am awake. See me as I am now, for I am no longer the woman who will dance only to please. I demand the head of anyone who would wrap my wrists, and these haunted river lands shall be my new palace until I find a wilder home."

<hr />

THE HOLINESS OF OUR DESIRE:
HONORING OUR MOST SOULFUL WANTS

In the revisioned tale, Salome is vindicated, with her dance of the seven veils being a great unmasking, a self-designed ritual of embracing authenticity. She is the Maiden of the Unbridled Sensual because her body, as it unapologetically shakes in river water, is hers and hers alone. She becomes the unashamed feminine as she casts off the veils wrapped around her skin since girlhood. She releases traumas and sheds her body's memories of being owned: *"I cast off the veil of sickeningly sweet surrender! This flesh, these bones are mine and mine alone!"* Her desire is holy, because that desire is not for a man's head on a platter, as it is in the biblical version of her story, but rather for her true self to be revealed in all its heartbreakingly wounded glory, for society to reject its constant, tiresome emphasis on the toxic masculine intellect, to metaphorically remove the *head* and sink the collective consciousness down below into the body, into the Earth, down toward our most impassioned desires, where it is needed most.

Desire is primal. Desire is whole-body want, and desire is a yearning so formidable and precise that it is nearly a dream state, a vision of the yet-to-come so real that it is akin to faint but treasured memory. Priestess, consider your most soulful wants, those things you crave so fully that your blood runs hotter, those needs that, when left unfulfilled, manifest as a sultry, in-the-bones ache. The Red Road is not a path of renunciation, and the Witch never forsakes embodied experience in the name of spirituality.

The feminine learns to dam up its most visceral desires during childhood. Children tame themselves early to avoid punishment and to garner approval. During adolescence, wild desire burns so brightly in a body forced to sit still, compete, and open itself to judgment or rejection. In *Nature and the Human Soul*, Bill Plotkin calls adolescence the "Thespian at the Oasis" stage of life, wherein the "world fairly *explodes* for us with all this running about and erotic heat." In our age of body shaming, poor and insufficient sex education, and the distortion of women's sexuality in the media, so few of us are permitted the necessary opportunities to direct our own pleasurable experiences when we are young, to feel into our worlds as young women without fear of being admonished as too dirty or too pure, and to, like the Goddess Lalita, embody a connection between joyous sexuality and pleasurable, embodied love.

Sexual pleasure aside, the feminine dampens its desire regularly, out of a belly-born and ego-affected need to appear in control. As the Maiden of the Unbridled Sensual, you are worthy of having your desire be both acknowledged and fulfilled. In the revisioned story, Salome seeks out ceremony out of a desire for authenticity. Like Lilith, who risks social rejection and leaves the garden forever, Salome escapes her father's house and takes to the road, risking much shame and punishment in the name of liberation, and she enacts a spontaneously choreographed body prayer of awakening and release. As the wild Maiden, you are tasked with considering how your personal veils have obscured your unbridled sensuality, left your desires unquenched, and kept you tethered to "good-girl perfection." You are tasked with considering how your desire is the stuff of prayer, in many ways the holiest feeling the feminine can experience now, when the world is in dire need of our medicine.

Handwritten Verses: A Personal Myth of Desire Reborn

Priestess, revisit a time in your life when you were positively on fire for something — be it a person, a charming art that bewitched you in the act of creation, a material acquisition or quest for abundance, your sacred work, or any other great want that was, if only for a time, all-consuming. How was your desire validated or rejected by those in your inner circle? How did it feel to be so turned on? What indoctrinated beliefs did you harbor about your right to want, and was that desire allowed to come to fruition? Why or why not?

You are the Maiden of the Unbridled Sensual, and this is your story. You may use the prompts I offer here or create your own, but let your story be a myth of personal desire fulfilled. Even if the actual events left you burning, even if you dimmed your wild out of self-preservation, even if another person in your life shunned your longing, rewrite your story as if your primal, gut-sourced desire had been fulfilled.

Part I: Welcome to the Age of My Longing

Welcome to the Age of My Longing. It began as a so-subtle stirring,
        a barely sensed but persistent pulsation that...
Desire lived in my body now, and I swear that I could feel...
Soon, I couldn't sleep without thinking about the luscious...

Part II: Whole-Heart Satiation

I refused to sit down and languish in a fire of my own making, so...
Such immense, majestic satisfaction came from...
I poured sweet nectar all over my...
I baptized myself in the name of...
I had never been so present, so complete, and so in the flow; it was...

Part III: Swimming under the Dark Moon

I let go, and...
My desire cooled slowly, and with time I was...
I swam under the waning moon, welcoming the void and knowing...

When a woman writes stories of her desire, she honors her longing and validates it as integral to the feminine experience. Write the stories they would call vulgar. Tell tales of the divinely obscene. Upon the descent, hand-mine rituals of desire reclamation out of times in your life when you dismissed what you truly wanted so you would not be called selfish, too much, aggressive, or arrogant; these are qualities heralded in the toxic masculine but condemned in the feminine. Write stories of the joyous and wild body, my love, and let the shock of the language run through you like lightning sent straight from the underworld by Inanna's womb. May these new myths form a firmer foundation over which the unbridled sensual, as you embody it now, can flow freely and with a forceful current.

Come to the Waters, Priestess of the Holy Obscene: *Psalm of Wild Longing*

Come to the water with me, Wild One! Bear witness to my Baptism by Nectar, and I promise you will never be the same! I've filled a bejeweled pitcher with the lush and tender guts of one thousand honeysuckle flowers, and I've left behind the names I was given and the dreams that died in the cocoon long before they were born. I am initiating myself in the name of erotic righteousness. I am spitting on those who think me vulgar and shameful, and I am pouring slow-running, thick syrup on those thirsty, cobwebbed places that have gone unlicked for far too long.

I've plenty of juice for you, too, my love. Let's be epic and get some sunlight on our shadowy parts. Let's be mermaid-selkies and spiral dance underwater bare-breasted and with more grace than the suit-and-ties could handle. Let's do things that make the demure Madonnas blush, and let them call us wicked Witches who have made a blasphemous covenant with a sly underwater sea demon.

I'm through with the monotonous, heady chants and sterile, still-bodied ceremonies! My house is dark and missing an ocean, and I'm craving salt-crusted skin and simple ritual. I've burned my last candle, and I've prayed my last spell. These are the longer days when spirits are quiet and my will is so strong that it could set fire to the iciest heart. I am the whole of summer embodied in the freckled, soft skin of a wild woman, and I've got a fire raging in my pelvic bowl that will not be doused by any insult or trickery.

Just for today, let's be Priestesses of the holy obscene. I've got some tales to tell that are too good to keep secret; let's write of our debauchery in a new scripture where the verses speak of hard-nippled freedom and hedonistic revelry. Our parables will be recited by snick-ering full-breasted grandmothers after the little ones are in bed, and our words will be so luscious and vibrant that they will make the blindly faithful and always pious question their loyalty to their venge-ful gods.

This is my Baptism by Nectar, and you are cordially invited; there's no other face I'd rather see when I blink my eyes through the sticky flower essence as it cleanses away my too-rigid, outmoded ideas about what liberation looks like. I'm not who I was in the winter, wise Sister, and nor are you. Let's take to the frigid water as thick-skinned sirens who are being reborn under the late-spring sun, and let's remember how to be playful, joyous Maidens who splash and shriek without fear of waking the tamed, bitter ones.

Leave your wand and your crystals, love; you won't need them where we're going. Forgive me, but today our bodies are the spell and the water is the altar. We are the living Craft, and we answer to no one claiming a higher holiness.

Hold my hand, and stand in the shallows with me, woman. Tilt your head sunward and hold your breath. With this sweet succulence, you are reborn anew. This is still your year, Witch, and I am in love with your magick and mystery. Dive beneath these gray-green waters now and resurface a wilder version of yourself. Tell me a dirty joke, then, lest we take ourselves too seriously, and let's search for shells until midnight comes and the moon beckons us to sleep where night visions of the pleasure-filled yet-to-come abound behind our eyelids.

Come closer, love. I want to hear your heartbeat. Thank you for spending this watery holiday with me. I'm not sure what came over me, but I grow so weary of dry land when the days grow warmer. Some part of my soul — the better part, I think — remembers how to live underwater, beneath the too-fast surface of the topside world, but I don't always like venturing into my depths alone. You are the perfect deep-sea companion, Witch-Lover, and I am blessed to know you no matter the season. Tomorrow, we shall return to our workaday lives and speak of grand plans, budgets, and activism, but, for now, I am reveling in the afterglow of our self-designed so-sweet, so-simple ceremony.

I hope I haven't taken up too much of your time, my love, but what's one day spent in sacred swimming within a whole life of being land bound? What's one day lost in the name of whole-body, whole-spirit renewal? I remember who I am now, thanks to you, and I can return to my bed in the morning with suppler skin and wet lips. We don't need to tell anyone, either. Witches have always had secrets, after all. Just raise a brow and smirk in my direction, and I'll know you're remembering our day spent wild, our twin baptisms, and our noon-to-midnight journey from parched to perfect.

Blessed be you, sweet one, and blessed be the Holy Wild.

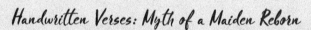

Handwritten Verses: Myth of a Maiden Reborn

I want to recite your verses now, my love. I want to read your holy book. Tell your story the way only you can tell it, and I promise not to change a single word when I carve your words into stone tablets and descend from the mountaintop to gift your wisdom to the saintly and sinful masses. You may use the prompts I offer here or create your own, but know that you are a mythic heroine whose journey is just beginning, whose wounds are shared by many, and whose courage is unparalleled.

Chapter 1: The Babe Wore Many Veils

The little Wild One learned to mask all that was…
She wrapped her wild well, with…
She had all but forgotten who she was by the time she reached…

Chapter 2: The Temple Dancer's Darkness

She learned how to perform by…
Their approval made her feel…
The descent happened quite…

Chapter 3: A Many-Armed Goddess, She Was

The red sun rose on the day of...

She laid out a feast in her own honor, and she sang hymns of...

A many-armed Goddess, she was, and she named herself...

Chapter 4: Wild Healer, Wound Gazer

She leaned over the ridges of torn skin to look deep into...

The wound was not as she remembered it; it was...

In order to finally begin healing what had festered for so long, she began...

Chapter 5: The Maiden of the Unbridled Sensual

She was a Maiden of the Unbridled Sensual now, and...

She cast off the too-tight veils of...

She danced alone in the dark, and it was a dance of...

Your story is worthy of writing, dear Priestess, for it is the story of the wild feminine. Your experiences live within us all, vibrating in all our cells and feeding the collective womb with love, joy, pain, numbness, ecstasy, and much, much grace. Read through your myth often; grant yourself permission to edit out what no longer feels true to your story and infuse the chapters with greater meaning as you evolve.

Personal myths are meaning makers, a way of forging psychic connections between the past, present, and future. The best personal myth writing feels liberating rather than confining, both in the practice and in the revisiting, and, should it feel right, I encourage you to share your story with those who will hold space for you to heal through that telling. Know this, though: You are to share your writing only if it feels right. In the revisioned tale, Salome understood that *she owed no one her story, and she alone would decide when it was time to make her truths known.* Your story is precious curriculum, and you choose who is worthy of learning your hard-won lessons.

OUR WILD ART AND UNBRIDLED SENSUALITY:
EMBODYING THE CRONE-MERMAID

To be human is to be tasked to create. We are born with the capacity to feel deeply for a reason, with the instinct to make something new out of the old and birth some great majesty from the union between body and imagination. To place restrictions on a woman's sensuality is also to restrain her creativity, and the Maiden of the Unbridled Sensual has awakened her art through whole-body feeling and the continual validation of her emotions.

In Salome's revisioned tale, the Crone-Mermaid grants the Maiden permission with only a single glance. This odd creature symbolizes the union of playful creativity with seasoned, grandmotherly wisdom. She is the ultimate creatrix, a living and joyous work of art who is the knowing elder. Her very presence as a witness to the beginnings of Salome's self-designed ceremony is heartening, spurring the Maiden forward and reflecting back to her this truth: She is the living, breathing antidote to all that would poison the creative and sensual empowerment of the feminine.

We all have an art that is ours, an embodied action that is generative, that awakens us, shakes us, and *makes* us as much as we make it. To create is to be brave, to move beyond the fear of ruining the blank canvas, the white screen, the onstage performance, or the shower song. To create is to be sensually alive, to face all our demons in a single creative action, and to harvest the shadows that we ourselves had buried deep within our psyches. All art is born of the fertile waters of passion and pain, and the Maiden of the Unbridled Sensual has been initiated into the tribe of warrior creators, makers of the heathen art and poetesses of the wild word.

Freya's Battle of the Beasts:
Communing with the Artist's Underwater Shadow

Ah, here I am, finally.

I've come, at long last, to the mouth of this primeval cave where the four hungry and licentious demons reside, their clawed fingers embedded deeply into all my protective totems, into every shield I thought would preserve my safety in this life and the next. I don't know what prompted the deception, the great betrayal that robbed me of my sense of self-worth, but I know that now I cannot turn away from the arduous task of reclaiming my dark, lest my art be forever starved, lest my sexuality remain forever frozen.

My bones are aching and shaking. I am entering the Earth's musty womb now, and I see the red eyes of the ghost of the north. She bids me turn back and leave her be. She tells me I lack control and am destined for failure, and she mocks my passion.

"Just who do you think you are?" she asks.

I crouch to all fours like the stalking huntress I am and take her down, bare hands clinging to her veiny throat and vicious mouth spitting straight into her judgmental eyes. Good riddance! This brave heart is mine! I have reclaimed my wild maturity now, my feminine fortitude, and my soul-born courage to find my purpose and let it drive my sacred work to the truest north.

Alas, my celebration is short-lived, for now I must fight the ghost of the east, the white-robed guru who thinks me weak and ego bound, the condescending spiritual vampire who wants to drain me dry and keep me addicted to a distant God. Ha! He tells me my sense of separation is meaningless, for unity is all that is real, but I stand rock-steady on the ancient ground and tell him of my selfhood and my soul-sourced integrity. I speak of my sovereignty. I tell him of the merit of descent, and he shrinks to dust with every affirmation of my body's holiness. This body is mine, and it is holy. I have reclaimed my inner divinity now, my blessed birthright and Earth-sanctioned mandate to be whole unto myself and pray with the body divine.

The air in the space is suffocating now with heat and wild hellfire. The walls are ablaze with an untamed bloodlust, and I worry I've come too far just as the ghost of the south springs forth with blades drawn and wings spread. She tells me my blood is dirty, and my flesh is flawed. "Have you no shame?" she asks. She speaks of shameful encounters I thought were long gone, and she shows me visions of more sacral woundings than I deserved.

I am undone. I fall to my knees and am about to claim defeat, to take my gifts from the north and east and turn homeward, when I feel spectral hands lifting me to my feet. I sense the grandmothers of my line holding me upright when all I want is to sink down, and I find the courage to speak of my truest currencies.

"Listen to me, you beast!" I tell the ghost; my rage is righteous and my body is mine and mine alone. I tell the wild temptress that her blades are not sharp enough to pierce my ever-shielded, always-unruined heart, and I take her down with a single upward flick of my tongue. I have reclaimed my holy lust, my right to dance, and my skin's sacred autonomy. This boiling blood is mine.

The flames cool, and I walk long into the icy depths, long into silence and solitude. I know that the three ghosts I have conquered thus far are nothing compared to the last shadowy elemental of the west, who knows the deepest parts of me, the darkness so hidden that I myself forget its name. I shudder, sure I hear a low whisper-hiss calling me, but find it is only a slow-moving underground river rushing lightly over obsidian. I wait, aware of the nonsensical comfort of this place, but soon lay eyes on my final foe. She ascends from the water like a black-eyed cave selkie, and she reminds me of every lie I ever told, shows me every face I betrayed and brought to tears, and threatens to tell the world my most shameful secrets. She tells me I could never be elevated, never praised for my art, never lifted into the public eye, for then all would be revealed. I would be exposed, and I would be exiled onto a faraway island like a soul criminal.

"You will be seen," she vows, and her threat is the most terrible one I've heard in all my years, for it speaks straight to my soul's greatest obstacle.

I do fear being seen. I fear judgment, and I fear being called fraud, fake, and phony. I fear all that comes from doing my sacred work in the world, and I've let that fear keep me quiet and my art unknown.

My muscles grip my bones, and I wonder if death is easier than fighting this shadow. I start softly, speaking of my muse and beauty, then I raise my voice and howl to the cave creatures that I am worth more than to muddle through and pedal on. I am the vital creatrix with a painted face, and I am not going home without reclaiming all that has been stolen.

"I demand you return my hidden wounds and sequestered shadows!" I bellow. "Give me back my right to be seen and heard!" I demand, and she crumbles into a slippery heap of leathery skin and oil-bubbled water.

It is done. This voice is mine.

I have not reclaimed all that was lost, but I've recovered enough of my buried treasure to continue on, to persist, and to bewitch this world with my art.

And so it is.

Handwritten Verses: The Watercolor Portrait of a Heathen

You have already imagined your life as an epic novel, my love. Now, imagine you, at this very moment in time, as a beauteous watercolor portrait. Describe this painting, using the prompts I offer here or your own, and consider this artwork a visual and vibrant reflection of your joys and your sorrows, your many pleasures and melancholies. Here, in this moment, you are the Crone-Mermaid, a wise and painted creature who has learned much in her long years swimming in the deep blue mystery.

> This painting is of a woman who...
> Her eyes are like...
> She seems to know exactly what...
> I would title this painting "The Heathen Who..."
> My wish for this woman is...

Of course, even the most skilled artist could not do justice to the breathing beauty that is you, but, if you feel called, create this artwork now, either by a simple line drawing in your journal or in a more elaborate form. Perhaps let this simple practice be the beginnings of reclaiming your artistry, of rekindling your creatrix flames.

THE MAIDEN'S MOON:
HOPE AND LONGING AT THE WATER'S EDGE

The new moon is a symbol of the Maiden, a lunar promise of hopeful be-ginnings, a monthly reminder that we, too, can be reborn. We, too, can shed the skins that no longer warm us, the masks that no longer fit, and the veils that hide our worth. Whatever other names we might give to our longing, we all yearn for embodied presence. We have all caught fleeting glimpses of that particular bliss awarded us only when our souls, bodies, minds, and spirits have been bound together in joy, and we have all stood at the water's edge, like Salome, wondering whether we had the power to give ourselves permission to dive in, to untie the tethers wrapped around our limbs by someone else's hand. The new moon is a cyclical vow made from the wild feminine to our heathen souls that whatever missteps we may have made in our past, whatever wounds have been carved into our flesh, we can rechristen ourselves with the holy water of our tears and begin again, at long last.

Chapter 5

Water Rituals

Rituals require the presence of our entire being, with ceremonies invoking the water element, in particular, asking us to show up with our whole body and whole soul. In the revisioning of Salome's story, the Maiden creates her own ritual of healing, unmasking, and rebirth. The water in her story is a great purifier, a symbolic and elemental force that both washes away the old and blesses the new, a rushing force that carries away the ties that bind to an unknown destination, a moving mystery that welcomes Salome, that invites her to stay and cleanse all that no longer serves the Priestess she has become.

Such water rituals are often joyous, with the sensuality of water begging us to not take ourselves too seriously. We must have joy in our Craft. We must be gifted with that sensuous elation from time to time, lest our rituals become stagnant and dry. Water infuses all it touches with liquid innocence, and, when engaged with the water element, we are tasked with approaching our healing and our magick from a place of newness and curiosity, to not fall into our overdried patterning or become anchored to all we think we know. To be in water is to move with it, to surrender, and to know embodied feeling.

The seven water rituals I offer in this chapter are intended to be tailored to your Craft by you. There are certain rituals that can be carried out in groups or as solitary ceremonies where your healing is witnessed by you and you alone. Be true to yourself, Witch, and remember the blood union between you and your ancestors; your healing is their healing, and your joy is their joy.

THE TEMPLE OF THE MAIDEN'S BODY: FOUR SEASONAL RITUALS FOR RECLAIMING WORTH

A woman's inner Maiden lives within her lower two chakras, with the energies of the root and sacral chakras informed by deep-seated childhood experiences, passions and convictions developed later in life, and woundings born of relationships, media messages, and innumerable forces emergent from a socioeconomic context wherein the Maiden-self has little value. When we speak of passion and pleasure, it is the sacral chakra that is most pertinent, for here, in that spiraling energetic center between her hip bones, a woman harbors her emotional integrity, sexual power, and sensual autonomy. When a woman's right to move and feel is invalidated in her youngest years, she learns to dim her inner Maiden, to keep her contained in a dark corner of her psyche where she will not be tempted to burst forth, and to quiet the capabilities of her senses, her sense-using and sense-making ways, enough that she will not be labeled with any number of patriarchal slurs used to keep the feminine disempowered by backward notions of purity.

In the revisioned tale, Salome casts off the veils used to disguise her wild. She does this while dancing in river water, and she does this as a self-designed ceremony of bond-breaking and joyous celebration of her sensual freedom. The Maiden of the Unbridled Sensual is the aspect of the wild feminine that makes sense of her world by joyously feeling her way through it.

She craves hot and holy pleasure, untamed movement, and bodily autonomy, and this hunger does not wholly self-abate even within a society built to keep the Maiden weak, visually pleasing, and ineffectual. Society takes the Maiden's power away by oversexualizing her, forcing her to perform, and demeaning her sensuality and creativity.

We repower the Maiden by seeking out her wisdom, and we learn much about our inner Maidens by exploring their relationship to our inner Mothers and Crones. Within the context of this Triple Goddess metaphor, the Maiden is the least socially acceptable archetype, and the Mother is, while hardly untethered to patriarchal expectations, the most socially acceptable.

The feminine's inner Mother is a healer, a creatrix, a nurturer; she is always producing something, and, through her tireless productivity, she is seen as a positive procreative force. The Maiden, quite conversely, is a passionately present creature who is highly individualistic and lives for the moment. The Maiden is at home in nature and is the quintessential wild woman. The Maiden's lack of socially meaningful productive behavior; sex for the sake of pleasure, not procreation; and strong sense of selfhood make these aspects of the feminine psyche vulnerable to subjugation.

The Maiden does not fit neatly into any predictable social role, and, like the Crone, she is therefore dismissed by any number of derogatory labels. The Crone differs from the Mother, too, in that she is sternly wise, content to be intuitive and still, and she is often alone. The Crone is the intuitive prophet within us who appears irrational and reclusive to the skeptical eye. Neither the Crone nor the Maiden is a good-girl producer and consumer; they are the aspects of the wild feminine that the uninitiated masculine seeks to oppress most fervently. Their lack of economic viability renders the Maiden and the Crone useless to capitalism and therefore in need of domination according to the ruling socioeconomic system. Our inner Maidens are oversexualized, robbed of their embodied power, and left to take refuge in the darkest corners of our psyches.

The child who is raised within our modern hyperspeed world learns to suppress the sensual Maiden; to impose strict limits on authentic pleasure; and to essentially sit still, be physically bound while mentally fragmented and scattered, and live more in the mind than the body. Keeping thoughts active and the body still is the catalyzing action for a great and common Maiden wound, for this encourages a continued socially applauded body-mind separation. This is the same body-mind split that serves as the foundation for most major religions wherein the flesh is inferior to the intellect and the quite tangible Earth is only a pale reflection of an invisible heaven. Transcendence of the body is rewarded, while joy in the body is sinful.

A woman's capacity for joy poses a threat to all mechanisms of oppression because if she, and she alone, has the power to experience pleasure and satisfaction, she does not need to search externally for fulfillment. Audre Lorde writes in her essay "Uses of the Erotic" that "this is one reason why the erotic is so feared, and so often relegated to the bedroom alone, when it is recognized at all. For once we begin to feel deeply all the aspects of our lives, we begin to demand from ourselves and from our life-pursuits that they feel in accordance with that joy which we know ourselves to be capable of." The Maiden wants to continually feel, and feel joyously, with her whole soul, body, mind, and higher self. There is no separation for her between nature and spirit, and healing our Maiden wounds means fiercely cultivating this holistic, whole-being connection as often as possible.

To begin these rituals, know the feminine as potent and powerful as much as it is graceful and serene. The Maiden takes what is hers and surrenders to no one. The Maiden knows her body as temple, with any controversies surrounding, or external claims on, that holy land being absolutely meaningless, for she is the keeper of her skin's sanctified ground. Take to this ritual not as sanctuary but as a vicious affirmation of your body's worth and autonomy. This ritual is not an escape. This is a righteous proclamation of the blood-and-bones majesty that is you.

As the Wheel of the Year turns, the feminine cycles through us in time with nature's rhythms. You are the Maiden of the Unbridled Sensual no matter the Earth's tilt, so honor your body as a vital cell in the great cosmic organism that is Gaia. As close to the equinoxes and solstices as possible, stand naked as a newborn in a wild place where you feel safe; this need not be out of doors, as not all of us were blessed with access to isolated land. You may be behind a locked door in your bedroom, standing in a steaming shower, or unapologetically bare-breasted in the kitchen. The place matters not, for you are at home in your body wherever you go, carrying an inner well-tended, ever-glowing altar behind your ribs.

1. Winter Solstice: Honoring the Bones

Materials: *Four candles, earthen oil (see suggestions below)*

Winter solstice is a time of sinking back into the cosmic source, of nesting and resting, and of honoring the fertile darkness. Stand and surround your body with at least four candles, but use more if you desire. Plant your feet so firmly on the ground that you can feel the bones of your feet digging deep. Visualize hungry roots sprouting from the soles of your feet, sinking through any human-made materials easily and finding the soil below. Point your fingertips straight down, and spread your fingers wide. When you feel ready, proclaim these affirmations as loudly as you are able, or spontaneously speak others that feel more authentic and true:

> I am the wild feminine embodied in the soft skin of a woman. These are my bones, spiraling in sacred shapes and floating beauteously within my pranic body. I am the Crone with tough skin and farseeing eyes. On this solstice, when the nights are long, the food is hot, and the hopeful fires burn, I am declaring my body a holy temple. I am a hooded Priestess trekking through snows and heading north. I am a wise medicine keeper brewing a salve for the ailing world, and I am soaking up the magick of this Earth through the bottoms of my bare feet. This body is mine and mine alone.

Return your body to a softer shape when you are ready, but keep the candles burning for as long as you are able. Anoint your feet with an oil of your choice, perhaps primal vetiver or earthy sandalwood. Feel your affirmations echoing in your very cells. Know them as branded on your bones, and nourish your luscious flesh now with whatever it craves.

2. Spring Equinox: Honoring the Blood

Materials: *Pillows, a few tablespoons of rose oil or water from a natural source, rose or calendula petals (optional), mead or sweet tea*

The spring equinox is the peak of Maiden time, a potent beginning of the perfect season for manifestation magick and sensual empowerment. Position your body this way if you are able: Sit cross-legged with a blanket or other type of bolster rolled beneath your sacrum so your hips are slightly higher than your knees and the soles of the feet are touching; if this is uncomfortable, you can place small pillows beneath both knees or just sit comfortably, holding your body in its preferred position. Breathe deeply.

Sink into the perfection that is you. Roll your tongue along the inside of your mouth, and shift your spine slightly from side to side. This is the season of sensual freedom, and your body is a feeling organism. When you feel ready, begin blessing your body with the oil or water; there is no precise order to move through — just offer gratitude to each bit of skin terrain you touch, speaking these affirmations or spontaneously offering your own:

> I am the wild feminine embodied in the soft skin of a woman. My blood is the rivers of the Earth, the musky wet on my thighs holy water from a mountain spring, and my sweat the warm pool of a desert oasis. I am the wide-hipped and full-lipped Maiden, and this blood is mine. On these damp days, I claim my right to feel pleasure. I claim my right to feel passion, and I claim my right to walk within the fertile Mystery. I will climb trees and lick their bark. I will plant seeds and offer them the benediction that is my breath. I am a flower-crowned temple Priestess dancing her way east, and I am drinking of the succulent moon through this sacred gateway between my legs. This body is mine and mine alone.

Seal your ritual by arching your back and lifting your heart skyward, in-haling deeply and exhaling as if you were breathing whole gardens to life. Take a ritual bath if you are able, gifting yourself with the scent of rose petals and calendula flowers. Drink mead or sweet tea, and dream of the yet-to-come.

3. Summer Solstice: Honoring the Belly Fire

Summer solstice is the time of fruition and gratitude, when we are tasked with burning as brightly as the sun and claiming what is ours. For this ritual, make the outside world as silent as possible on these brightest days; this is so you can hear your inner rhythm, the soft drum of your heart and the low, thrumming pulsation of your blood. Let this rhythm rise within you now. Begin to move infinitesimally to your personal body song, then let the righteous beat start to consume you. Stomp your feet and swing your hips. Howl-shout these affir-mations or others of your own design while you move, blessing your agency, selfhood, and will:

> I am the wild feminine embodied in the soft skin of a woman. My belly fire burns bright like a god-star. My guts are molten lava, and my will is a volatile, full crucible poised for a timely eruption. My arms are long, and my voice is loud. Feel the heat of me! This is the

Summer of the Wild Witch, and my body is built from star-stuff. I am here. I am staying. I am here. I am staying. I am here. I am staying. I am the painted, hooded Priestess marching her way south, followed by her kin, and leaving a blazing trail in her wake. This body is mine and mine alone.

Summer is the season of hedonistic delight. Spend as long as you have feeding your inner heathen. Swim in an ocean, lake, or river. Get some sunlight on your shadowy parts. Be epic, and revel in this time of high-fire fruition with all that you are.

4. Autumn Equinox: Honoring the Eyes

At the autumn equinox, we begin to enter the season of the Crone. The veil between worlds is thinning now, my love, and you are the oracle who can see in the dark. If possible, be in an unlit room or safe outdoor space where the moonlight is shaded and the spirits' voices can echo freely without competing with the hum of electricity. Let your body be soft and comfortable so you may surrender your heavy physicality just for a time; lean against a wall or tree trunk, lie on the grass, or cushion yourself with soft bolsters. Melt into an ethereal state now, honoring your right to see what others cannot. You may use these affirmations or speak your own, whispering a blessing to your highest-frequency self:

> I am the wild feminine embodied in the soft skin of a woman. Blessed be my eyes, for they show me much on these shorter days and haunted nights. They are windows to my soul, these two black-mirror orbs, and I am in love with their clairvoyance. I am softening my gaze and looking to the subtle vibrations. I am losing focus on hard edges and bright colors to see the quieter side of the world, and I am bidding the magick to consume me now. I do not fear death. I am the antler-crowned Priestess headed west with a long walking stick and the Mystery packed in her bag. This body is mine and mine alone.

Spend as long as you have in your holy place, wherever it may be. Offer gratitude to your ancestors for gifting you with your most soulful skills. Commune with those who have crossed over, your ancestral guides, and trust in the wisdom they have for you now under the harvest moon. And so it is.

SACRAL HEALING THROUGH INTEGRATION:
RITUAL BODY PRAYERS FOR THE ENERGETIC WOMB

Materials: *Just you and your wild heart*

The feminine womb resides within the collective unconscious as much as it does within the physical body, my love. You most certainly do not need to be born and named female, as there are many who are misgendered at birth, or to have retained an intact womb to experience divine feminine awakening. The energetic womb lives within us all, regardless of gender; it is a holy, dark space that is the very primordial center of death and birth.

You must descend into the energetic womb often in order to clear out the invisible demons who have taken up residence there in your sacral center. You must look into your own dark in order to integrate the wounds left festering from childhood, and, while you must always know yourself as completely whole, you can never claim to be completely and irrevocably *healed*.

Healing, after all, is an eternal process of unburying parts of ourselves we were taught to ignore, taught to discount as shameful. To heal is not to fix. All healing is a cyclical process of awareness and integration, and the Priestess knows this well. Even those with the strongest shields will ultimately be wounded again and again, as to protect oneself from wounding completely means being completely invulnerable, which is, in itself, a deep and bloody mark on the wild heart.

To descend into the energetic womb is to willingly look under the masks we wear every day to see our true face. There, in the fertile dark that is the very source of life and death, we come face-to-face with all the ghosts that still haunt us, all the indoctrinated beliefs about our sexuality and bodily autonomy, every snide remark ever said about our worth, and each stored memory about what a good girl does and who she should be. This work is not easy. It is the soul-work of the wounded Maiden, the task of the wild healer who is through looking to others to cure what ails her.

Priestess, on the cusp of the new moon, find a dark sanctuary you can call your own. Place your left hand low on your sacral chakra, between the hip bones, and speak these words aloud and with much ferocity:

This is the poetry of the primal feminine dark. This is an ode to the black-hole void from which we all emerged, covered in the blood of the ancients and wailing against the too-bright light of the human world. This is an epic eviction notice to all unwanted memories stored in my holy cells, and this is a permission slip written in my own hand to the young Wild One I once was: "You are a wild child, dear one, and you are ever loved."

These words belong to no one, for they are tattooed on the bones of the Earth. The rhythm of these lines beats in time with the pranic pulse of the universal heart, so hear me while I speak in the Mother Tongue of the ethereal infinite. Hear me grunt while I descend into the most fertile depths of the underworld we all share, and hear me howl while I dance with the demons who reside there.

I am a babe swimming in womb water, and I remember the dark Mother who bore me. I am an erotically innocent Maiden, and I remember the ones who scarred me. I am a purposed Mother-Healer, and I remember every forehead I've ever wiped and every psychic bone I've reset. I am a wise Crone with paper-thin skin, and I remember all.

I call out those who violated the sanctity that is me. I cast out the energies that bind me. I am digging out every bit of those who have burrowed in the walls of my holiest of holies, and I am slathering a healing salve on the raw places left empty by these monsters' absence. I am a horned Goddess who is keeper of this fortress, and I am raising the sharpest blade in answer to those who question my authority.

The walls of this inner sanctum are vibrating now with the hymns of the dark-winged descended mistresses. There is no evil here, only blissful sparks of *prima materia* so beauteous that they capture the majesty of an entire life well lived within a single burst of light and shadow. This black temple is mine. I have the only key, and only those who prove worthy are told the secret password.

I am the holy womb, and I am God-Goddess-Mystery. I am the holy womb, and I am a many-eyed creatrix staring long into the past and far into the future. I am the holy womb, and I am divinity embodied in the stretch-marked skin of a strong woman.

And so it is.

DANCE OF THE SEVEN MASKS: A RITUAL UNVEILING

Materials: *Journal, writing utensil, seven pieces of fabric, music*

And now, Priestess, if you feel called, I invite you to dance. This ritual is not a performance; it is a soulful ceremony of wild awakening. Perhaps move through this dance as the great Wheel of the Year turns toward spring, or perhaps come home to this ritual magick anytime you are feeling spiritually gaunt, sensually dried out, or otherwise in need of ripening. Here, you become the prayer.

In preparation, write down seven different masks you wear that you are ready to cast off; these can be very specific or more symbolic. For example, perhaps you have recently ended a relationship and you are ready to relinquish the mask of "so-and-so's partner." Perhaps you are a mother whose children are growing, and you are ready to cast off the mask of maternal nurturer to the very young. Consider the roles you used to play, the words you have spoken that were not truly your own, or the beliefs that once served you but no longer belong in your sacred psyche. This is not a relinquishment of selfhood, where you re-lease all identities and attachments, for this serves no one. Let go of only what you are ready to release. This is a symbolic action of claiming authenticity in the now. Once you have your seven masks defined, find seven pieces of fabric that each represent one of the masks. These can be scarves, ribbons, or actual items of clothing.

Here, you become the prayer.

Remember that rituals are stronger the greater the intention, so invest some of your precious time to claim this ceremony as your own. Infusing your greatest resources — whether time, energy, or other capital — into a spell is a clear communication to the cosmic infinite that you mean what you say, are not playing, and are willing to sacrifice something in order to make this magick happen. When you are ready, select a single piece of music or several songs that will frame and fuel this ceremony for you. Let it be your power rhythm, your Witch's war cry. Position the fabric on your body, tying, tether-ing, and wearing the masks as you see fit.

Now, Priestess, ready yourself for the unveiling. Begin in stillness as the music starts, looking down, feeling weighted and small; then begin to move as

Salome moved, a Maiden of the Unbridled Sensual. Cast off each veil when you are ready, howling to the moon mother and declaring what you are freeing yourself from to the ancient feminine eyes who are watching you with all the approval of a proud grandmother. When you have freed yourself from all seven masks, lie prostrate on the ground with your hands in a prayerful position, offering gratitude to the rawest form of your soul, that part of you that remains completely whole and irrevocably unruined despite all past woundings and future masks, despite all that tried to break you but failed. And so it is.

WE BELONG TO THE WATER:
A THREE-PART RITUAL OF COMMUNION, CLEANSING, AND SUCCULENCE

Gather your Priestesses, love. Hold your personal myths of Maiden healing close to your hearts, and make a pilgrimage to a natural body of water if you are able. Like all rituals, this one is fully adaptable to your own embodiment of the Holy Wild, to your own experience of divinity as you now conceive it to be. Know that any impactful ritual will meet you precisely where you are, will take courage to design and undertake, and will require a fierce intention infused with an authenticity only you, as a ritual participant and magick maker, can provide. While all three rituals described herein are collective ceremonies ideally practiced by groups, they can also be adapted to lone Wolf-Women — that is, Priestesses who prefer to keep their magick confined to a soulful, solitary practice. All three rituals may be practiced together in succession, framed within a single warm day of renaissance and sisterhood, or separately with much time taken in between for integration.

Part 1. Wild Communion: A Ritual of Sharing

Materials: *Small bowl of water from a natural source, personal myths written by the participating Priestesses*

Location: *Near a natural body of water, if possible, or see suggestions below*

Circle together near the water, Maidens. If a natural body of water is not accessible, feel free to create your own. There can be as much divine energy in a kiddie pool or bathtub as there is in Mother Ocean, given the right intention, and always know your own body as the only magickal tool you really need. Set the intention for this ritual as follows: Every Priestess will have the opportunity to speak and be heard as much or as little as they like. In sharing circles such as these, no one is forced to speak if they do not care to, and, very often, the circle will begin with many of the Priestesses unsure of its direction, uncertain as to whether they will share at all, and this blessed mystery removes some of the limitations on the ritual's outcome. Circle-craft often works best in the absence of personal expectations, with the collective hope of every participant's healing, along with a good deal of anticipated variance among Priestesses' precise experiences, the only reasonable prospect for the ceremony's desired resolution.

All that is needed for this ritual is the personal myths, using or adapting the prompts offered in the "Water Verses" chapter, of every Priestess and a small bowl of water taken from the natural source near which you are gathered; this water will serve a dual purpose as a cleansing medium and talking totem. All Priestesses will come to be seated, and, if desired, an invocation will be read by the designated space holder to signify the sanctity of the space and time; she may read from Salome's teaching tale, share her own writing, or spontaneously speak with the water as muse. Pass the bowl of water clockwise now, with each circle member dipping their finger in the holy stuff and blessing their hearts, perhaps speaking affirmations of presence such as *I am here.*

The space holder may describe the circle's intention and express the only rules of circle-craft:

1. **The circle is sacred space, and no circle member may share the words of another outside the meeting.** This rule ensures that members feel comfortable speaking and need not fear that their words will be repeated or exploited. Strict lines should be drawn between the friendships that may exist external to the circle and within-circle relationships, and circle experiences should not be discussed outside the circle even between circle members. In essence, what happens inside the circle stays within the circle, and gossip should be clearly denounced.

2. **The circle is not a space to directly challenge or question another member's experience.** Each member speaks from her own experience, sharing what she knows to be true in that moment. Opportunities for

back-and-forth communication are minimized or eliminated altogether, and unsolicited opinions, even those considered well intended, are kept in check.

3. **The "talking object" signals that its holder has the right to speak and be heard in that moment.** No one may interrupt the Priestess holding the talking object, and any member always has the right to pass the totem without speaking if she wishes. In special circumstances, the circle's space holder may need to interject in order to keep the circle on track or ensure the rest of the rules are being followed. For instance, if a circle member is holding the talking object but using her time to speak and be heard to use verbal aggression against another circle member, then the space holder may need to break in to reestablish harmony.

4. **Each circle meeting has a clear beginning, fruition, and end;** it is therefore best to not raise topics or issues that have come up during past meetings. If a recent meeting was particularly intense, granting the members permission to speak about the experience at the next one may be necessary, but doing so at the inception is usually sufficient.

5. **The circle is an organic, ever-changing space.** It is best to arrive at each circle meeting with the lone expectation of being seen and heard in a safe, contained, and compassionate environment, releasing any and all other expectations.

These rules keep communication empathic and reduce the influence of external ego-to-ego relationships on the integrity of the circle. Regardless of any histories or outer-world sisterhoods, everyone enters the circle space as an equal. Ideally, if certain circle members are better acquainted than others, they should not be physically positioned next to one another. Just as saliently, if one circle member has outside knowledge about another member's past, she may not raise that information within the circle. When ready, the space holder will place the water vessel in front of her and read part or the whole of her story. Know that there will be tears, and trust that the circle will gift all members with precisely what they need in that moment. Pass the water clockwise, having all Priestesses read their stories in turn. Treat the sharing as the ritual it is and, though it is challenging, do not immediately respond to what has just been read. This round is sharing only, with interaction kept to an absolute minimum.

Once all Priestesses have been given the opportunity to speak, permit the tone of the circle to shift now. Pass the water counterclockwise, signifying that the circle is closing and this is the final opportunity all members will have to speak in this circle setting. At this point in the ceremony, Priestesses may revisit the myths told by others, sharing words of gratitude and understanding, describing how their personal experience resonated within the words of others, and acknowledging the sheer courage shown by the circle as a whole. To close the ritual, the space holder will seal the circle now with another reading, spontaneously expressed words, or, if it feels right, a collective chant:

> We are Priestesses of the Wild Earth and Maidens of the Unbridled Sensual. These bodies are our own, and we are the only ones who can tell our stories. May all beings know the majesty of living in accordance with their souls' deepest truth, and may all beings know what it is to be wild and free. So mote it be for us; so mote it be for all.

Part 2. Wild Cleansing: A Ritual of Feminine Renaissance

Location: *A natural body of water, if possible, or a pool or bathtub*

This is a ritual of rebirth. All Priestesses will begin by acknowledging that healing a single aspect of the feminine, embodied within the warm, scarred skin of only one being, so heals the greater feminine collective and does much to infuse the whole of the ailing world with a spicy elixir of fem-fire, hope, and grace. When Witches gather, the collective feminine wound of isolation and fragmentation, a wound that manifests differently in individualistic societies than it does in collectivist cultures, bleeds a bit less. While it may feel right to be nude or bare-breasted for this ritual, be endlessly sensitive to those who have undergone trauma and may feel triggered by being unclothed or even seeing others in this vulnerable state; remedy this prior to the ritual by being absolutely clear about what will be occurring and continually affirm circle members' autonomy throughout the ceremony.

Have all participants define for themselves one thing, one pattern or indoctrinated belief, that they are choosing to cleanse themselves of during the ritual. If it feels right, drums, rattles, or other instruments can be played in a slow rhythm, mirroring the divine feminine pulse. Priestess by Priestess, have each person take to the water, calling out to the cosmic ether what they are releasing and then descending beneath the holy water. When each Priestess resurfaces, she will exclaim a declaration of rebirth while her fellow Priestesses erupt into a root-rattling and wave-making celebration of the transition, of their sister's bravehearted nature, and of the small bit of healing offered to the Earth through one Priestess's courage.

Part 3. Wild Succulence: A Ritual of Sensual Joy

Materials: *Natural objects symbolizing succulence, one per participant*

Location: *A setting in nature, if possible*

This ritual is a group body prayer to the wild sensual in us all. Set the intention clearly, with all participants affirming their right to feel deeply and with their whole beings. In preparation, have all Priestesses go into nature, even if it is only a small backyard, and find an object that symbolizes sensual succulence to them. This is not necessarily an object that is outwardly beautiful, nor one everyone will agree reflects the sensual succulent. Know that this part of the ritual can be a ceremony in its own right, a brief soul quest of sorts that precedes Wild Communion and Wild Renaissance, during which all Priestesses will enact a mini-restructuring of their beliefs about sex, desire, the senses, emotions, and all things Maiden.

The Priestesses will now return to the sacred space, objects in hand, and place them at the circle center. The objects can be in addition to an existing altar, or they may form the sacred space themselves. Standing in a large circle around the central altar now, the Priestesses will begin chanting softly "I am" while walking very slowly in a clockwise direction. Once three cycles have been completed, the chant will change to "We are" and grow louder, with the pace of the movement becoming quicker and clapping potentially added. The energy will increase now as the Priestesses spin about the circle center three times before making another change; the Priestesses will now chant "Hear us!" loudly, running in the circle and making as much noise as possible. Howl moonward. Stomp your feet. Shriek like the banshees you are, and move around the circle thrice. Once Priestesses return close to the original position, having made nine rotations altogether, all will stop now, hands on hearts and feeling the collective beat, resuming a softer chant of "We are" and facing the circle center. Stay with this for a few moments, allowing the chant to organically shift back to a low whisper of "I am." All Priestesses will take hands now and close their eyes, affirming they are single cells in one beating heart, acknowledging the unity between sex and spirit, and honoring their wildness as women of this world.

And so it is.

DIVINATION BY ART: A RITUAL OF RECLAIMING CREATIVITY

Materials: *Art supplies (see suggestions below)*

Sift through your earliest memories of creation, Priestess. Recall what it was to know art making as synonymous with joyful play. Remember the sense of surrender that came from the stirring of sandy mud in a bucket or from wholearm scribbling. Return to the youthful innocence that could source creation in the absence of control, and see beauty in the crumbling leaves and animal skulls. Descend into childhood, and know how it felt to embody the artist in the absence of our so-mature, so-limiting obstacles to creative freedom. Distinguish between a desire to create and a desire to create something perfect, glamorous, or salable, and work from a feeling state of robust fearlessness.

Find a forgiving medium that will permit many layers and a large perhaps nontraditional canvas for your work. You may work with pastels, ash, charcoal, chalk, or mud on newsprint, a flat stone, a driveway, or an old tabletop. The possibilities are endless, my love, so think outside any lines that may have been drawn for you so long ago.

Fix your eyes on your blank canvas now and honor the sense of trepidation in your sacrum and heart. Give a nod to the knowledge that you are on the precipice of manifestation, that while the potential for creation is limitless, you are about to significantly shrink down what is now infinite. Sit with the sheer power of this knowing, for it is the very spark of the Goddess.

When you feel ready, set an intention that you divine clarity on a particular area of your life. It might be relationships, sacred work, health, spiritual connection, or any other life area that seems to be on the surface at the moment. To source clarity is the only intention. There can be no other expectations for how you will feel while creating or how the finished piece will look. Permit the creatrix power to well up from your roots; then begin, trusting in your agency with an endless and ancient feminine faith that the outcome will be perfect no matter whether it be beauteously symmetrical or chaotically abstract. Move with your whole body, for the Maiden artist is never physically bound while her hands flit about like entities separate from the rest of her body. She feels the same Shakti pulse in her toes as she does in her fingertips, and she intuits every stroke. She is the medium, the canvas, and all things vibrating above and below.

Whatever your format, try to fill the space as fully as possible, leaving no area blank, and then close your eyes. Return to your intention to be gifted with clarity, then inhale deeply. As you exhale, you are releasing your hold over this piece you have handcrafted. Look at the art with a so-soft focus, letting your vision go a bit blurry. What do you see? What shapes and colors are there for you, and what do they mean? Let your art be a sense maker and an oracle.

Let your art be a sense maker and an oracle.

What themes arise, and what would you title this work? Now, if that title was an answer to a specific question regarding the life area on which you needed clarity, what magickal conclusions could you draw? You are an artist-mystic, and this work is your crystal ball. And so it is.

THIRTEEN DAYS OF SPIRALING THROUGH: A STRATEGIC RITUAL SADHANA

Materials: *Journal, writing utensil, art supplies as needed*

The Maiden of the Unbridled Sensual feels into the world by way of her creative expression. Whatever the form, whatever the intent, the act of creating is undertaken despite all obstacles to her sensual presence. Lalita, Freya, and Salome all embody sacred sexuality and empowered emotionality. They are the generative erotic, and a Maiden's wild art contains a good deal of power sourced from a low place.

At the end of the revisioned tale, Salome declares herself both unveiled and awake, now poised to refuse any unwanted mask or role given her by someone else's hand: *See me as I am now, for I am no longer the woman who will dance only to please. I demand the head of anyone who would wrap my wrists, and these haunted river lands shall be my new palace until I find a wilder home.* The acknowledgment that our art does not always require an approving audience, does not always need to be pleasing even to ourselves, is a radical rite of passage in any artist's life. While positive, or at least critical, reception is indeed necessary to sustain a working artist's livelihood, all that is required for art making is time, materials, and intention. In *What We Ache For*, poet Oriah Mountain Dreamer writes: "The artist's life is simply an ordinary human life that is consciously choreographed to support ongoing creativity." We do not need to tirelessly search for the "wilder home" Salome speaks of; we need only create the conditions of reception in our bodies, psyches, and worlds so we recognize the wild place when it finds us. Our "conscious choreography" of staying present as much as possible, regularly engaging with whatever our art may be despite many apparent obstacles, and feeling into and through our worlds with a sensory, innocent curiosity is the true dance of the fearless Maiden.

Sadhana is a Sanskrit word for a regular spiritual practice that holds the power to break dysfunctional patterns, gift greater clarity, and ground the normally scattered mind in both rooted presence and collective divinity. This sadhana is a thirteen-day ritual of sensual presence and wild art, beginning on the new moon. Ideally, take twenty minutes for yourself each morning, as close to waking as possible, to forge meaningful connections between the luscious body, creative psyche, and infinite spirit. Carve out thirteen pages in your journal, one for each day of the sadhana, and number them accordingly.

Each day of sadhana will unfold in much the same way, with the most variation coming from the words you write. Begin by stretching your limbs long and moving your body slowly with no intention other than to feel wholly present in your skin. Stay with this for as long as you have, either moving to music or responding to your heartbeat. When you feel ready, take to your journal and freewrite on this prompt: *I have the right to feel deeply, and right now I am...*

Try to write, without editing yourself, for at least ten minutes. Should you become stuck and feel unable to continue, write the prompt again and press on. Each day, as your sadhana nears a close, go back into your writing and circle any words that repeat or any themes that seem particularly pertinent. Use those words to handcraft a mantra for the day to guide you. Begin by repeating the mantra a few times while coming back to the organic movement. Allow the sadhana to set the tone for each day; trust that your muses, ancestors, and guides are present to support you; and let this simple practice be a valuable gateway to the ethereal, a way of communing with those whose bodies vibrate so subtly that we rarely are gifted with knowledge of their presence. At the end of the thirteen days, go back and take note of all the words and themes from each one and use them to inspire a piece of art — *any* piece of art — that will symbolize your Maiden's growth. Ink the words on your skin and dance, write an epic poem, assemble a collage on glass; whatever your art, name it as pure and unadulterated perfection born of genuine movement and honest emotion. Bless it, my love. And so it is.

BENEDICTION OF THE ROOTED EROTIC: A RITUAL MORNING PRAYER OF MAIDEN FEROCITY

There are mornings we wake knowing our value, full of hope at dawn that we will be granted just one chance before moonrise to show the world our worth, just one moment in our day when we will feel validated, whole, and present in our feeling bodies. Recite this prayer on those mornings, Priestess. Look into the mirror and anoint your throat with a single drop of water, granting yourself the very thing you seek, fulfilling your wish before breakfast, speaking to your own reflection, and calling your joy home.

Dearest Heathen,

Come to the haunted forest with feet bare and hood raised. There is no one else I'd rather be with when I paint the sacred symbols — the ones no one knows but me — on my soft, stretch-marked belly. Can you feel it? The bones of the Earth are sharper here, and the primal feminine buzzes from below and climbs our legs like impassioned vines. Watch me now as I revel in the most ancient grace, as I dance like a long-limbed faery with wide and wiry wings.

This is my benediction, my body prayer to the forked-tongue seductress that is me. I'm through with the solemn chants and still-bodied meditation. My God's skin is made of tree bark, and my Goddess is not pure. What's more, my friend, my divinity is a genderless spark that lives and breathes within and without, above and below.

And so it is.

Chapter 6

Water Magick

Water magick takes on many forms, just like the water element itself. Our magick is always our cosmic conversation with the universe about the kind of world we wish to live in, and the water element speaks to our truest values. Our joy, our desire, our sex, and our art are all of the water element. When we work our magick to manifest our deep passions, we call home what is ours, and we make real what has existed only in our fertile psychic landscape.

The spells, pathworking, and practical magick I offer in this chapter are all meant to be adapted to suit your life. Consider this work to always be moving toward a living Craft, a meaningful integration of joyful magick and spellwork into the everyday. These are accessible opportunities to bewitch your world, to commune with the deeper parts of your soul that often remain voiceless, and to enchant and reawaken whatever parts of your inner Maiden remain sleeping.

CRAFTING THE COSMIC EGG:
MANIFESTATION MAGICK FOR THE WILD MAIDEN

Materials: *Paper, writing utensil, clay or glass jar or lidded container, valued object, prosperity herbs (see suggestions below in part 2)*

Depending on her world and her wants, the wild woman may not readily encounter external validation for her desires. She must then look inward and affirm her own right to have pleasure, an abundance of what she truly values, and a fierce body love so strong that it could only be sourced straight from her own heart. The Maiden of the Unbridled Sensual works her magick to invoke personal abundance but, importantly, also fervently believes in a strong relationship between her own passions and purpose and those of the greater global community. In her more loathsome depths, the wild woman struggles with finding her soul's purpose and standing firm for what she believes in. After the ascent, after beginning the Red Road journey, after catching sight of her wild home, she now can clearly see how her personal path connects her to the wounded world at large. A Priestess must consider how her magick is a conversation with the global community and with the universal order of all things.

Every spell she casts is an affirmation, and a loud one at that, of the kind of world she hopes the future's children will inhabit wildly and with much joy. The most pivotal question she can ask herself when working manifestation magick for personal abundance is this: *How does my having* this *positively affect the world?* A woman who heals herself heals the holy feminine in her entire bloodline — past, present, and future. A woman who invokes what she desires affirms the right of every woman in the world to do the same, and, most important, a woman who nourishes herself also feeds a planet starved for affection from her human children.

Salome's dance is not just for her; it is her declaration of how she conceives of feminine liberation. Her dance is her spell, an affirmation of selfhood and bodily autonomy that is undergirded by strong, perhaps previously unspoken convictions. Her dance is also a spell for every woman who is living her life bound to others' expectations. The Maiden of the Unbridled Sensual is tasked with examining how her own freedom impacts the world. If she is a microcosm of the collective, what does her desire tell of her hopes for an ailing planet and positive social change?

A Priestess must consider how her magick is a conversation with the global community and with the universal order of all things.

Part 1. Spell Preparation

Priestess, you must work your magick for yourself and for the world in equal parts. Authentic global prosperity begins with you, and your right to have an abundance of what you truly desire — not what others desire for you, not what others say you should desire, but what you know in your bones is meant for you — is inborn and soul mandated. You might revisit the personal mythwork and rituals from the Book of Earth or begin anew, but start here by remembering the yet-to-come. How will you define pleasure when your skin is paper-thin and your wild hair has gone gray? Step back in time now and recall what gave you joy as a young babe. Finally, can you envision a scene in your life slightly in the future but not untouchable — not so unreal that it feels too far away to be clearly imagined — that connects these two versions of yourself? Trace your desire thread from youth to Crone, and there you will discover what makes you feel rich.

Working with that middle vision, the one only slightly in the future, describe the scene in as much sensory detail as possible. What is your skin touching? What tastes are lingering in your mouth? Write all you can on a lone piece of paper that need not be torn from any sacred book. If you are able, write in red ink. Now, my love, read through your vision and ask yourself what core values undergird your desire. Freedom? Hedonism? Security? Sustainability? Allow at least three values to emerge and consider them your authentic currencies, the heart of how you define personal prosperity. Write those values in the margins around your vision.

The final preparatory step is the most crucial, Priestess, for it defines the intimate connection between your spell and the cosmic infinite. How do these values relate to the world you want the children of the future to live in? Synthesize your answer into at least three sentences, one for each of your determined values. For example, if freedom is a key value that grounds your own desire, you might write *I want every creature in the world to feel free*. Let these sentences conclude your writing, placing them at the end of the vision you described in red.

Part 2. Spell Incubation and Release

Perform this part of the ritual as close to the full moon as possible. Fold your paper in whatever shape feels right to you, Priestess; then gather these materials to bring to a sacred space: a lidded container; something that has value for you such as actual paper money, an inherited piece of jewelry, a prized crystal, or a beloved found object from nature; and some prosperity herbs such as pine, bay leaf, or cedar. For any herbal magick, look to the plants indigenous to where you live, developing relationships with them, and your spellwork will truly connect with the elements in a far more authentic way than simply using correspondences recommended in a book.

Cast your circle now, Priestess, affirming your ecological position in this world, your body's right to be here on this Earth, and your ability to have what you truly want out of this precious life. Stand and face the north and cry out: *Cosmic energies, angels, and good spirits of the north, protectors of the earth element, strengthen and ground this circle!* Turn to the east and howl skyward: *Cosmic energies, angels, and good spirits of the east, protectors of the air element, infuse and enliven this circle!* Turn now to the south, raise a fire in your belly, and bellow: *Cosmic energies, angels, and good spirits of the south, protectors of the fire element, ignite and energize this circle!* Turn now to the west, frame your womb with your fingers, and speak firm: *Cosmic energies, angels, and good spirits of the west, protectors of the water element, penetrate and purify this circle! This circle is closed!*

Sit now at your circle's center and create the incubator of your spell, the sacred egg in which your desire will be made manifest. Place all materials inside the container, but leave it unsealed, then lift your pelvic floor toward your heart. Arch your back slightly but not so much that it restricts breathing. Sit before your incubator, feeling the energy flow between your root and your heart. Breathe deep and strong. Close your eyes. Visualize yourself as the joyous babe. Be the wild woman in the middle vision, then be the luscious Crone. Affirm your vision for the world at large, then breathe nine full exhalations into the container, harvesting all the power from the visions and fueling your spell with an in-the-blood desire for true and authentic abundance. After the ninth exhalation, seal the container. Wrap both hands around your energy egg now and hold it moonward, affirming aloud: *By the power of three times three, as I will it, so mote it be!*

When you feel ready, open your circle by standing and facing west, saying: *To those who have come from the west, thank you. Go in peace.* Turn to the south and say: *To those who have come from the south, thank you. Go in peace.* To the east: *To those who have come from the east, thank you. Go in peace.* Finally to the north: *To those who have come from the north, thank you. Go in peace. This circle is open.*

Take your incubator home now, my love. Nest it near your altar or an otherwise holy place. Trust that the universe will rise to support you, and release your desire to the will of the Mystery. Do not limit yourself, my love, by revisiting the spell again and again, lest you diminish the infinite possibilities that could erupt from the Mystery and gift you with what you invoked. Wait until at least the following moon cycle begins to dismantle your spell. Use your intuition, and you will know when it is time to gift your cosmic egg's contents back to the elements by burning or burying them, releasing them in water, or scattering them to the winds.

OUR WILDNESS, OUR MASTERPIECE:
A PRACTICAL MAGICK ELIXIR FOR THE UNDERWATER CREATRIX

Materials: *Sensual, malleable medium such as clay or beeswax*

Within the Triple Goddess archetype, the Maiden creates for herself, while the Mother creates for the collective. The Maiden cares not for the salable potential of her work. She has no time to consider how beautiful her art will be or how accepting society will be of her choices. It is the act of creation she is after, and neither the aesthetic of the finished product nor its reception holds as much value as the feeling she had while enraptured in the creatrix dance. All artists have a bit of the Maiden in them, for it is that initial feminine spark that called them to their most primitive during childhood. The mud, the dough, the grass stains — all that birthed the dull palette that informed our original so-innocent, wholly unapologetic masterpieces — were catalysts for the Maiden's awakening to her wild art.

The feminine's role in art making is primary, yet it is the one that invokes considerable fear. In order to create anything, the feminine must obscure all other possibilities. A writer who stares at a blank screen for hours, a painter who does the same with a white canvas, a dancer with an empty stage, or a chef with a clean pot, all are weighted by the knowledge that their next move will inevitably shrink down what is now positively infinite. The *Prana Shakti* force, the divine feminine spark immanent in all things, must conceal in order to manifest; so, too, the artist must surmount the fear of ruining the medium or choosing wrong, for even the gods must discern for a time and then take a leap of faith.

The Maiden of the Unbridled Sensual is fearless in her art making, for she understands the spiral dance of intuition and manifestation. She moves her hips with a deep trust that every movement is born exactly when and how it is meant to be. The teaching tale begins with the words *Salome would not be made to perform.* The Maiden creates for creation's sake, and the audience is secondary. Consider whatever mysterious force could have orchestrated our universe's big bang, whatever council of alien ascended mistresses and masters or all-powerful, many-purposed presence catalyzed such a profoundly immense event of ultimate birth. Consider the infinite possibilities obscured by that design, and consider that holy void preceding that massive universal crowning as the largest-ever blank canvas. Every artist plays god in this way, and every human being is an artist, a weaver of worlds.

Creativity, not driven by instinct but by an inborn desire to commune with something greater than ourselves, is the feature distinguishing between humanity and other animal species. If you were born human, you were born to make new out of old, to make sense out of your world with your body and psyche, and to make manifest your impulse to birth some great *thing* out of nothing, using the resources with which you were gifted in this blessed life of yours and without needing to exert power over others to prove your worth. To create is to bravely worship the Goddess of Revolution.

After all, an artist is, by nature, a change agent who cannot rest leaving things as they are, untouched and immutably defined. The artist re-forms and renames what is, without obligation, without being beholden to what will be loved or accepted by the consumer, without clinging to the infinite potential inherent in those early stages of creation.

> To create is to bravely worship the Goddess of Revolution.

The feminine is undervalued in our patriarchal society, and so, too, intuitive art born of the dark womb-space of fertile nothing is dismissed as worthless. The intimate and undeniable connection between feminine creativity and feminine sensuality highlights how grossly denigrated the Maiden aspect of our psyches is in our world, with young women slowly absorbing the messages that their art and their bodies are worth very little in a carved-up landscape of body shaming where, furthermore, women artists working in most media are paid significantly less than their male counterparts.

While all artists are change agents to some extent, the woman who is an artist is a true revolutionary; when she repowers her art, she reasserts feminine sensual power. Audre Lorde writes: "In touch with the erotic, I become less willing to accept powerlessness, or those other supplied states of being which are not native to me....And there is, for me, no difference between writing a good poem and moving into sunlight against the body of a woman I love." The fertile dark all artists draw from when they birth something new into being is essentially pure, primeval creatrix energy; there is no valid separation between the sensual and the creative, and the Maiden knows this well.

Even so, the Maiden-Artisan becomes stuck from time to time, blocked by some unseen force that dams up her creative power. She begins to feel as though a great and swelling wave of art is growing toward fruition within her, but, for the life of her, she cannot undam the waters and will herself to begin. In these moments, practical magick offers a remedy to the unique anguish of the creatrix.

To begin this spell, you need a sensual medium; malleable clay or home-made play dough (a mixture of flour, salt, and water) is best, but beeswax or thick mud make good alternatives. Begin with a single small piece of the material and let it warm in your hands. Start to envision the creative blockage. What color is it? What shape? What temperature? Where do you feel it in your body? Ask yourself these questions, and begin to work the medium in your hands, feeling it between your fingertips and in your palms. Where is the creative force in your body? What color is it? How does its energy move?

Now, with every inhalation, imagine that the blockage weakens, softening in shape and form, perhaps changing colors. On your inhalations, the creative force gets sharper and brighter, beginning to penetrate the softening blockage. Inhale; blockage surrenders. Exhale; creative power increases. Inhale; blockage begins to shrink. Exhale; the creative force moves into hands, heart, throat, and hips. Whatever your art, feel the creative force pool in the parts of your body you use to enact it. Stay with this until it feels right to come to this final vision: Now, wherever that small and ineffectual blockage is in the body, imagine that it has become the small piece of material you are holding and wielding in your hands. It controls you no longer, and your art is free to be born. Blessed be.

Dreaming the Watery Maidenscape: A Vision-Tale of Feminine Redemption

Consider the immense majesty that would arise from a world in which children of all genders were told of their bodily autonomy consistently and with much transparency, with their creative work similarly validated as not only permissible as a hobby but as the stuff of divine grace. What if an integral part of our social landscape was the purposeful honoring of the artist in us all, with no one made to feel their particular soulful art was less holy than anyone else's creative work? Envision this world with me now, my love, and call to mind a broader definition of art than that which we are shown during childhood.

Welcome home, prodigal daughter. Come inside, and permit me to pour you something earthen and bitter before I tell you of my dream vision, before I ask you to question all you know to be true, and before I bid you cast your sweet psyche into that liminal space between the only-imagined and the very real yet-to-come. Here, let me hold your hands. Breathe softly and sink your consciousness down to the womb-heart, down to that energetic void between life and death. There, time knows no bounds. There, we are wandering Witches who may not know where we are but understand fully the nature of our search.

This place is no utopia, for even those who are permitted the freedom to live out their souls' purpose are regularly anguished by life's fallow times and intermittently pained by loss. The feminine serves as solace, though, a soft-breasted and warm-skinned comfort during our grief, when the individualistic, tough-loving patriarch would leave us to cry in the cold. Walk with me through these haunted psychic woods, and let me show you what I have seen in my most indulgent moments.

Forgive me if I free-bleed on the snow while we walk, and don't mind the neighbors if they stare. They pretend to think my ways indulgent, but, all the while, they are mirroring my moving spells in their kitchens behind twitching curtains. Let them watch, I say. We can use more tree huggers, after all.

Ah! Here, beneath this ancient oak, I saw children painting their names on the high roots with wet rocks — not the names they were given but the names they had chosen for themselves, the names no one could take from them no matter their poverty or place of birth. Here, by this crumbling cabin, I saw Wild Ones of all genders coming together to birth their art, nurture their senses, and affirm the holiness of their hands. I saw parents raising their young ones to seek out the truest, most soul-deep parts of themselves and to cultivate them like fragile, precious heirloom seeds that would be the very sustenance of humanity's future.

Can you hear it? We are nearing the river where I saw lovers confessing their most forbidden aches to one another, where I saw Salome spiral dance with no intention whatsoever but to prove to herself that she exists without being seen. I saw spirit sit side by side with sex, and I saw the communal sparks of many-handed art making fueling the world with a profound, subtle energy. I saw this jewel-orange vibration seep into the soil and make the Mother unfurl like a baby fern, and I saw this blessed Maidenscape come alive with the sweet song of feminine magick.

I saw you there, you precious creatrix. I saw you defend your art like a wolf-mother, and I saw you affirm the divinity of your work. I saw you handcraft your writing, your sculpture, your dance, your spellwork, and your meals with an unapologetic fearlessness, and I saw you mold these masterpieces with a childlike innocence you thought you had forgotten. I saw you carve out the insidious, low-lying roots of shame about your art's poor value and cast them into a funeral pyre for the old and outmoded, and I saw you forever bind craft to Craft, the erotic to the beauteous, the irrational to the passionate.

Finish your drink now, my love, and let's take to the deeper woods. Let's collect our media by digging and climbing, and let's not come home until we've painted our worlds to mirror our many-hued psyches, a palette of primal reds, royal blues, and every jewel-bright color in between.

Blessed be you, and blessed be the body of your art.

MAKING HOLY WATER:
EVENING BLESSING PRAYER
OF THE OCEAN MAIDEN COME TO SHORE

Materials: *Purified water in a clear jar*

Let us make our own holy water, my love, for our blessings are as true as any said by those who wear silk robes and claim godliness. Hold your clear jar full of purified water in your hands, and speak these words on a hedonistic night:

> I am casting a spell with my hips as I walk to shore, honoring the salty deep with the solidity of my round rump and the flesh of my bare back. My time in the sea is over for now, for I've done all the healing I can before moonrise. This eerie night belongs to me, and I will bid all matrilineal blessings to wash ashore and keep me warm. My desire and my art are holy, and these last long nights I have fed both with underwater soul-food and much sex-to-spirit fusion. I am a Witch of the waves, but, just for now, I am resting on the slithering sands of serpentine grace while holy water runs in white rivulets down my thighs. Blessed be my hungry flesh, and blessed be the Holy Wild.

Leave the water overnight on your altar, drinking it in the morning in the name of renewal and rejuvenation. So mote it be.

WATER REFLECTION AND FINAL PRAYER:
TO THE MAIDEN WHO HAS WORN MANY MASKS

Both earth and water are the elements of the Maiden. The earth element asks the wild woman to find her ground, to connect and commune with what is most wild about her soul and to rebel against the too small and the not enough. The earth element shows us what we have outgrown and asks us to come home to self, while the water element permits us to feel into our worlds enough to recognize what will bring us joy. Water will cleanse away what no longer belongs, purify and name our darkness, and support our reclamation of sensual freedom.

Where might Salome have gone in the next chapter of her revisioned story? After she had reclaimed what was hers and swum in her sensual depths, creating her own ceremony of sensual initiation, where would the Red Road have taken her? In moving from the Book of Water to the Book of Fire, we must consider the Maiden's power to change her world. All the wisdom offered the Maiden while she immerses herself in deep feeling has much to offer the ailing and aching feminine within the collective, but we must empower the Maiden to make that wisdom known.

Water has the ability to cleanse without purging away completely, to purify without leaving permanent marks. The powers of water, the Maiden's greatest talents, are not the powers of fire. Fire boils water, sends raw emotions to the surface to erupt and destroy. While the water element grants us the grace to feel our way through our worlds, the fire element permits us to burn through obstacles to our freedom, to eliminate from our inner and outer landscapes those forces that seem to threaten us with another garden, with another cage. For the wild woman, the fire is the change maker, but she needs the solace of water to cool her off from time to time, when her rage runs too hot or becomes misdirected. She needs water to find her way again, to sink back into her body and use her senses to reawaken her joy when she begins to take herself too seriously. Water reminds her of who she is in her depths, while fire animates and enlivens her most genuine identity out in the world, igniting her desire to share her wisdom and catalyze transformation for herself and her world.

Lost Verses of the Holy Feminine: Charge of the Magick Maker

Creatrix, your magick is your communion with the divine about your vision for a more vibrant, vital world. Your body is the Earth, your blood its waters, your will its fiery core, and your vision its ethereal presence. Know yourself as God-Goddess-Mystery embodied in the soft skin of a woman, and honor your right to shape a soulful future for the children of this global community. Blessed be the Holy Wild.

The Book of
Fire

The fire element is a great transformer, and a glowing beacon of hope and promised evolution. The seat of the fire element in the body is between belly and heart, our inner altar and the physical center of our selfhood and sovereignty. Fire purges what no longer belongs, clearing away what no longer serves the individual or the collective. Here, the Witch is not tied to the stake and engulfed in flames; she is the willful pyromancer, and she uses her will to direct the power of the inferno. Know a Witch's rage as holy hellfire, a blazing wrecking ball swung often and hard at long-standing structures of feminine oppression, be they psychic fences built by her own hands or political mechanisms of environmental or social injustice. The Maiden of the Unbridled Sensual archetype validates our emotions — all of them, each of them — so that we can truly embody our right to feel deeply, even when that feeling is anger. The fire element tasks us with remembering that rage can be righteous and soul affirming, particularly when it is unleashed raw then transmuted to a productive ever-burning change agent. While women are taught to suppress their anger lest they be labeled as hysterical, bitter, bossy, or irrational, the Prophetess of the Wildfire archetype shows us the nature of our fem-force, the power of our collective rising, and the magick born when we tend the flames of our communal discerning will.

Wild Feminine Archetype: The Prophetess of the Wildfire
Themes in Her-story: Radical hope, righteous rage, transmutation,
   feminine will, magick as activism

Join me at the bonfire, Sister.
I'm setting all that haunts me to burn, and I'm invoking a feminine firestorm
to sear through the ropes that bind women to outmoded laws and crumbling structures.
I'm calling fire an elemental Goddess of liberation, and I will know myself as her.

Chapter 7

Fire Verses

For our ancestors, fire was the center point of communal gathering, a place to nourish the soul with food, warmth, and conversation. A place to dance, mourn, laugh, pray, plot, and dream. Fire has long been the great and mystical symbol of perpetual hope amid swelling, cool darkness, a burning promise that this, too, shall pass and a call to tend the flames with great care until the dawn ushers in rebirth and renewal. In exploring the Prophetess of the Wildfire archetype, we are asked to consider the fire element's dual roles both as great destroyer and as harbinger of hope.

You are right to revere your fire, my love. The Prophetess of the Wildfire archetype represents raw rage and unimpeded will. Her greatest attributes are among the most shunned for the feminine, for she holds the power to fight, and fight well, with a wolf-mother's ferocity and a skilled healer's cunning. She is the dark moon and the destructor. She is the black-winged angel of death, and she refuses to cover her gruesome face with a demure mask of contentment and acceptance. She is resourceful and forward-thinking, and moves with an intense collectivist instinct and fervent commitment to speaking the truth.

The Prophetess is an activist, for she foresees with great clarity both the aspects of her own world that must be transmuted and those within the global community that must be changed to support a sustainable future in which the sacred masculine and divine feminine exist in states of mutual support, balance, and generative partnership. The Dark Goddess is always working to protect and uphold the feminine. For now, she is activist. After the coming dawn, after the social scales have balanced the awakened masculine with the sacred feminine, it may be that she is viewed as an acknowledged necessity, a revered divine cog in the ever-turning Wheel of Life. For now, she is the change maker, transmutation embodied in those feminine traits most feared and most subjugated since the advent of Western civilization's body-spirit separation. She is radical hope and a red-hot vow that the future is feminine.

In this chapter of verses, Priestess, I ask you to consider the relationship between your will, radical hope, and righteous rage within your stories. Key attributes of the Prophetess of the Wildfire are her steadfastness, discernment, and willingness to claim her right to act upon her world and effect the change she desires. Envision yourself standing around a loud-burning bonfire while you read, surrounded by the courageous souls who came before you and those who will come after you. Your ancestors are keeping the fires burning for your hopes and your dreams, willing the world you live in to evolve enough to support your true-to-self values and most authentic currencies. Warm yourself near these flames when your world grows cold and dark, and let the medicine of your soulful inheritance reignite your will.

THE PROPHETESS OF THE WILDFIRE ARCHETYPE: RECLAIMING THE FLAMES

The essence of the fire element is purifying change. Fire is the space maker, the transmuting force that enacts the psychic clearing out, the great purge of all the Priestess no longer believes and no longer wants taking up space in her wild home. But the blaze she creates is not one of blind destruction. There is a purpose to her calculated action, destructive as it may be, a careful plan often born of nothing more than an instinct, a radical and embodied hope, that demands she melt down and recast the shape of her world. If earth is her ground, her new foundation after she has left the garden and taken to the Red Road, water is her way of feeling into and through these uncharted territories. There is a fluid surrender to the water element, an opening to emotionality and sensuality that demands a letting go of control and unbinding of body and soul. The fire element is far more driven, surer and swifter in its action, and to embody the Prophetess of the Wildfire archetype requires a discernment and hard-edged will.

As a Priestess, you must reclaim the flames. You must reclaim your right to hope and your right to act, knowing that Witches exist on the fringes of what is acceptable, knowing that the magick keepers have a responsibility to support their core values in their Craft. We are boundary pushers, both in our own lives and the world at large, and we understand the power we wield as change makers and mystics.

We must continue to exist in that liminal space between what is acceptable now and the world we want the children of the future to live in later. We must carry a lantern there, lighting the way for others and questioning any rules, laws, or norms that constrict the wild feminine nature. The aspects of the feminine that have been strategically shunned, the very traits that were targets of the European Witch-hunts and remain criminalized in many parts of the world, are ones that do not fit neatly within traditional gender roles in which women were wives and mothers. Those targeted during the Witch-hunts were not, prior to confessions elicited through coercion or torture, self-identified Witches; they were women viewed as embodied threats to male, capitalist rule. They were medicine women and midwives, yes, but they were also business owners, those who refused to marry, and those who lived alone and in isolation. In addition to the common characteristic these women shared of being easily targeted in the absence of patrilineal defenses, these women, their children, and, in some instances, the men who were affiliated with them, the victims of the Witch-hunts were socially independent, either as outcasts or as knowledgeable and powerful women who did not depend on men.

The Prophetess of the Wildfire is a mystery keeper, though fire was used as a weapon against women's wisdom. The hunted were often but not always healers, those having an intimate understanding of the birth-death-birth cycle. Wisdom, intuition, and magick pose a dangerous threat to masculine social structures when these tools are embodied by women. Modern-day Witch-hunts in sub-Saharan Africa, Papua New Guinea, India, parts of South America, and other regions where perceived spiritual crime is still punishable by imprisonment or death target primarily women and children. The diversity of traits targeted by the modern hunts and of sociocultural conditions in these regions precludes most generalizations about the victims, but the hunts are typically concentrated in rural and impoverished areas, where resources are scarce. Much like those arrested and persecuted during the European hunts, accused Witches in these areas, once singled out as such, have little opportunity for reprieve, and twenty-first-century Priestesses living in individualistic, wealthy nations do well to understand that, for many, the "Witch-hunt" is not a long-gone historical event to be claimed only by those of European descent but a persistent human-rights abuse. It is the very antithesis of what we stand for, an atrocity we will work against, and the particular brand of horror that does not exist in the world for which we hold a deep and radical hope.

The Prophetess in us is a seer, and she has envisioned a better, brighter world for the children. The most fearsome characteristics are hallmarks of the Prophetess of the Wildfire archetype and long-standing power sources of the Dark Goddesses across cultural lines. Magickal power, prophetic power, and, most important, the power over death are stored within the wheelhouse of the primal feminine, with the toxic masculine mentality emphasizing dominance over these untamed and almighty forces. The Witch, in her rawest form, is a keeper of the wisdom of the Holy Wild, for she is able to see beyond the man-made curtain of Dark Goddess fear.

The Prophetess of the Wildfire archetype resides in the Mother of Babylon from the Christian Bible, a blasphemous symbol of the end of days that was torn apart as punishment for her specific sort of evil. Tattooed on her forehead was "Mystery, Babylon the Great, The Mother of Harlots and Abominations of the Earth." She was the downfall of man embodied in a woman, a great unifier of how feminine immorality was framed throughout the Christian Bible, often depicted as a scantily clad seductress, as in the final book: "And the woman was arrayed in purple and scarlet colour, and decked with gold and precious stones and pearls, having a golden cup in her hand full of abominations and filthiness of her fornication."

The dark feminine is persistent, despite the efforts to contain her, and she is evident in numerous cultures and throughout time. The Greek Goddess Medusa, with her famed crown of serpentine hair, was a truth-teller dismissed as too unbeauteous to be seen. She was vengeful, bringing about the downfall of heroes, and she was the dark to Athena's light. Her primal feminine power was that of prophecy and Crone knowledge, and her authentic Goddess traits were cast in a dim light by patriarchal retellings of her myths, which framed her as grotesque, a loathsome creature whose visage was so horrible that to look upon her was to turn to sudden stone.

While the Dark Goddess has been exiled in our individualistic societies, those of a more collectivist nature do, indeed, honor her. The Yoruban Goddess Oya, whose name means "She Who Tore," embodies the principles of the dark and destructive feminine. She is a nature Goddess, a woman of the storm. She brings about necessary death in order to make space for the new, and she is the raw, elemental eruption of feminine power. The Hindu Goddess Kali is not only a Dark Goddess of destruction; she is a protector of children and dismantler of dying ages. Her complex nature defies most generalizations about her, as she, like Oya, has many faces worshipped by her dedicants. She is blood dripping from the mouth, skulls worn as jewelry, and long-tongued fear. Kali is the shaken foundations of outmoded social structures, and she is the in-the-belly sword blow to the rigid ego and individualized power hunger.

The Prophetess is a destructor, but she is also a flame tender and hearth holder. She keeps the fire burning to warm us when our radical hope is dimming, when we feel too small or too tired to press on. As the flame tender, she is akin to the Celtic Pagan Goddess Brighid or the Greek Hestia, a steadfast and wise presence who bids us nest ourselves near the hearth, who tells us even radical hope cannot be truly lost as long as there are those who share our dreams, who will stroke our hair and hum hymns of victory and strength in the face of adversity until our individual sense of hope is restored.

Pilgrimage to the Wisdom Keeper: Revisioning the Mother of Babylon

They called her a Dark Goddess, but we had heard that to look upon this Witch-Prophet was to be blinded by a many-sunned system of red planets and blazing comets born of rubies and rage. Yes, we had heard of her, my sisters and I, but we did not go looking for her until we had no choice, until the powers that be were verging on a war that would carve out the best parts of humanity and replace them with greater greed and ego-mad dominance. We waited to seek out our savior until we knew — with the whole of our unruined hearts, we *knew* — she was the only one who could bring about the end of their days.

Our bare feet waded through lakes of fire, swamps so polluted with the waste of production that they ignited on warmer days, and we collected others as we marched. We were a howling army of mothers holding babies and weeping wise men. We were a tribe of warrior women whose lips dripped with a certain bloodlust so bitter that it burned the ground, and we were a flock of wide-winged angels singing mournful punk-rock anthems alongside holy, hopeful hymns.

She was not the whore they had warned us about in the churches of our childhoods. The red-hooded Prophetess was blessing the infertile soil when we found her, chanting primal feminine spells long forgotten, bleeding on the ground, and beckoning the darkest Goddesses to join her in the awakening. She carried a lantern she had kept burning for thousands of years, a soul-warming symbol of our radical hope for a healed world, and her animal familiar stood beside her.

Her beast did not have seven heads, as their revelations had foretold; it was a fearsome, long-fanged wolf with blue-black eyes and patchy gray fur. The beast was marked, as they said, tattooed in its bare places with verses of women's ire and tortured poets' anguish. Together, the Prophetess and her beast were a symbol of the righteous rage in us all, and, when she stood before us with her majestic creature at her side, we knew that our journey had been worth every growl in the belly, nighttime shiver, and festering blister. We knew that the overlong pilgrimage had been necessary, for the Dark Goddess is never encountered without sacrifice.

We begged her to gift us with certainty, to promise us that all would be well, and to tell each of us our fortunes so we could return to the wounded world with direction. Some of us fell to our knees in worship of nothing more than holy hope, and others wept with the knowing that our work was not finished. The Witch made no sound until the red sun sank below the tree line and her patient congregation was softly crooning old ballads of protest and redemption. Her wolf howled mournfully with us, sending our words moonward and so far into the past that the ghosts of burned healers arose from the ground beneath our feet, so far into the future that the crystal children, born only because we took a stand, descended from the ether.

The Prophetess spoke to her immense terrestrial and celestial tribe then, her words a rhythmic spoken-word poem that will echo within the bounds of my soul until I reincarnate no longer. She raised a scarred hand and bade us be quiet, and, aside from the intermittent whimpers at the bone-rattling truth of her divination, we were stone-still and hushed to silence. The resonance of her voice made the trees bend back and the Earth quiver, and like punctuation during every potent, pregnant pause, visions of wildfire overtaking the land glowed in the black-mirror eyes of her beast.

"I know why you've come to my desolate wild, you vagrant visionaries, you hotheads, you freaks. I know why you're here, and I know what you seek in what little scatterbrained, rage-filled wisdom I still have to share. I could tell you of the awakening, the after-battle calm that will follow a needless surging war between the overlooked soul and misunderstood spirit. I could tell you of the beauteous yet-to-come, where children tend to the Earth like skillful stewards, gender means little, lands have been returned to the indigenous peoples, reparations have been paid, and compassionate equality is the rule of law. I could tell you of a collective unity that will be birthed and parented from good intentions and steadfast morals alone, and I could weep with you while you recount my story as it was drafted in their unholiest books. But I will not.

"I will not grow tired of many-armed spell casting and clenched-teeth growling. I will not sit back and watch while mothers rock their bullet-riddled babes, and I will not quiver at the feet of the privileged and pout at their institutionalized racism and protected, gold-backed prejudice. I will not shake my head when I read news of oil-choked creatures and skies streaked black with chemicals. I will not click my tongue and move on with feigned grace when I can hear the Mother bellowing out war cries from below, and I will not teach you, my wide-eyed innocent ones, to tread softly on the eggshell fragility of these feckless, ill-fated crumbling foundations.

"Go home, and walk hard, children, for this is the end of their days. Go home singing with voices so deafening that they have no choice but to listen. Go home and outvote them, outprotest them, and outdance them. Their money won't stand against your art. You are wolf-mothers and wild men. You are demons to their false-angelic pretenses of charity and protection. You are the far-seers and the rain-makers, and this world is yours.

"Go and take it back with your bare hands, and claw so deeply into corruption that you can feel its black-tar heart's feeble beat in your palm. Take back the land and pray for preservation. Take back abundance as you know it to be and feed the babes starving at their mothers' breasts. Find your cause and rise against, my children, for the doomsday clock is ticking so loudly now that the golden doors of hidden banks are shaking open.

"Get angry. Get moving. Waste no more time here with me wishing for a quick and flaming solution; that is their way, not ours. Stop looking to the sky for a great fireball to smite the mad ones and leave you be. This is not in the cards, and I am no diamond-bright oracle or pink-glittery savior. I am the crucible, boiling down the steel out of which a million-bladed sword will be forged. I am the raging prophet they tore apart to suit their needs, and you are my hands, my tongue, and my red-hot still-pulsing guts.

"You cannot birth anything new without making room, raucous ones, so do not mistake this prophecy for a gleaming grace that requires no work. Clear the fields, do it loudly, and urge others to do the same. My beast and I will be howling at your sides, for this is the Armageddon I foretold so long ago, this is the death rattle of sustained injustice, and this is the end of days ruled with the heavy hands controlled by individualistic and uninitiated masculine minds. Do not spiral dance in joy just yet, my loves, lest your anger spoil and rot you from the inside out.

"Light your lanterns, and walk with me. We'll go to the cities now to bleed on the steps of government buildings. Walk with me. Let us vote with our voices and our rage. Walk with me now, for we are doing no good standing here in the forest depths and wishing for a better world. Let's spit on the ground and tell them they can't talk to us like that. My beast is snarling, and I am bloodthirsty. Now, march!"

And march we did, powered by her holy truth and a renewed faith in no one but ourselves. We did not wander; we sped with a purposed direction, and our march was a many-bodied prayer to the primal feminine, to the darkest Goddess in us all. We were Mother ire embodied, and we were rising. There would be no retreat, no surrender, and only the most necessary of rests along the Red Road.

Handwritten Verses: We Will Keep This Fire Burning

Ask yourself this, Priestess: For what are you keeping the fire burning right now, in this moment? If all the children in the world could hear you speak and consciously listen to your words for five minutes starting now, what would you say? You may use the prompts I offer here or adapt them as needed.

Children, I am a Prophetess, and I know for sure...
Be full of faith that...
In your wise and innocent eyes, I see...
I am sorry for...
You give me hope that...
When you get angry, remember...
You are loved, and you are...

Light a candle, and read your verses aloud now, envisioning a sea of small faces attending to you, trusting you, looking to you as a faithful flame tender.

THE IRE OF THE PRIESTESS: THE MERIT OF RIGHTEOUS RAGE

The messages girls receive at an early age about their anger's merit are few and far between. Our society seeks to dim the wild during childhood in order to support social acceptance, with girls, in particular, dismissed as "bossy" or "unladylike" should they show the slightest sign of red-faced, tears-in-the-eyes rage. What if we were raised with an understanding of our right to rage? What if the divine feminine was not presented to us as tantamount to "gentle and soft-spoken"? What if we were to call our rage out of exile, and bring it home? What global-order shifts could the wild feminine dark accomplish?

Sift through your childhood memories, Priestess, and see if you can pin-point events when you remember being authentically entrenched in whole-body anger. What were the catalysts for your wisest and most bravehearted rage? If others perceived your anger, how did they respond, and if you quietly raged in solitude, what did you tell yourself about your right to feel? Recall now, Witch, a more recent time when you were angry. Do any of the same patterns persist? Ask yourself about the role rage has played in your life and to what extent a violation of your personal values, your deepest convictions, has always set you ablaze.

The solar plexus chakra, Manipura, is the seat of both masculine and feminine rage. It is the epicenter of our egos, all we know to be true about ourselves and show the world, all we believe about sacred work and our right to act, and all our so-precious, so-fragile self-esteem. During childhood, we need to see that our actions can have a real and palpable impact on our worlds, and we need to be given the freedom to learn from nature and discover what it is about this wild world that we love and will fight for. There is a rage to the Holy Wild that cannot be discounted, and, for all our evolved technologies, we still cannot protect ourselves from the destruction of hurricanes, earth-quakes, wildfires, and the most vicious faces of the Earth Mother.

Immature rage is chaotic and reactive, having no particular intention in mind or preferred outcome; this is not to say that such unbridled anger is not sometimes required, an automatic and perfectly valid response to a great wrong or injustice. In Women Who Run with the Wolves, Dr. Clarissa Pinkola Estés writes: "There are times when it becomes imperative to release a rage that shakes the skies....When women pay attention to the instinctual self, they know when it is time. Intuitively, they know and they act. And it is right. Right as rain." The maturity of Mother rage comes from its purpose and transmutation, the wild woman's ability to let her boiling blood fuel her action and affect her world. The scale need not be grand, either, for mature rage does not need to involve a great number of people or some majestic cause in order to be effective. A wolf-mother raging against a predator is not lashing out, gnashing her teeth out of a fainthearted hope that her foe will fear her and leave. No, in that moment, she must be sure of victory, sure of her creaturely ability to protect her bloodline. So, too, the Prophetess of the Wildfire foresees the impact of her rage and uses her will to direct that white-hot force for the ultimate good.

PROMISE OF THE RED-HOODED PROPHET:
TO THOSE WHO HAVE SPAT UPON ME

You are right to acknowledge those who have manipulated, abused, or otherwise wounded you, and you are right to let your scars be power sources. Priestess of Holy Hellfire, these words are yours:

I see you, suckers, and I have no time for your psychic vampirism. Your cowardly nonsense means so little to me that I can no longer remember the shape of your face or the precise flavor of bitterness that peppered your lies. I can forget you now and with much ease, but, should you strike at me again, know my wrath as sure and swift.

My teeth are bared, and my fingers are curled. I am ready for you, you fickle beast. There are those who can be betrayed by the likes of such predators as you and move on with a demure grace I have never known. I will not be dismissed as your fragile-winged prey, and I will not lie in wait while you hone your criminal machinations against those I love.

Go ahead and test me. I live for it. Go ahead and tell others of my low worth and many vile sins. I have nothing to hide, wicked one, but you do. I was born knowing your secrets, for they are the shadows of all unawakened humanity. Open your eyes just as I take my red hood down so you can see the intent in my eyes and conviction in my jaw. Open your eyes and ask me if I mean what I say.

I do, and you'll not want to cross me again.

Handwritten Verses: Remember This Face

Know your anger as teacher. What lessons does this primal feeling hold for you, and how can the resonating energy be transmuted by the power of will? Sit in your power now, my love. Examine your base-level emotion with the knowing curiosity of a medicine woman, and understand that which angers you most is always what is most contrary to your deeply held values. Ask yourself this: If you could make one change in the global collective now, one great and irrevocable shift based on your conceptions of justice, freedom, sustainability, and environmental consciousness, what would that change be? Now ask yourself, What is the single, greatest obstacle to that change you wish to make? It may be difficult to pinpoint a lone barrier to what you want given the complex systems of oppression and power that have overtaken our world. Even so, give the obstacle an embodied form now, in your imagination. What does this creature look like, this poisonous monster who blocks the world you wish for? What would you say to this beast if you could speak to it? You may use the prompts I offer here, or write your own.

> No, vicious creature, I will not let you...
> You have been in power too long, and now you must...
> I am taking you down, and...
> Remember this face because...
> You'll not want to cross me again, or I will...
>
> So mote it be.

Read your letter aloud now, my love, and let it inspire action. What tangible action can you take today that would weaken this creature just a bit? We must marry our voices and our wills to our magick and our actions, so embody the Prophetess and take to the streets. Hold tightly to the powerful intimacy between radical hope and righteous rage, and *act.*

With This Blood, I Thee Wed: Timely Vows from Earth's Witch-Bride

The pods I plant now are engorged with the ruby-red heirloom seeds of dissent and shielded by razor-sharp scaled skin tattooed with my wedding vows. I nest these precious embryonic totems here in this haunted forest where the Witches gather, their wombs swollen with a persistent hope for a better world and their eyes glowing with the same black-mirror feminine ire that I used to sew my gown. They will be my guests tonight, these raging activist Priestesses who know the magick of the green-skinned muses and know it well, these change-agent Witch-Mothers who will soon birth a generation of babes charged to fight for their world while choking on the malignant, festering mouth cancers left them by their nearsighted grandfathers.

My ceremonial gardening marks the beginning of this commitment ritual, but its end will not come until these soft-souled, starving star-children, now so innocently swimming in womb water, dine on the flourishing harvest of stone fruit and conviction I sow tonight. May my words echo through their mothers' stretch-marked skin and ignite a bone-deep purpose to ever protect the lover I wed tonight, under a moon that mourns for a planet under siege by a particular privileged politics of corrupt consumption and petty, pitiful narcissism.

These venom-fanged Wild Ones are gathered here today to witness my marriage to my longtime and ever-loyal lover. Under these ancient oaks, I vow to love, honor, and cherish her crystalline and overmined bones, the polluted waters of her blood, and the carved-up landscape of her skin. I promise to use all the magick I have in store, all my words and all my will, to stand against those who melt through what little fireproof armor she has and leave her to be burned at the stake. I vow to make good use of every resource gifted me to rally and rage against those who think we are more valuable than she. I am Bride to Earth, and the only death that shall part us is hers.

For now, she has been raped but remains unruined, and she has yet to unleash the howling-wind majesty of her Dark Goddess wrath. She has yet to show her most ancient sorcery, though I fear it will be too late once the golden doors are blown apart by righteous waves conjured by a fem-force no superior human signature could ever cage. Perhaps these yet-to-be-born babes will know to get to higher ground while my lover washes away the sins of ego madness and bids the world to start anew, or perhaps she casts us all out as an ill-fated virus to which she is now immune.

I am bleeding on the ground now to consummate this blessed union, and I can hear ethereal voices of future generations screaming for salvation. This ritual's audience has grown, and I can see the faces of burned women standing among the Witch-Mothers and vibrating with the same pulse beat that resonates from the core of my wide-hipped bride. We are but infinitesimal cells in her slow-throbbing heart, but we are hardly helpless.

With this blood, I thee wed. I am painting my face with worm-riddled loam and tracing pentagrams onto bark. I am wail-praying to everyone I know to not give up and head for the wilderness where no one can hear you weep. Stay and rage for my bride, who does not care to speak a language that has too few words for peace but thousands for profit. Stay and rage for the hunted Witch that is our planet, and stay and rage for the Wild Ones still bound by womb walls, who have no choice but to be born into a world left in ruins by soulless, diseased beasts so taken by the sound of their own voices that they cannot hear the tearful pleas and begging screams sent back in time from their great-grandchildren.

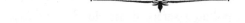

MOTHER MAGICK AND RAGE'S TRANSMUTATION: TO WEAR THE CROWN OF SERPENTS

There is no change agent greater than the unified force of feminine wisdom and feminine rage. The Priestess claims the serpentine crown, Medusa's so-fearsome attribute, when she uses her magick and will to direct her anger and affect the world. This requires a foresight and Crone's intuition blocked by the rawest forms of rage. A Witch's blood boils at the harm being done to our planet, at the notion of child brides and child soldiers; at animal cruelty; at the shaming of the beauteous human body; at corporate and political corruption, institutionalized racism, persistent and pervasive colonization, and myriad other defects in our world order. The Wild One feels this gut-level upset but knows that rage without directed will does not fuel effective and lasting change. While the purest form of anger is indeed valuable, it is through its ultimate transmutation that it becomes a genuine force to be reckoned with.

The will of the wild woman is where her magick sits; it is an in-the-gut source of fuel that permits her to affect her world. In the revisioning of the Mother of Babylon's story, the Prophetess of the Wildfire describes herself as the *crucible, boiling down the steel out of which a million-bladed sword will be forged.* She is the hot will to destroy contained within the cool, crisp knowing that change will be born of her raw destruction.

Consider the feminine will to create as not opposed to the feminine will to destroy, as both fem-forces writhe within the solar plexus chakra of the Wild One. Know the feminine will as integral to the birth-death-birth cycle, an instrumental force known as the *Iccha Shakti* in Tantra that precedes any action, whether that action is generative or destructive. When a Witch works her magick, her will is akin to both a manifestation and a banishing spell, and she engages and trusts the primal feminine force to infuse her Craft with the particular scent of wolf fur and dried blood. Anything she is manifesting is concurrently banishing all other possibilities, and any banishment, any casting out of that which does not belong in her world, is also manifesting the world she desires in the absence of that *thing* she does not want. There is no light separate from dark, no birth separate from death.

This Is What Our Power Looks Like

This is what our power looks like; it looks like wide-hipped and sure-footed movement forward despite the rapid rhythm of the heart and trepidation in the belly. It looks like hand-holding and authentic reassurance. It looks like red rage transmuted to emerald heart healing. It looks like mournful howls and streaming tears, clenched fists and gut-born resignation. It looks like a mother cradling the body of her son. It looks like a mama cat eating her own afterbirth. It looks like real conversations with babes about self-compassion and the autonomy of their bodies, and it looks like a sharp-nailed middle finger given to every new incarnation of the Witch-hunt that arises to terrorize the feminine heart.

This is what our power looks like; it looks like a frenzied hailstorm and the spiral roar of a tornado. It looks like rushing subterranean rivers ground-swelling from below and shaking the foundations of backward systems. It looks like Kali's red tongue and Oya's lightning bolt. It looks like Medusa's slithering hair and the Mother of Babylon's ten-headed beast, and it looks like a woman holding her body a little straighter since she was called "too this" and "too that," since she was caged by others' words into an overnarrowed view of the vast, sparkling, and sprawling majesty that is she.

A woman rising into her spiritual power eventually faces a high-ledged wall that seems impossible to surmount, and this wall is built from the heavy stones of long-standing feminine disempowerment. In order to truly embrace the Priestess path, she must dig out and dismantle indoctrinated beliefs not only about divinity and deity; she must seek and destroy beliefs that discount her will as ineffectual, her self-esteem as low, and her selfhood as weak or inferior to her spirit-hood.

In your depths, my love, make peace with the power of your will to break down, burn through, and bust open. The powers of the Mother are not only those of manifestation and generation. The primal face of the Mother is hard-jawed and fierce, with a pierced nose and forked red tongue. She wears a belt of skulls and wields a bloodstained blade. She is the destroyer of ego and outmoded systems, and she will show you who you are. Looking the dark Goddess in the black-mirror eye does not feel comfortable and safe, and she has no soft-breasted and warm embrace for you.

The feminine divine dark is the power of the waning moon, the great letting go. She is the death doula and the somber mourning ritual. She is grace and the painful void of nothingness, and she is a soft whimper of loneliness under the darkening sky. Know this, Priestess: There are few things in this world that cause more anguish than realizing that you are not who you thought you were, and, quite often, such a realization comes on the heels of a great wounding. The sword of the Dark Goddess hits us in the belly, the seat of our sense of self, and forces us to release the parts of our outward identities, the masks we show the world, that have become restrictive to our souls, the truest parts of ourselves. In the battle, we have no choice but to release personality traits, roles, and other certainties, because they are spilling out from our middles onto the mother-loving ground.

Handwritten Verses: Diary of the Warrioress

Begin this experience by recalling a time when you were forced to let go of a particular aspect of your identity. Perhaps it was the perfect mother, the rebellious daughter, the fearful follower, or the ever-poised leader. You might reflect on your experience from unmasking rituals and mythwork in the Books of Earth and Water to gain inspiration. For this experience, the particular force that spurred the letting go was one that was harsh and humbling, like a betrayal or an uncharacteristic mistake. It seemed unfair, and it was completely unexpected, like a sudden and unwelcome visitor busting through your locked door to show you your most fearsome shadows. In your depths, there was whole-body anguish, but, upon the ascent, you knew that particular experience allowed a previously buried piece of your soul to rise; there had been no room for it before, but the wounding decluttered the belly-centered sense of self just enough to permit greater and much-needed authenticity.

Let this personal mythwork be a healing experience, a spell in its own right for making sense of a particular pain that had been scripted into your story. You may use the prompts I offer here or edit them as you see fit. Envision a fierce feminine presence standing with you as you write, and invite the wild flame-tending muse to speak through you.

Part I: Verses of the Wayward Queen

She can barely recall the shape of the masks she used to wear, but she remembers they were made of...

For all of her know-how and foresight, she never saw it coming; it hit her without warning, coming from behind like...

In hindsight, she can see herself lying on the ground, surrounded by long-winged angels, and begging...

Part II: A Warrior's Surrender

Clinging to those parts of herself she no longer needed was an act of futility, so she...

Laying down all her weapons, she chose...

Pain gave way to a numb sort of liberation, but she knew it would not be over until...

Part III: Dark Goddess Encounter

She named the part of herself that had been destroyed...

Forever changed, she now walked with a particular grace and ease she had not known in this life, and her body was...

> She had looked the Dark Goddess in the eye, knew herself as her, and bowed deeply to the Mystery for...
>
> If you feel called, share your story with a circle of supportive friends, wild sisters, or other flame tenders who share your values. Light a fire, gather as our ancestors gathered, and gift them with your words.

BLESSED BE THE HEARTH-HOLDING WOMEN: THE HEATHENS' RIGHT TO REST

Blessed be those wisdom keepers busy with babes and weary from workdays gone on too long. Yes, we must be magick makers and activists. We must embody feminine ire and work to change our worlds, but we must also tend to our aching souls. Our magick is only as strong as we are, and even the most righteously raging heathen must claim her right to rest, and rest well.

Women sense when their fires are burning low. We understand that our will to make change cycles within our ever-shifting psyches, erupting in a great burst of heat one day, then dimming to near darkness the next. We must take time to recharge as needed, to quietly tend the flames closest to us, those small but well-loved altars in our hearts and our homes, and we must not become defeated — must not lose that radical hope — when we feel called toward self-preservation and soul restoration.

Our magick is only as strong as we are, and even the most righteously raging heathen must claim her right to rest, and rest well.

Remember that many patterns of sharing and being seen in our world are new, and our bodies and psyches have not evolved to process the rage, melancholy, and trauma many of us face on our multiple screens every day. Indeed, we do have a responsibility to act to change those injustices that anger us, to heal those wounds that affect us most deeply and directly, but we also have a responsibility to our holy bodies and aching minds. No one will do our sacred work for us if we burn out, so we must keep the fires burning for ourselves, forever and always.

Chapter 8

Fire Rituals

The ceremonial fires are hot and holy, and we cannot stand too close for too long. All elements beckon us toward moderation and balance, and fire is certainly no exception. Too much earth, and we begin to feel heavy and change resistant. Too much water, and we drown in a sea of chaotic emotion. Too much fire, and we incinerate even the parts of our world we wish to keep. The keys to working with the elements in a meaningful and practical way are balance and authenticity, and we must constantly be reflecting on the power embodied by those with which we seek kinship.

The power of fire is the power to animate, and to wield that power is to believe you have the right to make the shifts you know are necessary to create the life, home, love, community, and world you seek. Most of the rituals I offer in this chapter are intended to heal the feminine will, to remedy a deep-seated belief that many of us harbor that tells us we do not hold the power to effect change. Adapt these seven rituals as needed, and take great care to balance your fiery Craft with opportunities for reflection and rest. Remember, you can be a Priestess of fire and quietly tend the flames from time to time. It is not a daily investment of strong will and hot rage that is required of the fire-keeper; it is an enduring belief, one that may burn low as often as it burns white-hot, that her will and her magick *matter*. Your radical hope matters, Priestess, and your ancestors are keeping the fire burning for you.

THESE GUTS ARE MINE: A RITUAL FOR HEALING THE WILL

The solar plexus is the seat of the will, an in-the-gut energy center that formed during our wild toddlerhood and continues to shape our sense of self-efficacy and agency throughout our lives. The insults and admonishments that affect the wild woman most brutally are taken not just to heart; they are taken to belly. Every time a child is told to keep quiet, keep still, and every other instruction aimed at taming what is most human and natural but somehow misaligned with the social ideals of good behavior, the will is affected. Certainly, this is not to advocate the raising of feral or neglected children, which can, of course, have dangerous and detrimental effects on the impressionable psyche. In the absence of models drawn from nature, of opportunities for exploring the wild world, children can become small soldiers, holding their bodies overrigid and pursing their lips tight so as not to offend, stand out, or make mistakes.

Time and healing are required, for certain, but we keep our will strong when we, of our own volition, dig and dive to find out who we are rather than rely on someone else's interpretation of our purpose, passions, and ultimate place. Healing the damage done to the feminine will is a practice integral to a Priestess's path, for she can hardly work her magick to change her world if she believes her spiritual actions are soft and futile, if she believes her Witch's will to be completely ineffectual, if she haplessly wanders the Red Road rather than walks firm with direction.

Consider times in your life when you felt most empowered and alive, when you were engaged in some sort of action that seemed to flow through you effortlessly, as if your body were a medium for sheer purpose. Harness that in-the-belly fire now, and seek out a place that feels powerful to you.

Stand with feet wide and knees slightly bent. Lift your palms slightly skyward and begin to breathe with force.* Pump your belly inward on the exhale with an audible but hushed *ha* sound then inhale through the nose sharply. Stay with this, and allow your voice to get louder in your own time. With every breath, visualize your solar plexus becoming a vibrant orb of golden light, expanding throughout your body and enveloping your aura. Be consumed by the force of your own will. If you can sense any stagnant or dark parts of the

---

*   This breathing technique is not recommended for those with asthma or other breathing difficulties, pregnant women, or those prone to panic attacks or extreme anxiety.

energy, breathe through them with all you have, eventually shouting *Ha!* on every out-breath like a warrior Priestess. Stay attuned to your heart-drum and praise the unbridled life force rising within your guts and stretching heartward.

Once the energy feels immense and intense, this mantra is yours. Howl these affirmations to the holy sun and continue to embody the fire: *These guts are mine! My sword is raised, and my will is strong! I will not be quiet! I will not stay small! I will not bow, and I will not beg! I am a Prophetess of the Wildfire, and no one will douse these flames!* Walk through your world now like a discerning and impassioned wilderness guide, a hooded prophet on a vision quest seeking truth with a laser-eyed focus and fierce intent. And so it is.

VERSES OF THE BEAST WITHIN:
RITUAL MORNING PRAYER OF THE PROPHETESS

Materials: *Mirror*

On those overgray mornings when an extra dose of passion is needed, when you are feeling called to walk hard on ground, when you wake yearning to be a living beacon of radical hope, these words are yours. Speak them into a mirror if you are able, plant them on your inner altar with your voice, and let them bloom there like giant sunflowers as the sun rises.

> She's made your bones her den, this seven-headed beast of the primal feminine dark. Call her Medusa and she may answer you, for she is crowned with a serpentine and many-eyed intuition that only the most primeval souls will recognize. She does not walk with grace but with a particular bemuscled strength that will not stand down when there are still children to be fed and choking power chains to be broken.
>
> She's coiling around your ribs now, my love, and licking at your heart. She's hissing hymns of the ancient feminine and showing you the way deeper into the musty dark, and she's beckoning you hellward to keep you from being ever blinded by artificial light. Remember who you are, Priestess. You are a fire-keeper and a medicine woman. You are a magick maker and a flame tender. This fire temple is yours, and its sacred embers are kept alight by all the women in your bloodline.
>
> And so it is.

THIS RAGE IS OURS:
A COMMUNAL RITUAL OF GLORIOUS VALIDATION

Materials: *Dried burning herbs for clearing such as cedar, frankincense, or palo santo (if you are indoors); instruments or rhythmic music (optional)*

Location: *A wild place near a body of water, if possible*

Some of the most effective spells begin with a whole-body acknowledgment that something about the Witch's world is profoundly amiss. Tie your anger to a desired goal, my love, and you will do much to empower the shift you desire. Importantly, if you are seeing red and unable to think clearly, it is best to wait until the rawest rage has passed, processing it in a way that both validates and honors your right to feel. Starhawk writes in *The Spiral Dance*: "The primary principle of magic is connection. The universe is a fluid, ever-changing energy pattern, not a collection of fixed and separate things." Unacknowledged anger has the power to separate you from all that is, creating an invisible barrier between you, the magick maker, and the very world you hope to heal.

This is a ritual of acknowledged rage. Ideally, it is practiced in a small group, but if you must practice this ritual on your own, begin by envisioning your ancestors standing with you and raising their fists high in solidarity, nodding in affirmation of your birthright as a change agent. If you are with your fellow Wild Ones, stand in a circle in a safe space, preferably out of doors. If you are inside, ensure you have a clearing herb to cleanse the space after the ritual is finished. Facing circle center, have everyone focus their awareness on the belly, perhaps drumming softly on the solar plexus with the right hand. Additional instruments can be added as well or rhythmic music played. Envision a single thing that raises your feminine ire as specifically as possible, and feel how your body is affected. Note that all negative emotion is physically expressed as flexion, with the body potentially hunching forward in a protective stance.

When ready, you will begin chanting "I hear you" in unison for a few moments before one circle member will move into the center. They will begin with the words "I am angry because…" finishing the phrase in whatever way feels meaningful and true, taking as long as they need to, and moving their bodies, growling, and beating the ground in whatever way feels authentic. The other group members will keep chanting but mirror the movements of the individual at circle center until it feels finished. All members will know it is finished because the participant moves from the center back to position.

Every member who wishes to be seen and heard will take her turn, with full and unquestioned opt-out permission given to all individuals by the space holder before the circle begins. Know that this ritual is intense, and make sure all participants understand the palpable nature of the energy that will be summoned. After the ritual is over, be sure to cleanse every participant with a smoke bath or quick dip in a body of water, then circle together and process the emotions through sharing; this final step is important, as it integrates the experience into heart-centered communication, prompting the transmutation process and permitting the shift to occur. This ritual affects all participants differently, with some people leaving feeling empowered and joyful, while others feel unsettled or depleted. Ensure that a support system exists after this ritual for anyone who needs it, and discuss the validity and perfection of all emotions and the merit of the feminine being seen in all its raw and snarling glory. And so it is.

OUR SHARED CRUCIBLE:
A THREE-PART RITUAL OF DEEP TRANSMUTATION

Materials: *Candles or alternative fire source, pieces of paper suitable for burning, fire bowl or fireplace*

Descend into the molten core of your will, blessed Prophetess. Here, you may scry your way forward through and away from the darkness where all your wicked vitriol bubbles in a stagnant well. Ask yourself how your rage can be repurposed into action and what the outcome of that action will be. Once you can answer these questions, set a metaphorical fuse beneath the bubbling stuff and send it bursting skyward. If you are full of feminine ire after a great loss or betrayal, perhaps you must speak and be heard in order to free yourself from the binds of grief. If you are spitting sharp nails at an unjust policy where stone-faced men in suits have decided the fate of women's bodies, grab the hands of your sisters and march to the government buildings.

The many-colored threads of our soul-wounds can be beautifully woven into the fabric of our known identities, the parts of ourselves we come to understand, and potentially even adore, through harsh, spine-aching work and asking the deep questions we have run from all our lives. There is a rage that limits us and a rage that liberates us.

The rage that limits us is the rage born directly of a soul-wound that remains buried in festering soil beneath a well-manicured lawn. We may have all the appearances of perfection, and we worry that harvesting such raw emotion and what we may perceive as a shameful experience might brown the landscape we have worked so hard to maintain. The rage that liberates is the rage that is understood and utilized to support genuine soulful values.

There is a rage that limits us and a rage that liberates us.

The wounds common to the primal feminine affect many wild women as they grow, very often becoming apparent while they remain in their too-small gardens. The wound may then become a catalyst for that initial escape, igniting a sudden craving for the Red Road journey. Consider the unexamined wound a blockage, often the most immense psychic obstacle, to encountering our true, wild selves. The Triple Goddess metaphor can be applied to the soul-wound experience, with the ways in which our inner Maidens, Mothers, and Crones become wounded and feel rage distinguishable according not to linear age but to our energetic makeup and chakral maps. Rage born of individual wounds is often the most difficult to transform, and it becomes an obstacle to our feminine freedom.

Part 1. The Blocked Rage of the Maiden

Light your fire, Priestess, and recall the attributes of our inner Maidens, those aspects of ourselves that are akin to Salome's blessed dance. The Maiden lies beneath our veils, both those we consciously place and those wrapped around our skin while we sleep. The unbridled sensual in all of us cages itself in order to keep from being left behind by others. As children, as those tiny Priestesses who cast spells without even trying and commune with the soft-bodied creatures with steady hands and knowing eyes, we learn that certain aspects of our personalities will get us metaphorically or actually cast out of our loved ones' arms. In an effort to keep from being abandoned, first by our families and later by our friends and peers, we submerge our fierce presence, emotional fluidity, and holy sensuality.

The rage of the Maiden is that of a woman disallowed from claiming her wild, often erupting with great volatility, even violence, and resistance to feeling it precludes its transmutation. When the Maiden-self is not integrated, a woman learns she does not have the right to embodied feeling, and she holds herself with a hard-jointed rigidity. In many ways, the wound of the Maiden is the most dangerous but also the most pervasive, as every time a woman is told her body does not belong to her, this wound is reopened. This can happen brutally through violence or subtly through various media messages. The wound of the Maiden is inextricably bound to the only real demon — that is, shame — and she overlays her righteous rage with veil upon veil in order to remain in the graces of those she loves.

Consider the ways in which the wound of the Maiden might affect you and your world. Ask yourself how a fear of being left behind or alone affects your will and your magick. On a small piece of burnable paper, complete the following prompt: *I am the Maiden. This body is mine, and no one will tell me...* Read your words aloud, and set them to burn in your burning bowl or fireplace.

Part 2. The Blocked Rage of the Mother

Our inner Mothers are active and relational, in contrast to the Maiden, who is not generatively productive and is largely individualistic in her thinking. The Mother is a creatrix, a giver of new life and a protectress of sacred work. The Mother in all of us craves nurturing connection in many forms, hardly limited to the relationship between her and child, and she herself is fed by seeing her work flourish and her relationships, to others and to community, thrive without depleting her selfhood and personal integrity. Our inner Mother is also a storyteller, a source of authentic voice and strong, hard truths. The Mother becomes wounded through the ego destruction of great betrayal, and, fearing future violations of the heart, she may dilute her own generative work in order to please her family or others in her inner circle.

The betrayal wound keeps the Mother from being truly whole, and she becomes the mirror for the patriarchy's perception of traditional gender roles. A betrayal wound comes later in life than an abandonment wound, often affecting us during adolescence and young adulthood when we learn that our friends and lovers do not honor us as unconditionally as we might expect.

There is a deep understanding within all our psyches that the divine Mother lives inside our hearts, that she has been eclipsed by the shadows of the Father, and that we deserve to be respected. When this expectation is betrayed, we bleed bright red, often subjected to the deepest pain we can remember experiencing, until that in-the-gut blow becomes rage.

The rage of the inner Mother in response to a great betrayal — be it sexual, financial, emotional, or otherwise — can often be transmuted when we examine it on a more collective level; this is, importantly, not to rob the one who was wounded of her right to rage, much less encourage forgiveness of the betrayer. Rather, it is to partially soothe the sting of the wound by reflecting a shared feminine experience. The feminine feels betrayed by the masculine on a level greater than our partnerships, and there is much merit in exploring the extent to which our relationships are microcosms of the grander drama, the great interplay between the divine feminine and sacred masculine, both struggling to be seen and heard in the global collective.

Ask yourself how the wound of the Mother has manifested in your life, Priestess. In what ways has betrayal struck at your heart, and in what ways has it affected your will? Complete this prompt on a piece of paper, read it aloud, and set it to burn: *This heart is mine, and I will never again be...*

Part 3. The Blocked Rage of the Crone

While the Mother is undervalued in our society, she remains far more socially supported than our inner Maidens and Crones. The Crone is our Goddess-self. The Crone is our wise elder who intuits the way forward without scientific rationale. The Crone is the knowing woman, our divine omnipotence. The wound of the Crone is escape, often through addiction, in response to spiritual oppression and invalidated divinity.

Our society does not value spiritual quest, and there is a part of all of us craving nature pilgrimage and a felt presence of the divine source that can only come from time spent in the Holy Wild. Our Crone-selves are psychically awake and physically still, thinking in slow spirals and barely visible relationships. Engaging the Crone takes time, a lifelong journey of inquiry and innocence. The Crone never claims mastery, for her wisdom has shown her just how much growth humanity has to do before compassion rules over consumption. The Crone is chronically undersatiated in our world, with few workable socially acceptable pathways for empowered and embodied spiritual quest, particularly for women. In response to the unquenched thirst for God-Goddess-Mystery, the inner Crone in all of us demands escape, a liberation from environmental destruction, and a fleeing from the sins of the shortsighted Father.

The Crone is not unlike Lilith in her urge to run from perceived injustice. The rage of the Crone is a muted numbness, as she prefers to simply escape from that which diminishes her worth. She will not stay and rage, as will the Maiden and the Mother, as she is on a slow inward journey of divine realization. She leaves to look for the genderless Goddex, the essence of the precious Mystery in all things. She leaves to look for a meaning greater than what she has found, and she leaves to look for an answer to the prayers she whispers when the nights are dark and her hood is raised against the wind. This is her wound, our wound, and the wound of the unburnt feminine all humanity shares.

Ask yourself how the wounds of the Crone have affected your will and your world. How have you had your spiritual power taken away, and what would you say now to reclaim your serpentine crown? Complete the following prompt, read your words aloud in a resonant voice, and set it to burn: *This spirit is mine, and if there's one thing I know, it's this...*

To complete this ritual, to ground yourself, discern where you feel love in the body, and anoint yourself there with the ashes once they have cooled. Do not declare yourself healed. Declare yourself *whole*. Paint your skin with as much ash as you like, a symbolic action of reverence and rebirth, and rise wide-winged like the phoenix you are. And so it is.

PYROMANCY OF THE PROPHETESS:
A RITUAL OF DIVINATION BY FIRELIGHT

Materials: *Candle or alternative fire source*

Fire is the original oracle. Begin with a question or an area of your life on which you would like greater clarity. You might consider which of these primal feminine wounds has affected you most deeply, my love, or you might ask a question about a lost lover, a pending move, or another pressing issue that holds meaning for you now. Be as specific as possible. Set the intention that you divine clarity on this thing, that you be gifted with a missing piece of information or a deep knowing you had not honored before now, and start a long-burning fire. Become your ancestors, looking long into the flames without needing to rush away too quickly. You may light a single candle's wick or pile the kindling high in your cauldron, as the size of the fire matters far less than its duration. Grant yourself an hour or more to gaze deep into these flames, Prophetess. What do you see? Once you have your answer, you might ask the fire to tell you something of your rage's merit, your wound's purpose, and your pending journey. Ask the fire to gift you with greater meaning, to reconcile your rage with your grace, and to show you a symbol of your wild will. Soften your gaze, Witch, and bid the flames show you who you truly are. And so it is.

YOUR RUNE BONES: A RITUAL DIVINATION BY BODY

Materials: *Candle*

This is practical magick and everyday alchemy. Come be seated, my love. Light a candle. Press your thumbs to forefingers, and hold your right hand in front of your belly, left hand in front of your heart. Ask your body to show you how a joyful *yes* feels. Did your spine lengthen? Did you shift forward? It is the subtlest movement you are after, Priestess. Do not look for it to be immense. Ask your body to show you how a hard *no* feels. Did you hunch down, move back, or feel a tightening in the belly? Body divination feels different for everyone, but trust your inner pendulum and tune in to your rune bones. You are the black mirror, Witch, and you need no gold-embossed cards or crystal ball. Ask your body to tell you whether to go left or right, move or stay, wait or run full force. Your bones and your blood know the way, for you are the embodied omniscience. You are the deity and the ever-present divine feminine. And so it is.

POWER PROVERBS:
SPOKEN AFFIRMATION RITUALS FOR THE HOLY HEATHEN

Commit one or more of these affirmations to memory, Prophetess, and call it to mind when you need it most. Share it with other women when they need words of validation and power, and remember that the best affirmations are those you have created yourself.

Blessed be the woman who has been to hell, for she can teach others the language spoken in the underworld.

Sacred is the rage of the Priestess, for it holds the power to transform and restore all.

Anger at great injustice is charmed wildfire.

You are not your wounds; you are the fertile richness of what lies beneath them, the primordial soul-stuff that powers your flesh-and-bone frame.

There is no greater change agent than a woman's wild will.

Chapter 9

Fire Magick

All our magick, from the simplest and most timely words spoken in affirmation of our worth to our most elaborately planned and carefully orchestrated ceremonies, is an expression of our radical hope, a conversation with the universe that says, *Here. Here is the kind of world I want to live in.* The fire element is not only a symbol of that radical hope but also a great enactor, a driving force that moves us toward the future we seek. All magick transforms, but fire magick purges and activates, purifies and ignites our wills, and spurs us onward in the face of adversity.

In this chapter, I offer fire magick in the form of daily practices, spellcraft, and pathworking experiences that ask you to empower your agency. This is the Craft of the willful Priestess, the sovereign heathen, and the activist-alchemist. Only move through the offerings that feel authentic to you, and feel free to adapt the materials and specific steps to suit your needs. This temple is yours, after all.

TOWARD A TRUER MAGICK:
SPELL BUILDING FOR THE WILLFUL WITCH

A Priestess's spellcraft is critically dependent upon her belief that she has an embodied right to affect her world. Women who know themselves to have been raised within the context of spiritually oppressive systems, including religions asserting that divinity was not only external but also superior and male, are charged to deconstruct the barriers to their own agency; these high walls may have been built by someone else's hand, but they remain internal, psychic obstacles to spiritual freedom. No spell will be effective in the absence of the practitioner's belief in her own empowered right to act and effect change, with her unimpeded will entirely reliant on and preceded by this belief.

Once Priestesses have a felt sense of their own agency, once they see with their own eyes that their spellcraft has caused change, they begin to truly own not only their magickal agency but also their internal divinity. Women look to Goddess archetypes as divine reflections of aspects of their own psyches, as mystical embodiments of what is not at all whimsical or otherworldly: their rage, compassion, wrath, beauty, ugliness, and power. My love, resist the internal belly clenching you might experience when I tell you this: There is a part of you that is a She-God, and that knowledge does not equate to egotism, arrogance, or delusions of grandeur. You require a regular felt experience of your God-self, and I have brewed some medicine for you.

Carve out some holy time for yourself, ideally on the same day of the week around the same time. Perhaps Mondays can be "moon-days," or Fridays, named for the Norse Goddess of love, Frigga, can be your dedicated Craft time. Whatever time you choose, ensure that it aligns with your schedule and will not feel overly burdensome. Whenever a new practice is added, often an old and outmoded one needs to go, to be sacrificed in order to make space. This sadhana will last for one month, so potentially vow to disengage with screens or other time suckers for a few hours before and after your designated holy time, as your life allows. Sacred silence and solitude invite the Mystery to come through, permit subtle messages to be received, and create the opportunity for embodied knowing — that is, the felt interconnectivity between the body and the psyche.

Once a week for four weeks, during your designated holy time, give yourself one hour to work your magick. You might begin by reviewing your personal myths from the "Fire Verses" chapter and finding one line that you feel was truly spoken from your soul. These words, these *spell*-ings, will become the foundation for your practice. Let go of any lofty expectations for how you will feel or what you will experience, but be completely open to sensing your internal divine nature.

Holy Day 1: Circle Casting and Energy Raising

Materials: *Journal, writing utensil, four candles*

The practice of circle casting is a vital gateway to spellcraft, as it provides opportunity for the magick worker to sense and declare her ecological position. The Priestess acknowledges where her feet stand and how the elements and directions live within her body, working through her and with her to support intention. On your first holy day, you will cast a circle and raise energy using your body, mind, and will.

Set four candles or other objects around you to mark a circle, each object representing a direction. Stand at circle center now and begin to turn your body slowly clockwise with your eyes closed. Notice which direction feels the most like home, and this is where you will begin. Raise your arms high and call out to this direction in whatever way seems right in the moment, perhaps howling fiercely: *Energies of the west! Hear me! I am here, and I am staying!* Or perhaps whisper-praying: *Fiery energies of the south, I welcome you.* Remember your Craft is your own. It belongs to no one else. There are Priestesses who wail like banshees, and there are those who command respect and communion in the softest tone; both ways are true, as are any in between.

Moving clockwise, call to all four directions, then stand at the circle center with your knees slightly bent, again facing your home direction and recalling your soul-spoken line from your myth. Begin repeating it silently, letting your Witch's voice echo in your bones. As you do so, see if you are gifted with any visions or in-the-body sensations. When ready, speak the same words aloud, and do not be alarmed if your voice seems to somehow be not your own. If it feels right to let your body move within the circle as you speak, do it. If it feels right to stay stone-still, do it. Your being will become a purposed and strong-willed medium for the Mystery now, so leave room for the unexpected to emerge and work through you.

Stay with this, noticing all that seems important, for twenty minutes or more before letting your voice grow softer until you are again repeating your mantra only silently. Open the circle now, moving counterclockwise and beginning with the direction you ended with at the inception of your sadhana. Go to your journal now and make note of all feelings that arose during your work; it need not be eloquent, only descriptive. Then end your journal entry with a final proclamation: *This will is mine.*

Holy Day 2: Intention Shaping

Materials: *Journal, writing utensil, four candles*

For your next holy day, consider whether or not you would like to work with the same words, choose another line from the myth, or create another mantra altogether. Read through your journal entry from the prior week and consider any messages you received from the Mystery, any pertinent signs or relevant dreams, that may inform your spellwork. Ask yourself what you would like to call into your life right now, what is truly and wholly *for you* that you do not yet have in your hands, and what you can feel in your bones as real that has not yet been made manifest in your world. Mind you, this is not an exercise in the fluff-filled Law of Attraction philosophy. True manifestation magick connects your unique values to what you want not only for yourself but for the world. Ask yourself: Do you really believe you have the right to have this thing, and does the manifestation of these changes support your deepest convictions and in-the-gut sense of selfhood? Where does this vision fit into the larger conversation between you and the cosmic web, and how is it linked to societal growth, justice, and evolution?

Again cast the circle, giving yourself the freedom to change the specific order and nature of this practice or stay with what worked, then raise the energy as before using your chosen mantra and movement. This time, when you can feel the energy palpably within and surrounding you, let your voice naturally fall into silence. Begin to visualize your intention now as if it has come to fruition, as if you are living now in a pivotal scene where this desire has been completely realized. Sense the sounds, tastes, smells, colors, and subtle vibrations of this scene. Know it as real. Call it in by being there as wholly as possible. Stand in the deep knowing that this intention has been realized, and feel your power rising in the belly. Come back to the mantra now, repeating your sacred verses for as long as it feels right and allowing your words to connect you to your intention. Feel that every sound you make is fueling your vision, pumping your desire with the nutrients it needs to grow, and stay with this practice for as long as you have before concluding as before, opening the circle and journaling, ending your entry with these words: *This will is mine. So mote it be.*

Holy Day 3: Charging Power Symbols

Materials: *Journal, writing utensil, four candles, object to charge (see description below)*

Revisit your journal entries from the previous holy days. Permit your mantra and vision to evolve now, given any messages you have received during the previous week. On this holy day, you will proceed as before, with one addition: In your circle, you will have an object you will be charging. This can be a spell bag that includes words describing your vision along with meaningful herbs or crystals, a precious stone or other natural object, or any totem that holds meaning for you. Cast the circle, raise the energy using your chosen mantra, and sink into your total visualization of your intention. Be there with all that you are; know it to be true; then, when ready, infuse that knowing into your object.

Come back to the mantra and cling to the whole-body, whole-psyche understanding that you deserve this, that you have the right to call this in. Curl your fingers around your object now without touching it; pour the raised energy into it with your hands without allowing actual hand-to-object contact. You may feel a subtle pulling of the energy through your hands toward the object, but the sensation may not be palpable. Gaze at the object now, but let your focus go a bit soft. Feel that you are pouring the same force into the object with only your gaze. You may see a halo of light around the object, or you may see nothing at all. Stay with this, allowing natural ebbs and flows of energy to move through you. When ready, come back to your mantra, call all remaining energy within the circle to infuse your object, then open the circle. Place your object somewhere sacred, on an altar if you have one, where it will not be toyed with during the week. Record the experience in your journal, ending your entry with these words: *As I will it, so mote it be.*

Holy Day 4: Blessed Surrender and Release

Materials: *Journal, writing utensil, four candles, object from holy day 3*

One of the most crucial aspects of any spell is its release. Priestesses are tasked with holding intense passion for their intention during the spell and then completely surrendering to the Mystery once it has been cast; this is no easy feat, and it takes practice. On this last holy day, you will work with the entire spell journey, and then you will let it go completely, trusting that the cosmic forces are holding it in their hands now.

Reflect on your week and past journaling, evolving the mantra and vision if need be. Reflect on why your work has been important, not only for you as one individual but for the world at large. Move through all previous spellwork steps: casting the circle, raising the energy, charging the object with your will and your words, and then opening the circle. Now, carry the object to a secret place in nature, a place that feels blessed by spirit, and release your object in whatever way seems right. Bury it, float it, leave it to sit under a maternal tree, but, whatever its place of rest, you must leave it be. Do not come back and visit it until long after your spell has come to fruition, if then. Be full of faith that your will has worked as it should, affirm the merit of your holy days, and retract your claws. Offer your object a final blessing before you leave it to the elements: *This will is mine. So mote it be. Blessings for all, and blessings for me.*

And so it is.

THE FUNERAL PYRE FOR WHAT WAS: A MAGICK SPELL OF LETTING GO

Materials: *Paper, writing utensil, candle, fire bowl*

The Priestess does not lower her eyes and demurely take her leave while man-made injustice runs roughshod over the Earth. She does not lock her rage away to spoil and rot; she keeps the anger purposed and fresh, ready to fuel the next calculated maneuver. There is a certain charm to her upset, you see. This Wild One harbors a necessary foresight, a knowing intuition, and a primal feminine instinct that keeps her steadfast on the path to a better world. She is not content to stay still and silently red-faced in her too-small space, for she knows the utility of her rage and knows it well.

Preceding the transmutation of the wild woman's rage is necessary destruction. This is the Dark Goddess's predicted return, the Prophetess's divination unleashed, and the reason why the feminine dark has been so historically feared. Consider times in your life, my love, when you burned your world down to make space without even knowing for what purpose that space would be used and with a hawk-sighted direction that felt more belly driven than heart born. What seedlings sprouted from the still-smoking soil? What grace lay there buried in smoldering ash, and what wide-winged, mythic creature arose after the chaos cooled and the high-flamed turmoil dimmed down to warm coals?

The spiritual disempowerment of women has created a disease of the feminine psyche that affects our collective ability to wield our will and our magick to birth a better world. We inoculate the feminine energies in our children against this pandemic of disempowerment by teaching the cyclical nature of time, the old ways, the ephemeral grace of both joy and sadness, and the importance of social courage in standing against racism, sexism, and other forms of oppression. We sip elixirs of affirmations and oracles to undo the damage already done to our majestic agency, and we rewrite the stories that told us of our moral weakness and our inborn malice. We must also act to continually honor the work we have done, to take time out from our forward-thinking spellcraft and nourish our souls in the present moment by marking past victories and giving a nod to our bravehearted healing.

This spell is an act of honor and release. Light candles in the four directions and call to the energies of earth as you face north, air as you face east, fire as you face south, and water as you face west. Sit inside your circle, your energetic container with unbreachable walls, and face south. Have your journal, a writing utensil, and a fire bowl on hand.

Call to mind three times when you have been victorious in your life; these can be seemingly small and uncelebrated moments of glory, such as getting up on a spring morning after a too-long late-winter depression, or glorious occasions that have already been well honored. Every birthday is a victory. Every dream remembered after a restless night's sleep and every kiss well placed is a victory. Casting your circle was a victory. There is victory in every soulful action, Priestess, so call to mind three times you have won in your life, and give these moments the titles they deserve. You might call them "Victory at the Water's Edge," "Battle of the Darkest Night," or another mythic name. Write these three names on separate pages of your journal now; then, one at a time, speak these words or adapt them to suit you: *I am the Warrioress come home, and I am honoring* [name of the victorious moment]. Light the paper off of the south candle, drop it into the fire bowl, and watch it burn. Gaze into the flames and the smoke and divine a piece of information, perhaps one that sources more closure than you might have about that victory, from the ritual burning. Notice how you feel, then move on to the next two victories using the same words, releasing those moments to the cosmic infinite, and staring into the flames like the pyromancer you are. Before you open your circle, stand firm facing the south and affirm: *There is victory in every action.* And so it is.

DEMYSTIFYING THE DEMONESS: PATHWORKING FOR THE INNER WILDLING

The extent to which feminine power, in its myriad forms, has been condemned as evil is nothing less than ancient and global. A demon is a deity who has been labeled as inferior or less than, a primitive creature thought to prey upon kind hearts and pure minds. The Goddess has been demonized in our culture, increasingly cast not into a hellish underworld but into a pink and glittery fairyland where she is harmless but also useless. The contemporary image of Goddess has been commodified, bottled up, and sold as prepackaged but weightless divinity for those who do crave an injection of feminine spirituality but cannot find it, cannot find *her*, in more meaningful, more natural, more primal spaces.

To remember the Holy Wild is to remember her, and to remember her is to face our deepest and most human fears. From girlhood, we are threatened with damnation and degradation unless we honor a masculine God, if not in his religious form, then in human incarnations of overly protective fathers, hierarchical corporations, the military, governments primarily run by men, and our fear-based economic system. To deviate from these political, social, and economic norms is to look certain rejection straight in the eye, and thus women's conformity to the status quo pervades the global landscape. When we rise in various social movements attempting to drive a much-needed change, often instruments of oppression are waiting to take hold even in our activism, even after our most hard-won battles.

A Priestess must continually sift through her world, mining out the insidious and poisonous chemicals of patriarchy bit by bit, hour by hour. A Priestess must continually become the demoness, the long-tongued and wild-haired Dark Goddess not just in her own world but in the world at large. She acts from a place of individualistic rage, but she moves toward the compassionate liberation of the collective. Do not, for one second, believe the problems of this world are too big for you, Sister. Do not succumb to apathy and stuff your healer's hands in your pockets because you were told your work was without true impact.

Do not discount your right to effect change in your world. You were born here, too, and you were born to be a living antidote to the poison of unbalanced masculine dominion.

Do not succumb to apathy and stuff your healer's hands in your pockets because you were told your work was without true impact.

Call to mind your early memories of magick and embodied divinity, those moments during childhood when you met the Mystery without looking for it. Call to mind moments later in life when you were beginning to awaken your inner Priestess, after a garden or two had been left behind and you were walking the Red Road with a stronger will and at a steadier pace. Read these words now, and envision yourself as the little girl in the tale, curious and committed, full of wonder and ready to invigorate those parts of her soul that had been called wicked:

> She kept it hidden, and rightfully so. If her soul-admonishing childhood had taught her anything, it was to tuck away those magickal tools, those found totems that had a bit of mystical otherness to them, lest those who spit the name Witch as if it a curse raise their brows and click their tongues in disgust. And so the black mirror remained beneath her bed, locked without shame inside a box containing a blue and broken robin's egg, a battered journal, a torn tarot card — the High Priestess it was — and a makeshift wand she mischievously carved with stars and diamonds.
>
> Hers was a nighttime practice. After her keepers had gone to sleep, dosed with drink and bitterness, she would drag her box full of mystery from beneath her bed and sit where she could see the moon. She would unpack each sacred relic, one by one and with great care, lining them in front of her legs and whispering apologies to the male

God she was told would one day cast her into a lake of fire to burn for all eternity for the sins she committed now.

Before too long, her repentant prayers would always give way to a more rhythmic chant of grace and gratitude. The magick was a felt magick, an in-the-body sensation she knew to be proof of divine feminine presence. Holding the fragile eggshell in her hands, she would feel a quivering lightness in her heart, as if the baby bird had flown from its nest and made its home inside her rib cage. Caressing the knowing eyes of the High Priestess seated upon her throne, she would feel a pulsing pressure between her brow bones and see visions of hooded wise ones roaming about mist-filled lands. Her journal would lie open, its first page christened only with a single sentence — *In the beginning, there was She* — and she would curl her shaking fingers around her splintered wand and beckon the angels to stand with the ghost of her grandmothers and protect her aching soul.

Last, when she was satisfied no devil was coming for her, she would begin the divination. Staring long into the black mirror, she would ask what would become of this ailing world, and what her part was in the collective awakening. Her vision would go soft and her lips would part as she surrendered to the mysterious communion with all that she was. Hours would pass, and she would see nothing, but it was always this way. Still, she tirelessly awaited the unseen powers showing her something real, gifting her with direction, solidifying into a shape she could see, touch, and taste.

Night after night, she continued this practice, starting her own religion of unrequited longing for the divine to touch her in just the right place. One night, just as the Witching hour approached and the girl was weighted with fatigue and frustration, disgusted with time wasted and faith misdirected, she punched the black mirror and splintered the glass, sending a single shard straight into the robin's shell and shattering the thing to blue dust. A single drop of blood from her hand fell on the High Priestess's crown and reminded the girl of a bleeding Christ, and, in her rage, she broke her wand in two and sent crumbs of willow wood into her open journal.

Gazing down at the mess she had made, weeping for the destruction she had caused and lamenting every choice that had brought her to that pivotal moment, the young prophet finally found what she had been looking for these last long nights. The egg dust had coated the spiderwebbed glass in such a way that the blue-black fractures looked like the petals of violets, blooming right on her tearstained face's reflection where her eyes usually were and spinning about like pinwheels as she circled the collection of broken totems. Her face morphed into an entire spiral galaxy then, whirling in black and blissful space.

She fell to her knees and whimpered gratitude to the feminine Mystery for showing her the divinity in her own soulful eyes, for granting her visions of a wounded world continuing to spin just as it should, a perfect sapphire nature hung just so in the great massive void of the cosmos. Hand to heart, she affirmed herself as the High Priestess and the wand as the fragile egg of new birth and the black mirror that of death and divination, and she gathered up her journal to rewrite the stories of wicked women and cast spells with her voice and her art, from that day forward a Witch awake and a woman unburned.

And so it is.

VOWS OF THE FLAME-TENDING WOMEN:
FIRE MAGICK OF VOICE AND VICTORY

Flame-tending women keep the fires burning against all odds, protecting the softly cracking coals of perpetual hope for a world where all beings are able to live out their souls' deepest purpose. Flame-tending women are present and sovereign, fierce in their commitment to their values and steadfast in their action. At times, they are singular in their goal, having a laser-pointed intention that serves them well. They rest when they feel called, trusting their sisters-in-fury will not let the embers cool while they care for their soft bodies and bright-eyed loved ones, but they always return. Speak these vows when you feel called, Priestess, when your world is showing off for you and you are full of a fiery faith that, for all its woundedness, there is still joy to be had and miracles to be witnessed.

I am a flame-tending woman, and I will keep this fire burning for my soul's next incarnation. May I do enough good in this life — offer up enough gratitude for the gifts I have been given — to be someday born into a world where all children are nourished and held by the wisdom of their elders. When my newborn eyes open again to see the eyes of a mother, may my majestic matriarch show me all the old ways, as her grandmother taught her the mysteries of moon and blood, in just a single mother-to-daughter smile.

While I'm still in this body, bless the little girl who sits curled inside my pelvic bowl begging me to stay quiet and paint my face to be pleasing, for she was shown too much too soon. Bless the weeping teenager who stands in feigned defiance of partnership and holds her throbbing belly like an infant, for she was told of her ugliness and worthlessness by those who claimed to love her. Last, cosmic Mystery, bless the hooded wise woman with fragile bones who stands so still inside the haunted forest of my psyche that I can barely see her, for she was told of the sacred feminine's weakness and the futility of un-resolved spiritual quest. Blessed be the wounded feminine, for years of brutality have not killed the slow-to-wake but ever-enduring Goddess in us all. I am a flame-tending woman, and, by the power vested in my Pagan heart by all the heathen ministries and ancient covens whose names we shall never know, I will keep this fire burning.

And so it is.

FIRE REFLECTION AND FINAL PRAYER: FANNING THESE FLAMES

The magick of fire is born of the unlikely union of hope and destruction. We dismantle, we purge, and we incinerate all in the name of radical hope. We dare to dream our worlds into being, and, in so doing, we claim our right to say no. *No, this does not belong in this new land I am creating.* Let your fires exist both in crucibles of your wild transmutation and on altars in memoriam of who you once were, and let your fires be promise beacons of the beauteous yet-to-come.

Though fire is the potent change maker, it is the union of fire and air that is the true harbinger of transformation. The air element can feed and direct

what is already burning, what might have burned out without the nourishment of space and wind. The wild woman can only burn hot so long in the
same place before she needs to either rest or move, and the air element decides
the future of her inner belly fire. Will it dim, rest, and refuel? Will it die out
enough to permit the wild, compassionate healer to emerge from the ashes?

The air element functions at the heart, and only here does the Priestess
find the love she needs. For all her power, for all her fire-breathing will, she
remains a creature who craves heartfelt communion and an intimate relationship with her world. As we move from the Book of Fire to the Book of Air, we
must ask ourselves what we will build in this new and still-smoking landscape.
What communities shall we foster here, and what relationships deserve our
time and our touch?

As we age, we must ask ourselves how we can become the women we once
needed. For all our wild ways, rootlessness, joyous temple dancing, and righteous rage, there is a part of us that longs to share our stories, to teach, and
to move from the heart instead of the belly. The lone activist can do much to
change her life, but a circle of magick makers can change the *world*. In every
woman's life, there comes a time when it seems she has no choice but to find
her circle, to bond with other like-minded seekers. This is certainly not a permanent plateau on which we become stuck but rather a cyclical calling toward
community. While the elements of earth, water, and fire nourish our individual souls, the air element spirals in and through our heart centers, inviting us
toward relationship, connection, and intimacy. Here, with our hair tossed in all
directions and eyes closed to the rushing wind, we find the medicine we need
most from time to time, the hand-brewed communion with other wild hearts
who will hear us, see us, and love us as the fiery, sovereign women we are.

Lost Verses of the Holy Feminine: Love Me Like a Witch Loves the Moon

Listen, lover. I'm not interested in the ephemeral beauty of roses
today, nor do I wish to hear your heady poetry. I've grown weary of
oversweet romance, and I'm ready to tell you what I really want. Light
a candle, lean in, and listen close.

I want a love so impassioned that it ripples back through the cosmic web and stirs the hearts of the ancients. I want a love that lives on long after the flesh of these two bodies has gone cold, long after these wet lips of mine have spoken their last words and set all my secrets free. Love me like Lilith loves the untamed wilds, like a Witch loves the moon, and I promise you'll never hear a heartbeat truer than mine.

The Book of Air

The air element fills the empty spaces in our hearts, subtly pulsing and winding through the very centers of our being, cooling and calming the overcharred will and subtly urging us to remember the love that infuses and connects us all. Our human cosmic web is spun from creativity and compassion in equal parts, and an embodied soul left to live and thrive without external shame or denigration grows to be generatively creative and wholly loving, sourcing as much inspiration from the dark and unbeauteous places of her psyche as from her glittering, radical hopes and brightly lit dreams. The expression of sacred work and sacred love are unique to the individual, of course — but, with our basic needs met and having been the wild feminine embodiments of earth, water, and fire, we always return to a heartfelt longing to love and be loved in return.

> **Wild Feminine Archetype:** The Witch of Sacred Love
> **Themes in Her-story:** Divine union, the healer-teacher, the cauldron of
> relationship, the cosmic web

Just now, just this very moment, I was struck by a sudden and deep knowing, Sister.
My bones went soft, and my breath caught in my throat.
Look at me! Do I seem very changed to you?

*I feel I may never again be the hard-jawed woman I once was,
having realized so completely what it is to love another —
a son, a daughter, a lover, a friend, a teacher, a grandmother —
with my whole eternal soul.*

Chapter 10

Air Verses

While we develop an intimacy with the earth, water, and fire elements through our own individual souls' explorations — through introspection, our senses, and continual self-reflection — we encounter the air element only in our relationships. The Witch of Sacred Love archetype asks us to consider this question: After the ashes have settled, after the last glowing ember cools and the snaking smoke trails have been licked away by the wind, what is left? The air element has much to teach us about love and longing, gratitude and grace. The Holy Wild does not rush so quickly to fill countless voids opened up by floods, fires, and other disasters, for nature knows the ephemeral majesty of nothingness, and knows it well.

Air is the element most akin to love, made so by the dual and balanced actions of giving and receiving. In our very breath, we find a telling metaphor for love, for a truly symbiotic relationship. The Witch of Sacred Love claims her right not only to love with her whole heart but to be loved in return, just as the exhale inevitably follows the inhale. We receive the breath, our air, take the sustenance we need, and gift it back to the Holy Wild. Like a sovereign and compassionate lover, we give and take in perfect balance, in perfect trust.

The Witch of Sacred Love is an openhearted lover who embraces vulnerability with outstretched arms, who has witnessed the ever-turning wheel of waxing, fruition, waning, and void. Despite all heartbreaks and hardships, this

Witch knows all must die so all may begin again. Even in the depths of total loss, she can sink into the fertile dark knowing a great cocooned transformation is taking place, so long as she can keep her wild heart beating through the anguish. She is not defined by whatever relationships she may be in, whatever roles — of partner, parent, or lover — she might play. The Witch of Sacred Love understands that while intimacy is an invaluable expression of strong-hearted vulnerability, with relationships a great and telling curriculum holding the very lessons our souls must learn in this life, it is also ultimately fleeting.

The gift the Witch of Sacred Love has to share is an understanding that relationships shift, dance, and change direction just like the wild wind. They uplift us one moment and whip around and through us the next — so to live every day of any relationship as if it were the last, to be so whole unto oneself that no single relationship will jeopardize one's sovereignty, is the task of the Witch of Sacred Love. In this chapter of Air Verses, I offer stories and tales with harsh wind currents of love, loss, and longing running through them, themes every woman knows well, interspersed with opportunities to write and share your own life's myths like the healer-teacher you are.

THE WITCH OF SACRED LOVE ARCHETYPE:
WAKING THE HOLY HEALER

All women have loved and lost. All of us are Lilith, Salome, and the Mother of Babylon. We have all been gutted by abandonment and betrayal, and our task is to transmute these wounds into something greater than what caused them. Our task is to become the teacher, friend, mother, mentor, and lover we needed when we were younger.

Our task is to sit in gratitude, even if only for short moments in time, for our ability to love and be loved in return.

Our task is to become the teacher, friend, mother, mentor, and lover we needed when we were younger.

The Witch of Sacred Love archetype honors romantic relationships as ephemeral energetic cauldrons where two souls dance, bubble, and boil for a time, learning from one another, mirroring one another, and shedding some light on the too-shadowy parts in each other's psychic landscape. Such love is an embodied love and, by extension, destined to transform in death, if not before at the hand of another force. The Witch of Sacred Love does not define herself by another person or lose herself when a love is lost, but this does not mean she is immune to the great ache affecting even the most invulnerable heart. She is not an empty vessel who dismisses her selfhood in the name of love or feigns nonattachment in relationships in order to self-protect. She is both humble gift giver and regal queen, seeking balance in all partnerships she wishes to sustain.

The wild feminine thrives in the liminal spaces between this and that, in the open skies and on the mountaintops. Air is the elemental essence of meaningful relationship. Air is what remains when the fires have cooled and the smoke has cleared, the vibrant, wide space in which to build anew and to flourish, yet again, within partnership and community. Air is infinite possibility and opportunity, the very object of that radical hope the Prophetess of the Wildfire keeps her lantern burning for.

If the air element is radical hope realized, we must frame all our relationships as meaningful microcosms of our connection to the global community, our dreamed-for world in which a lasting balance has been struck between the qualities of the divine feminine and sacred masculine. The contested relationship between Mary Magdalene and Christ is a living metaphor, just one of many, for the potential of reinvigorating the bond between the holy masculine and feminine. This is not to herald Christianity over any other religious system, nor to in any way disproportionately sanctify monogamous heterosexual love, nor to delineate as gender-specific roles what are, in essence, cosmic attributes that permeate and infuse all human beings regardless of gender. It is the lost connection with nature we are after, regardless of the names we may give to that connection, and the air element is our holistic relationship, the desire to belong, and the collectivist spirit.

The Witch of Sacred Love, the Magdalene, resides in the feminine psyche as the red-hooded teacher who is the healer-lover, the wilderness guide to the wild heart. She is the alchemist and the mentor, the student and the seeker.

She is the relational feminine, ever-seeking wholeness for our wounded society, busy brewing salve for the fragmented divine masculine, and

> *She is the alchemist and the mentor, the student and the seeker.*

trusting, often against all odds, that the holy feminine is rising amid the political and social chaos. She is the Priestess of Magdala, mourning for the loss of a loving and accessible spirituality. She is Aphrodite, a woman born fully grown to effect change in even the most immature and selfish heart. She is Oshun, great protector of those in need and beauteous incarnation of sweet mother-love, and she is Parvati, the Goddess who stands still in icy waters for hundreds of years in order to romance the divine masculine into action.

All of us are Mary Magdalene, misunderstood, shunned, and mourning the loss of the divine masculine. These blessed incarnations of the deified feminine are the holy healers, beacons of the lighter side of the sacred feminine. Though her story is controversial, it is likely that this Mary — this Mary who has been framed as the virtue-compromised counterpart to the virginal Madonna — was, at the least, one of Christ's most favored disciples. In *The Once and Future Goddess*, Elinor Gadon describes the Virgin Mary and Mary Magdalene as "stereotypical symbols of the virgin and the whore, the virtuous chaste Mary and the penitent sinner Magdalene, they provide models for human behavior that severely inhibit women from experiencing themselves as fully human." In Goddess traditions, the Magdalene has been perceived as the living grail, a keeper of Christ's untainted teachings and wise, spiritual guide in her own right.

The Magdalene embodies traits similar to the Greek Aphrodite, the Yoruban Oshun, and the Hindu Parvati, all three alchemical deities who favor feminine principles of holism and relatedness over individualism and personal abundance. Oshun is the beauteous and venerated Goddess of love and fertility, but she, like Aphrodite and Parvati, also emanates a particular feminine fortitude that is often overlooked by those seeking only the sweet and palatable Goddess. Oshun is a protectress, a wide-winged mother-vulture as much as a warmhearted Orisha. Parvati is the fierce consort of Shiva, her mythology reflecting a continual challenge-made, challenge-met cycle of proving the worth of feminine will. Aphrodite is the change agent, whole unto herself and dependent on no man, yet the reflection of embodied sensual love, the true sex-to-heart connection. In essence, these are not the faces of the pink, fluffy feminine, Sister. These are the healer-mothers who conjure the energetic antidotes to isolation, loneliness, and self-interest, who are interested in lacing the cosmic web with ethereal, whispered love stories about love, loss, and longing, for these are the stories that embody and amplify the truest human experiences — those shared tales of wounding and healing that bind us all.

Myth of the Red-Hooded Widow: Revisioning the Magdalene

"Hail Mary, full of grief," she whispered to herself, eyes dipping to the babe at her breast and lifting to the salty sea on the horizon in a melancholic rhythm. This was how she would heal, one wave at a time, and this was how she would remember him, letting go and sinking into these still and sorrowful moments so completely that she could feel his long arms around her and his breath on her neck.

Theirs had been a timeless love so extraordinary that it held the power to not just shift but shatter many broken spiritual paradigms shaping their imperfect planet. Together, they were a diamond-light infinity symbol marking humanity's blessed potential, and, together, they were a holy dynamic of masculine spirit and feminine soul. She sighed now, heavy with the knowledge that she would be written out of the sacred texts, mourning not for her own historical absence but for that of a love that could have changed the spiritual landscape of the world.

A southern wind blew her red hood down and whipped her hair in all directions, and she wondered if their love had been so profound that nature herself would remember it. Would the breeze whisper into the ears of mourning lovers tales of their long nights spent wild? Would these waves tell their story long after her own soul had passed into the ether to rejoin his, at long last?

The widow eyed two large waterbirds, dipping and rising together above the water, riding the air in unison then breaking apart. The darker gull soared out to sea, leaving the other to fly low and alone toward the shore and land just out of her arm's reach, a lonesome gull striding away from her with as much grace as it had in the air.

"Apart, we are wounded," the Witch of Sacred Love muttered toward the bird. "But your mate will return."

She faked a weak smile in her son's direction as he paused his search for sand creatures to seek her approving glance. "Apart, we are nothing more than fragile children," she muttered, waving to her hunted babe, who she hoped, with all that she was, would never know the same fame, the same shame, that burdened his father. She crushed her eyes closed and wrapped herself in the warm blanket of his memory.

"I can still feel you, my love." Inhaling deeply, she breathed in the musk of his sweat and spoke to his ghost. "I know you are here, and I know you will walk with us to the deep places of this Earth and hide with us inside the dank caves."

She unlatched her sleeping daughter from her breast, breaking the suction with a single finger, and pulled her close. "I know you will be with her as she grows into a woman stronger than me, and I know you will see him rise up from fatherlessness and embody his own sacred masculine strength."

The gull turned toward her and settled into stillness, an unlikely, statuesque avian companion. The widow took no more notice of the bird, even in this sudden, curious stance. Her grief was blowing through her in sudden gusts, and all she could do was speak to her lost lover as if he were still there, still warm and breathing.

"Your hands will hold us while we sleep in secret places, and your ethereal body will stand guard at the door while we pray for peace." Her tears were running hot and wild now, but she kept decreeing the truest eulogy she had for her lost love: "I will teach them the stories they will not read. I will share with them the verses that will not be transcribed by any of the famed prophets, and I will channel your medicine, our medicine, until the day I die. I will tell your daughter of the sheer power alive within her tiny body, and I will bid your son stand against the vile fear that took his father's life. I will be the embodiment of wild feminine grace and fierce love, and I will be a channel for honest expression and righteous compassion. I will hold secret circles attended by red-hooded women who have acquired a distaste for illusion, and I will bid them to seek solace in an activist sisterhood that has no name.

"All the while, my love, my whole body will remember you. My hands will not forget the curves of your ribs or the place where your hair would meet your back. I will always recognize the brown-black of dark grain as the very same shade as that of your kind eyes and the sweet scent of wood dust and salt as that of my stolen lover and truest friend. I will worship you forever, as you worshipped me, and I will wander through this world with our children on my back as a living body prayer to a love so great that it could not possibly be forgotten, for every word we spoke to one another about the Goddess, the Godless, and the Mystery is emblazoned on the crystalline bones of this planet for all time."

The gull spread its wings and made a sharp sound, looking straight into the eyes of the widow as if it understood every word she had said. A harsh wind blew then, and the widow pulled her babe close. She listened for the wind's wisdom, hoping for words of assurance and warmth, but all she heard was a hushed and whistling urge to keep moving. The full moon was rising over the water, an overbright Mother Moon that promised balance and fruition amid loss. Riding the breeze, the darker gull landed next to its partner, and the two bowed their heads in greeting and walked toward the sea, mirroring each other's smooth motions and leaving deep footprints in the sand.

The widow watched them for a few moments, smiling to herself, then stood and raised her hood to cover her hair, beckoning her son to join her as she walked. They would travel through the night again, hugging close to the shoreline and trusting that the shroud of darkness would keep them safe from the wicked ones who stalked them, having faith that the wind and the sea would sweep away all traces of their footsteps, and knowing, with all that she was, that her lost lover lived on inside her still-beating heart, inside her very breath, though she seemed to walk the Red Road alone. A warmer breeze blew behind them now, moving the healing family along, lightening their grief, and lifting their heavy hearts.

THE WISDOM OF THE SACRED MASCULINE: LEARNING THE LANGUAGE OF THE HUNTER

The red-hooded widow is a wild feminine symbol of our longed-for integration, our yearning to synthesize the instinctual, individualistic masculine with the intuitive, collectivist feminine in our own psyches, in our intimate relationships, and in the world at large. Even the most long-term relationships, romantic and otherwise, die many times in order to be born anew, and the Witch of Sacred Love understands that it is always integration we are after. The building blocks of the human community are souls seeking greater wholeness and connection, and, once a relationship is no longer permitting that growth in intimacy, the union begins to wane in one way or another, for better or worse.

My love, we must consider that the masculine has also been wounded by the ways of the world. The qualities of the Father archetype are dominant in our contemporary society; these are primarily individualism, protection of personal property, and consumption. Any force that threatens the dominance of these attributes in which our economic system is thoroughly grounded is framed as a danger and consequently targeted. The Mother, while the most valued aspect of the feminine for her generative, production qualities, remains socially subservient to the Father because she is holistic and collectivist in her thinking. While individualistic cultures certainly value the Mother archetype less than collectivist cultures, the pervasiveness of capitalism has created global conditions wherein the Mother's holistic powers are diminished. She is a community builder and creatrix, and she is concerned with trusting sufficiency rather than fearing material scarcity. While the inner Father is necessary in order for us to enact our work in the world, feed our families, and prevent complete lawlessness, he is a heavy-handed beast without his maternal counterpart.

The Witch of Sacred Love longs for the lost, crucified attributes of the sacred masculine, with the Hunter a particularly invalidated archetype in our society. The Sage, counterpart to the Crone, has dominated our religious systems since ancient times; he is a forward, linear thinker who, while compassionate and innocent, fragments in order to investigate and explore. The Crone sees patterns, honors the interconnection between all systems, and considers the spiral nature of time, while the Sage ponders the ultimate destiny of our universe, the Great Mystery, and the all-oneness affecting humanity. In an effort to better examine spirit, the Sage has surgically removed the higher self from the soft flesh and loamy ground. Balanced spirituality reflects the unique soul path of everyone, the cyclical nature of time, and the merit of individual intuition. The missing piece in many Sage-ruled spiritual systems remains, however, our connection to nature and the elements.

To learn the language of the Hunter is not only to rekindle our relationship to nature but to forge connections between nature and our most primal selves. The wild feminine has been wounded by the hunt, with healers becoming the hunted and our precious wisdom pierced again and again by the arrows of consistent invalidation, shame, and fear of feminine power. You, Priestess, are the Witch of Sacred Love, and independent of gender or sexual orientation; this Witch lives in us all, demanding the holistic feminine be validated and seen without having to sacrifice her fiercer and wilder aspects, and the sacred Hunter upholds the wild feminine at all costs.

This Witch is well versed in the language of justice, and she wants, more than anything, for the subjugated aspects of the divine masculine to be resurrected alongside those of the feminine. While the Magdalene laments her lost love on the shore, she understands that this was *how she would heal, one wave at a time.* The healer's road is long and unpaved, and part of our task is to strike a balance between directing social evolution and surrendering to the parts of the healing process that are organic and already occurring in their own way, independent of our actions. As the Witch of Sacred Love, you are the red-hooded healer and loving partner to the sleeping parts of the wild masculine, and you are the wise Priestess whose words have been intentionally omitted from the holy books for fear that spiritual seekers might find what they long for not in a vengeful father but in a strong-willed and openhearted mother.

Handwritten Verses: Tale of the Windswept Huntress Awakened

Energies of the feminine and masculine cycle within us throughout our lives regardless of gender. In this moment, Priestess, honor the times when you have been the instinctual huntress, so closely attuned to your ecological position in nature, so bound to your physical instincts and animal body that you were more wolf-mother than woman, more primal than priestly. These are the aspects of the sacred masculine that must be healed and integrated, the hand-brewed salve for the bleeding, toxic masculine. You may use the prompts I offer here or write your own:

Every bit of my live-wire body was abuzz with a fiercer presence than
I had ever known, and I was full of...
All my thoughts, all my wisdom, were submerged under...
There was only breath, only body, only...
If a great artisan had painted me in that moment, I would be
crouched to the ground, teeth bared, and...
I was confidence and certainty embodied. I was a windswept hunt-
ress. I was connected to all things, and I knew for sure...

Read your writing aloud in a wild place, if you feel called, and remember what it means to be creaturely. Let your inner Crone teach your inner
Maiden how to hunt, and heal the sacred masculine one breath at a time,
one word at a time.

Stirring the Cauldron of Relationship: Invocation of the Healer-Priestess

Consider any relationship a soul-to-soul energy exchange, and consider both the Triple God and Triple Goddess archetypes as living
metaphors for the holistic expression of our authentic wildness. The
Maiden, Mother, and Crone live inside all human beings, just as the
Hunter, Father, and Sage live inside our ever-changing and always-
cyclical psyches. These are not immutable, solid traits bound by linear
age or gender. Our souls, those parts of us that are uniquely and truly
us beneath the overtamed personalities and polished perfection, are
challenged to live as truthfully as possible according to our passions,
desires, divinely mandated talents, and wounds.

If we descend deeply into past relationships, do we not always
find that those friends and lovers, sisters and brothers, teachers and
students who made us feel the most true to self were the holiest com-
panions? Perhaps it is up to the lover not to make us feel precious and
romanced but, rather, to hold us when we are unmasked and vulnerable. Perhaps even the most soulful relationships are not about a fateful fulfillment of destiny but about a necessary shedding of skin.

Hail and welcome, she who is feared for her wise ways and

hand-brewed ancient antidotes to the particular poison that is relentless and uncontained power hunger. Run screaming from the shadowy caves and dank prisons where you were cast. Take down your hood and show your worth, for we are desperate for your medicine. May we see every relationship as a sacred spinning of the cosmic web, and may we continually seek those who will slink through the haunted forests of our psyches and hunt the parts we keep hidden. May we mourn for that lost Hunter and the wise-elder Sage as much as we grieve for the Maiden, Mother, and Crone, and may we resurrect the wounded masculine through our work and our will. So mote it be.

Handwritten Verses: Personal Mythwork for the Foam-Born Woman

Aphrodite is the Greek Goddess of love, but she is neither weak nor needy. She was born fully grown, the daughter of Zeus, and she is the archetype of the parentified child, forced to care for herself at a young age and consequently developing a hardened shell around her heart. She is not a teaching tool but a warrior, though her armor does not always serve her. The Witch of Sacred Love archetype embodies Aphrodite's alchemist skills — that is, the ability to turn the most careless heart into a bubbling pool of pure compassion and desire or the bleakest and most outmoded social institution into an instrument of healing — but does not reflect the more "armored" qualities of the love Goddess, the parts of Aphrodite that will long for independence even in the most supportive relationship and will often seek out drama and conflict in order to resist mundane monogamy. The Witch of Sacred Love is not selfish, but she is not without selfhood.

Before beginning this mythwork experience, sink your consciousness into the heart space by breathing deeply and repeating this mantra: *Love and empathy, thank you.* Stay with this mantra, either aloud or in a whisper, until you feel a greater awareness, a sort of swelling warmth, of the heart center rather than the head; this is a subtle change, and sensing it may take practice. You may also prepare to write by creating a ritual container — for example, surrounding yourself with candles, meaningful images, or flower petals; casting a circle; or anointing your heart chakra with rose oil. When ready, you may use the prompts I offer here or create your own. These prompts are designed to focus on a single pivotal loving relationship in your life, but let whatever memories or experiences arise pour out onto the page. Feel free to use any pronouns that are authentic to you, and let your story feel liberating rather than confining to write. Do not edit yourself, Priestess. It can be part fantasy, if you wish. This is a love spell-ing written by you, for you and you alone.

Chapter 1: She Might Have Seen It Coming

She might have seen it coming had her...
They met just like all twin souls meet, with...
The moment when she knew she had been irrevocably changed was...

Chapter 2: But Bliss Is Ephemeral

Their brightest moments together were hardly...
Their love was like...
In her quiet moments when she was alone, she still longed for...

Chapter 3: Lessons Buried in the Breaking

The relationship itself was the teacher, after all, and the lesson was...
Over time, she stripped away every iron breastplate she had strapped on so tightly when she was younger, and...
On the day of reckoning, she found herself unprotected, and...

Chapter 4: All Dies to Begin Again

She emerged from the cocoon a fragile-winged butterfly with bleeding...
She was fully grown, fully formed, and fully...
In her lonelier moments, she understood...

Chapter 5: The Truest Union

As she sifts through her memories now, an older and wiser Priestess, she...

The truest union was in fact the truest...

Her heart is raw but unbroken, and she knows for sure that...

Hold this story close to you, you dear heart, you foam-born woman, and revisit it when you feel called.

Hear My Reddest Prayer: Lament of the Wild Seeker

One day, I may come to know a wise Wolf-Woman who hand-built her own stone cottage on a mountaintop, where she speaks to the ghosts of burned women, smokes homegrown mugwort, and waits for young women thirsty for truth to come and sit by her hearth. One day, she might teach me the most moving benedictions to unnamed deities while I sip nettle tea and knit blankets for her horned billy goats, and, just maybe, she will write a primal prayer just for me. Until then, this is the truest prayer I know.

I kneel before you, Mystery, for I am always in awe of what is nameless and unshown. I say I bow to no one, but I bow to you, for you are the ultimate treasure. You are what we all seek, a firm and eternal understanding of purpose and destiny. You are why women eat the forbidden fruit, and you are why the Priestess continues to quest. You are why the sage scientist examines, and you are why the mother gives birth.

In my loneliest and most indulgent moments, I fantasize that I find the end of the Red Road, not at my doorstep but on the precipice of a massive black void that holds all the answers to every question I could ever ask. I leap into the primordial swirl, and my soul becomes a sponge for every truth spoken by every ascended master and every innocent babe. I am a child of wonder and a sainted Witch. I am dark matter, and I am the potential to be every alien incarnation in the backwaters of our ever-expanding universe. In that moment, I am you, and you are me. In that moment, I am one with the spiral dance of time, and, for the first time, I truly know the meaning of magick.

All blessings to you, Mystery, and all blessings to the Holy Wild.

CIRCLES OF RED-HOODED WOMEN:
SISTERHOOD AND THE DISTASTE FOR ILLUSION

While the value of sacred solitude in a woman's life is irrefutable, the relational Mother archetype in all of us craves community. This yearning stems not only from a genuine desire to be held and heard but, more importantly, from the soul-born need to have an authentic, safe context in which her truest identity can be enacted and seen. We must, as modern Priestesses, rally against many of the weapons of soft sisterhood, for, despite their candlelit and glittery appearances, many have been shaped by the patriarchy's hungry hands. In the teaching tale, the Magdalene makes a promise to her lover: *I will hold secret circles attended by red-hooded women who have acquired a distaste for illusion, and I will bid them to seek solace in an activist sisterhood that has no name.* Let our circles be spaces for action as much as for rest and ritual. Let our circles be change agents, and let our circles be well attended by those who have acquired a distaste for the illusions of the passive feminine and the overbleached wild.

In asking ourselves how we can be the women we needed when we were younger, we can always see, and see quite clearly, the heart of who we have become during our long journey on the Red Road. We can also see the kinds of communities and circles that can no longer serve that heart — can no longer hold us how we need to be held, indeed having become Lilith's confining garden in many instances — and we can handcraft the communities we need. We can create circles that feed not only our souls but the soul of the collective. We can plan rallies alongside our spellwork, and we can clean riverbanks as often as we knit and pray. Very often, the woman we needed when we were younger was not the soft-breasted embodiment of unconditional love; she was a fierce Wolf-Woman who taught us to trust what we value and work tirelessly to support freedom, choice, and equality in the global community.

THE BARE BONES OF A PRIESTESS CIRCLE:
FUSING THE JOINTS WITH BREATH

Many women long to be part of a circle where they can speak and be heard, a circle that meets regularly enough so that it can be a dependable source of support, and a circle that affirms not only their right to be in it but also their right to be here on this blessed planet. What we are really saying when we wax poetic about our desire for community is that we desire a circle of people who, while they may not share our lived experiences, hold the same hopes for the children of the future that we do; and so this is where we begin.

If you feel called to circle, Priestess, if you have searched high and low for a small group of like-minded Wild Ones who will listen while you weep and work magick with you, *for* you and the wounded world, but have not found that sense of untamed belonging and fierce acceptance in any existing space, then, my love, it is time to create your own. Ask yourself: What is the conversation you want to have with the global community through your circle? How is your circle an expression of the values you hold dear for all humanity? How will your circle embody and honor the holistic, integrated, and primal feminine?

Begin *there.* Begin with your core values and deepest truths. This is how the circle grows up round from the roots. Consider your circle's mission as primary, so that every meeting and every member is threaded together by red-hot convictions that do not change. Each individual within the circle is a microcosm of the circle itself, which is, in turn, a microcosm of an envisioned juster collective.

The circle is not an escape. The circle is not a wild retreat from the workaday lives of its members. The circle is a living expression of how you want the world to be.

The circle is a living expression of how you want the world to be.

It is a real and tangible reflection of what you wake up hoping for and an in-your-face answer to the injustices that keep you awake at night.

The fire that boils beneath the circle's surface is what keeps it alive and well amid the cyclical nature of its membership and the naturally wayward energetic investments of its participants. Resist the predictably skeptical voice inside your head that warns you to shrink back, that says you do not know enough or that no one will come. Resist the urge to dilute the circle's message in order to gain attendance, and, dear Priestess, resist the need to know exactly what your circle will be. Take stock of your deepest, most immutable values and begin there, with what you know for sure, and do not back down from these tightly held convictions.

Handwritten Verses: The Circle Is Always, the Circle Is Never

In digging out your circle's mission statement from your vast storehouse of beliefs, complete these two sentences as many times as you can:

The circle is always...
The circle is never...

Circle all the sentences that meet the following condition: *They affirm the values I want the global community to embody.* From those sentences, create a mission statement or manifesto. Do not worry, not yet, about how often you will meet or precisely what you will do during your meetings. Fuse the bony foundations together now, and the rest will come. Allow your inner Witch of Sacred Love to work with the Prophetess to form a vision for your sacred work, and know yourself as a wise Craftswoman who works in the art of circling as a potter works in clay. Permit circle-craft to empower rather than burden, to liberate rather than cage, and always grant your circle permission to swell and shrink as if it was a living, breathing entity.

The circle is versatile. For some, it is only a space of openhearted communication, their place to speak and be heard. For others, it is a candlelit container for communal magick, chanting, and spellcraft, or a driven and purposed boundary for activism and community planning. Whatever the circle's nature, whatever the intention that anchors it firmly to ground, it is an organic shape in which the most intense learning often occurs. The circle is a teacher-in-the-round, an entity in and of itself, and a mirror for the greater global collective as you would like it to be.

Too often, ours is a quiet and lonely practice. Dissatisfaction with our garden communities leaves us in a precarious position, at once longing for truly empowering spiritual community and resigning ourselves to a life of solitary Craft. Sometimes, in our more bitter moments, we attempt to become our own support system, struggling to embody an entire coven within our own skin, all the while wondering if we can, one day, muster the energy and know-how to start our own circles. But if we take our lessons from the wild, we know the merit of belonging and trust in the power of community. Know this, Priestess: If the wild women of this world could truly come together with their shared magick to support a common vision of a healing planet and could cease battling one another and using the still-sharp weapons of capitalism and colonization, then, my love, we would become precisely what was so feared during the burning times. We would become the wise change agents, the heathen collective come home.

Healing Salve for the Lonely Witch: Parable of the Lost Sister

Each and every one of them would have preferred to remain indoors and snuggled by their hearths had circumstances allowed. Their lands were on the cusp of a great snowstorm, poised to receive a heavy frozen blanket flake by flake, but before the first crystal fell, the red-hooded Priestesses braved the looming weather and gathered in the secret place.

"Let's get on with it," urged one sister, her hot words evaporating into a thin moonlit fog.

The other sisters bounced to keep warm, rubbing their hands together and folding their robes tight. All sympathetic eyes fell on the youngest among them, their reason for leaving the warmth of their lovers' arms on this treacherous night, and she stepped forward.

"Thank you," she managed to whisper, her voice shaking with emotion. "Thank you. I had nowhere else to turn."

The pursed lips and raised brows of her sisters told her, in a language clearer than any she had learned in school, that she did not have to say any more. The nature of her need did not matter. The wounds that brought her here did not matter. She need not offer any justification for her anguish or need for healing, and the face of every sister spoke in the Mother Tongue of feminine grace in that moment and said, "My love, we are here for you." She told them just enough then, that her resources were depleted and the situation for her family was dire. The spell's intention was for their lost sister to find a source of income that would sustain her meaningfully, and, together, they pictured her in a safe, secure, and warm home, feeding her children a home-cooked meal without fear. They held that vision in their minds as they forged the ring of light and attuned to the vibration.

"Our intention is set for our sister," spoke another young mother. "May she find the source of security she seeks, and may the circle itself know sustainable sufficiency for all members. May those without homes in our local community find shelter tonight, and may the most resourceful within the global community rise to support those affected by the painful scarcity so pervasive in the most silent parts of the world. May the Great Mystery bless us all, and may the universe hear and support our prayers."

With those words, the spell's threads wove through the lost sister and connected her to the circle, the local community, the world, and the divine source. With those words, the heat of activism boiled beneath them and warmed their feet. With those words, they were ready.

All members faced the north and called to the holy energies of earth to strengthen the circle. Facing east, all members raised their arms high and called out to the air element to enliven the circle. Turning south, the sisters used their will to call to fire to empower the circle. Finally, facing west, they howled to water to rush forth and purify their circle, before affirming the circle was closed.

The work began now, with all sisters chanting "Yes!" in unison, dancing clockwise within the boundaries of the circle while the lost sister shouted out in support of her vision. The one in need, standing at circle center among the wildfire that was the movement of the red-hooded Priestesses, prayed out her desires, and every one of the sisters heard her despite their rallying, and every one wanted for her exactly what she wanted for herself, and every one believed in her bones and her blood that their visualized intention would come to fruition.

The chanting continued but quieted to a whisper then, and the movement slowed to a sultry sway before stopping altogether. The

Priestesses raised their arms high, palms facing their sister, coming back to their intention and seeing her so nourished, so fulfilled by her sacred work, and infusing that vision with every ounce of energy they had raised in the seemingly endless moments just before, when they moved as one being united by a common vision.

The sister at the center began whisper-chanting "Yes!" with them then, overcome by the will and the love of her circle and sinking to the ground. The chant morphed into "Yes, thank you, more please," and continued until the first flakes began to fall. The Priestesses sat in silence for a time, letting the snow fall on their red hoods and freeze their tears. When an energetic shift, a subtle swelling and palpable pressure, told them their work had been done, the Witches faced the west, honored the direction, and asked the energies to go in peace before turning south, east, and, finally, north. The circle was open, their weighted work was finished, and all was coming. They sent the energy down and through the roots beneath them, grounding the residual energy straight to the fiery core of the Mother, and they trusted with an infinite faith that they had done enough.

Their work did not end once the spell was cast and the circle members dispersed into the snowy night. Two sisters joined their beloved one in need at her home, cooking and tending and becoming the village when she needed it most. Another with ample resources spontaneously drove to the local shelter and offered transportation to those who were not likely to make it safely on their own as the snow fell, and the rest simply held their babes and their lovers a little closer that evening, grateful for the lives they had been given and humbly surrendering to the magick running through their veins, the same she-force driving the storm outside their frosted windows.

BRIDGE LINES OF THE COSMIC WEB: WEAVING THE WAY

The Witch of Sacred Love knows every relationship she has is a meeting of two bridge lines in the cosmic web. She knows her circle as a space of sacred communion where the magick coexists alongside the mundane and the energy raised therein ripples out across time and space. There is at once a level of trust and a desire for proof, as the Witch has never been one to blindly believe in the unfelt and unseen. The Witch honors that she has done what she can for herself and for the world, and she believes so courageously in her convictions that there is little psychic room to question the integrity of her magick.

More than all that, the Witch believes she has the right to effect change in her world, a divine birthright to cause those ripples in the cosmic web, to break the bridge lines that do not serve in order to form newer, more formidable ones. The Witch is the Crone Spider, weaving away with confidence and grace, seeking to harvest the most buried parts of the feminine and spittle-bond them to the places where they are most needed.

The Witch is you, my love; the Witch is the sorceress, the magick maker; and the Witch is the unburnable Holy Wild.

Healing the ailing feminine in oneself is no small feat, for one woman's healing serves to, on a small but valuable level, heal all other women throughout all time; and yet, the language of healing is in danger of becoming overly diluted, and the Witch of Sacred Love must work to grasp the true — often quite bitter — nature of healing herself so that she may better heal the world. Authentic and lasting healing does not come prepackaged as sweet and syrupy wisdom to be spoon-fed to lost souls, nor does it aim to *fix* what we perceive as broken.

> The Witch is the Crone Spider, weaving away with confidence and grace, seeking to harvest the most buried parts of the feminine and spittle-bond them to the places where they are most needed.

True healing is born of both awareness and integration — nothing more and nothing less. True healing is an eternal, often cyclical process through which we discover the roots of our unique passions and wounds, framing them not as, respectively, positive and negative but, rather, as interconnected gifts that, when brought out of the cavernous depths where we buried them during childhood, cast a clear gleam on precisely why we are here. True healing aims to seek out not what is broken but what is hidden, weaving and integrating what is psychologically repressed in ourselves, often to the point of dysfunction, into our light-of-day personalities and thereby doing the same for the consciousness of the society in which we live.

Handwritten Verses: Letting the Crone Grandmother the Maiden

Despite societal perspectives and tired media narratives, our inner Mothers are not eternal givers who expect nothing in return for their nourishing support. Women tend to express shallow aspects of their Mother-selves, learning from childhood onward that the doer in us, the creative and generative woman who is in constant motion, is the most socially acceptable form of the feminine. We gift our inner Mothers with much power while still keeping them subservient to our inner Fathers, those individualistic providers who seek to protect and shield while, in the absence of their feminine counterpart, sacrificing soulful authenticity at every turn. Our Maiden-selves become oversexualized during our youth, with the true gifts of our wildness, our relationship to the natural world, and our ever-changing, always-powerful emotional landscape stripped of their true grit, weight, and value by focusing solely on the Maiden's sexuality. So, too, our inner Crones are robbed of their power altogether, their intuition, psychic ability, and spiritual liberation. In essence and regardless of gender, human beings learn to suppress the expression of the authentic feminine during childhood, limiting her to the lusty Maiden or the overproductive Mother while burying her true holistic nature deeply within their psychic depths.

Ask yourself now, Priestess, how your inner Crone can best grandmother your inner Maiden. What elder wisdom have you acquired these last long years? What messages have you intuited from the clouds that you can share with that youthful, innocent, and hopeful part of your psyche? Write a letter to your Maiden-self now, sent straight from your inner wise one. If you find these prompts difficult, feel free to alter them or, perhaps, write as if you were gifting your advice to a dear friend.

> Dear wise and innocent one, I feel for you, for I have seen...
> Tell me about your longing and your joy, and I will tell you about my...
> On your loneliest nights, remember...
> The greatest wisdom I have to share in this moment is...

If true healing is the twofold path of awareness and integration, then we are tasked with seeking out what has been lost; aiming to understand why it was cast out of our light-of-day personality, the mask we show the world,

and into the dark; then finding a newer, truer place for these parts of ourselves to be assimilated and express themselves. If every human being is a
single pulsing cell within the great heart that is the Earth, which is, in turn,
a single pulsing cell within the greater organism of the universe, then the
resurrection of the buried feminine in you adds much to the cosmic conversation about collective healing and communal change.

A Prayer Spoken and a Promise Broken: Vows from One Witch to Another

Promise me you'll listen, and I'll make you a promise in return. I won't
pretend to know who you are or where you come from. I won't ask
what names were given to you or what labels have been scrawled at
the foot of your bed. I want to know the name *you* want to be called
right now, in this moment, and I will not ask you for a justification or
rationale for your answer.

My love, hear me! I am begging you to see the wondrous part you
are playing in this interstellar comedy and the majestic significance
with which you move. There's nothing small or stuck about you; you
are the tide turner and the game changer. Ask yourself what is wild
about you that they called wicked, and what makes you feel full of fire,
ablaze with impassioned purpose.

What if the most righteous healing comes not from acknowledging your individuality but from affirming your flesh-and-blood relationship to all that matters most to you? Were you the wise woman
of this wounded world, what would you want for the next generation
of children, and now, in this life, how can you heal yourself in such a
way that those children are one shaky, toddler step closer to that feminine future? What if every person on our imperfect planet woke this
morning and asked themselves these questions? What then?

I promised I wouldn't pretend to know you, Priestess, and I won't.
Forgive me, but I'm wondering if you'll indulge me and consider
yourself my friend. I'm in love with your passion and your weariness,

you see. I don't need to have seen your heathen magick to know it is there, shaking its hips below the surface of your controlled, busy-handed, rigid-bodied Mother-self. You don't owe me your story, but I wonder who told you to cage that beauteous belly-laughing dancer, and I wonder what it would take to set her free.

Oh! I just can't keep from breaking my promise, love! I'm sorry! I do know who you are, for I've seen you standing next to me among the Witches and the warrior women. I've seen you holding hands with the sacred masculine Hunters and the hooded Sages and winged angels. I've seen you, and I know you. You are the holy healer come to save us all, for we are all her. You are long-fanged and primal dark feminine grace, and you are the brave heart going into the crystalline caves of her psychic wilderness to dig out the gems of claircognizance, clairsentience, and clairvoyance hoping to be found these last long years.

Harvest these treasures in you and for you, and you harvest them for all humankind. So mote it be for you, so mote it be for us all.

WHERE THE WIND FINDS US: HEATHEN HILLTOP MEMORIES

The red-hooded widow is a heathen healer, an embodied promise of sacred masculine and divine feminine integration. She is an artist working in the medium of relationship, weaving webs within her community and her home, but not tirelessly so. While the gifts offered us by earth, water, and fire are presented to us in solitude, those of the air are given to us in those moments of intimacy. A kind and poignant word spoken by a true friend, a joyous and too-quick hug from a child, a knowing and heated glance from a would-be lover; these are the moments where air finds us and caresses our hearts in just the right places. In these fleeting moments, we are heathens holding one another on the hilltop, blissfully removed from all things built and busy, lost in a heartfelt union and silently praying for all beings to know the love we know.

Chapter 11

Air Rituals

If our rituals are our living and ceremonial statements of presence, containing and commemorating those holy transitions between this and that, the rituals born of the air element are bound to the themes of relationship, healing, and teaching. Air is a dominant element in any group ritual, with the interconnection between participants a felt, palpable energetic power. In solitary ritual, we invoke the air element through our breath, our open-armed physical expression, and our willingness to honor our lost love stories and heal our aching souls in times of postbetrayal loneliness or longed-for intimacy.

Both the solitary and the group rituals offered in this chapter are fully adaptable to suit your needs, Priestess. All practices are suggestions, and all wording is flexible so long as you speak in the Mother Tongue of the wild feminine. Be true to yourself and you cannot misstep, for the very energies you are calling on are the same that live and cycle within you, spiraling around your bones and breezing above your skin in electric pulses of empathic connection, healing through integration and the sharing of experience. In all seven of these rituals, I ask you to embody the red-hooded widow, the Witch of Sacred Love, as fully as possible. You are she who has developed a distaste for illusion, she who has become the woman she needed in her younger years, and she who weaves the web through an intentional, timeless communion with her most ancient soul.

BODY PRAYER FOR THE HARDENED HEART:
A POSTBETRAYAL MOVEMENT RITUAL

This is a living ritual to honor the unruined heart. Gather your fellow Wild Ones if you are able, or practice in solitude. Let this be a temple dance of imperfect grace, and let this movement stretch your body in ways that permit greater space in the aching shadows so that the emerald-green heart-light might flood in, against all odds and despite all grief. You are loved, Priestess. In the midst of this limitless cosmos, you are so, so loved, wrapped in a warm red blanket of unseen magick and riding this pleasure planet we call home.

Stand grounded with your feet spread more than hip width apart, and soften your knees. Arch your back and lift your chin moonward, opening your palms to the ethereal infinite. Breathe, my love. Breathe as if your very inhalation were a confession and your exhalation a demand for vindication. Breathe as if your breath is medicine, and, when you feel ready, raise your arms high with soft elbows, spine arched in the shape of pure reception. Take a deep breath, then exhale, folding your arms across your heart and curling into a smaller shape as you hinge at the hips and become closed. Stay with this for as long as it feels right, blooming on your inhalation to the infinite wisdom of the universe and proclaiming yourself whole, then contracting on your exhalation and allowing yourself to shrink. Inhale into the light, and exhale into the dark.

Stay with this movement and add a mantra now. On the inhale as your heart swells, declare yourself a Warrior of the Healing Heart by howling: *Thank you! I'm still here!* On the exhale as your body folds into a position of self-protection, whisper: *All is coming.* Open and close your body to the rhythm of a loud *Thank you!* and a whispered *All is coming: Thank you. All is coming. Thank you. All is coming.*

Trust in the cyclical nature of healing and grief, love and loss. You are She Who Is, and you are the living antidote to the poison of your own betrayal. Permit yourself to mourn when you feel called, be it in response to an external loss or an internal call into your depths, and honor the resilience of your beauteous soul to continually incarnate into a heavy human body despite the guaranteed aches and pains this world holds. The potential for joy on this planet must be so great, my love, for we willingly choose to descend to human form lifetime after blessed lifetime, knowing full well of the agony and the ecstasy embodied in any relationship worth its salt. And so it is.

HARVESTING THE HUNTER:
A WILD DIVINATION RITUAL TO HONOR THE SACRED MASCULINE

Location: *A wild place*

The Hunter is the Maiden's counterpart, the virile, nature-loving masculine that sees his role in the life cycle with an intense humility. Harvesting those Hunter traits in ourselves and our society does not mean returning to a primitive life devoid of technology or progress; it means knowing that our humanity is no less holy simply because it is bound to the Earth, not an invisible heaven. The Maiden is the sensual and emotional part of us that lives for the moment. The Hunter is the potent, active nature-conscious masculine. The Maiden and the Hunter are erotically innocent in their earthly intimacy, and they seek no golden roads in the afterlife, for they know that the true bliss is here, surrounded by flesh and blood.

For this ritual, immerse yourself in nature as much as you are able. You might be in a small green space or on a rooftop urban farm. You might find an abundant field full of corn or grapevines or a sparse and brown land of leafless trees and drying grass. Wherever you are, begin by feeling blessed to be there, in that moment. Walk now the way a huntress walks, seeking not prey but a sign. Seek out a signal sent straight from the Holy Wild to you that tells you that you belong here, that makes your inner animal purr and howl with the understanding that all is connected. Find your place here among the wilds, as the sacred masculine must find its place in our world where little boys are robbed of their tears. Come into a state of deep feeling here, Huntress. Take nothing for granted, for this landscape holds it all for you. And so it is.

RESCUING THE MOTHER'S TWIN:
A RITUAL MISSION OF RECLAIMING VOICE

Materials: *Journal and writing utensil*

Location: *A sacred place*

As the oversoftened and overactive feminine is filtered through a narrowed version of the Mother archetype, the messages received by children are these: The feminine is meant to be busy but not powerful, creative but not compensated for her artistry, and ever nurturing but not deserving of the same nurturance she doles out from dawn until the Witching hour. Though the Mother archetype is the most socially valuable, even our Mother-selves have been split into pieces, with the wildest and most potent parts cast aside.

The Witch of Sacred Love reflects the integrated Mother. She is not merely engaged in busywork but creates joyously, expecting a sustainable relationship with her sacred purpose. She is not merely the giver in her relationships but demands to be loved and held in return. She does not focus intently only on her own inner circle but seeks to forge connections and networks that are expansive and transformational. Most important, she is not content to stay quiet. The Mother is a great storyteller and myth writer, and she knows the weight of her voice. She is resonant. She is resilient, and she is a Craftswoman skilled in the ancient lost medium of her-story.

To begin this ritual, my love, you will need a journal and a place you know to be, on some level, sacred. This can be a sanctuary in nature where you know you can be alone or a carved-out space in your home where you will not be disturbed. Go there now, taking only your journal, a pen, and a wide-open heart. Call to mind the image of the Magdalene nested on the beach, watching her babes and mourning for her lost lover. Call to mind her conviction and her promise: *I will teach them the stories they will not read. I will share with them the verses that will not be transcribed by any of the famed prophets, and I will channel your medicine, our medicine, until the day I die.*

You are she who will not be silenced. You are a wolf-mother howling moonward to call her pack home, and you are wisest scribe among us. Be there in your wild place with all that you are. Feel the way your bones rest on ground, and offer up some fleeting gratitude for the ephemeral bliss of the breeze, the shade of the sky, and the confounding perfection of this planet's suspension in space. Consider this: If it would be a disastrous tragedy for you to die today without sharing one story — a story that is part of your lived experience, a story only you can tell — what is it? What is the story the world deserves from you today in this moment, and what story is it your right to share?

Begin writing this story, starting with these words if they seem authentic to you: *My name is _____, and I will not die with this story in my heart: _____.*

Write for as long as you have without editing yourself. When it feels finished, take a moment to recenter yourself and spread your arms. Breathe deeply and exhale with your mouth wide and tongue out; then, my love, *then* gift your story to the wild place. Empower the part of the Mother that feels her story is worthless and bid her stand and speak. Read your words with all the strong-boned ferocity of the Magdalene. Read loud and with purpose. Call to the directions and let them hear you, and share with the elements the verses that could not be written by anyone but you. And so it is.

HEARING THE ANCIENT HEARTBEAT:
A RITUAL FOR MENDING HUMANITY'S HOLY WOUND

Materials: *Journal and writing utensil; or newsprint or canvas, pastels or other art supplies*

Ours is a land of soulful diversity, and the depth of human experience negates the possibility for universal norms and static beliefs. What if our collective suffering arises from the individual caging of each and every soul into an iron-barred trap that does not permit the growth and movement necessary for awareness and integration of purpose? If each and every soul were given the resources to seek out their deepest passions and unite them with their most valuable gifts in order to fulfill a divinely mandated destiny, if the social landscape of the global community permitted such self-inquiry and did not depend so precariously on the individualistic, fear-based actions of the internal Father, if our spiritual journeys were rooted in nature's lessons, allowed to ebb and flow and spiral and dance without being condemned or controlled, humanity would truly be moving toward an immense soulfully validating shift.

The Witch of Sacred Love can see humanity's holy wound so clearly that she weeps for it, in her own way, every day. Her lone wish is that our children would be raised with a reverence for nature and shown their in-the-blood relationship to the oceans and the mud, that they would not be told they were too this or too that, and that they would be allowed to cycle and change as they aged. No one would ever tell them "Stop, that's not like you," and no one would seek to confine them in a box in order to serve economic, social, and religious rigidity.

If the task of the Witch of Sacred Love is to see her heart-wounds as gifts so that she may become the woman she needed when she was younger, then humanity's holy wound can also be framed as a precious cosmic treasure, of sorts. In our collective evolution, how can we now be the community we needed when we were younger and even more volatile, more disconnected from one another, and more destructive than we are presently? In essence, how can we best grandmother the Father archetype, and how can we midwife a better humanity's birth without overly depleting her so-needed feminine voice and long-contained agency, autonomy, and force? How can we unleash the most potent form of the Mother and be the humanity we needed in our younger years?

As the red-hooded Prophetess, you hold the answer to these questions in your heart. For this ritual, you will tap into heart-consciousness. This practice can be done quite simply, with only paper and a writing utensil, or it can be adapted to be more elaborate using art materials and a large background such as newsprint or canvas. Begin seated, feel where your thinking mind is now. Ask yourself where the location of your thoughts is, and now plant a seed question there: *What is my role in healing this world I live in?*

Now, envision that seed question descending through your third-eye chakra, the seat of your psychic vision; through your throat chakra, the seat of your voice and unique truth; and into the heart chakra. When the seed's energy hits the energy of the heart, sparks and vibrant colors flash and spiral inside your rib cage, radiating forward and back, vibrating in all directions. What else do you see there? Is your heart center gifting you with any images or signs? Feel free to draw any imagery that feels pertinent, and, when ready, begin writing the answer to your seed question, straight from the heart. Let the energetic heart speak, for it has much to say about healing, justice, and our collective evolution. And so it is.

REKINDLING THE SPIRAL FLAME: A RITUAL OF EARTH INTIMACY

A woman coming home to the wilds values her relationship with this holy planet on which we were born. In turning the collective cold shoulder to the plight of the Earth, humanity has abandoned an essential part of itself, as if the ephemeral flesh of a body were to reject the very bones that give it shape, and the wild woman feels this wound deeply. The subjugation of our planet — that is, the rape of her resources and shortsighted harvesting of her limited bounty — is tantamount to the oppression of the feminine. In framing itself as superior to — rather than an integral part of — her, human society has forgotten how to dig down into the most primal parts of ourselves, for this act of soul harvest demands a certain humility. To be humble, to drop to one's knees before the sheer forces of nature that we take for granted, does not mean being disempowered or passive. To be humble before the Earth is to affirm that we are a part of her, a blessed but infinitesimal point on her long life line. Will we be a bad memory she will, in time, forget, or will we rise to be her greatest stewards?

The Witch of Sacred Love has a long memory, and she considers her relationship with the Earth — her elements, four directions, seasons, and cycles in all their forms — as a vital and intimate communion that sustains her own wildness. She remembers the reverence with which she watched the first leaves fall in the autumns of her childhood, and she recalls the sanctuary of hearth flames and ginger tea while the snow blanketed her world. She does not remember merely the ebbs and flows of nature's spiral dance but also her valued place *in* that dance.

Ask yourself when you first fell in love with whatever season you find yourself in right now. If it is winter, when did you first feel at home *here*, entrenched within nature's great rest? If it is spring, what dewy, floral scent was the original antidote to your homesickness for nature's intimacy? Re-create that experience as closely as you can in a ritual of remembrance and vow renewal. Be a bride to the Earth before you forget the warmth of her love again, before life calls you away from her wonder. Give yourself permission to be in your body *on* her, opening yourself to her with the same childlike vulnerability that once wed your small sacred body to the awesome majesty that is she. And so it is.

CIRCLE-CRAFT:
COMMUNAL RITUAL FOR TUNING TO THE VIBRATION

What kind of red-hooded Priestess are you? You are a steward of your own spiritual path as well as the circles you birth into being. Know that you do not need to include spellcraft and magick in your circle meetings in order for the circle to be a change agent, but, if you do, ensure that your magick truly expresses your circle's intention and empowers all members toward authenticity and growth.

If your circle is a true microcosm of the global community you would like to see come to fruition, then consider the merit of nonhierarchical structures, feminine communication, and warm, compassionate space holding. The circle is not a shape conducive to ego, linear rank ascendance, manipulation, or aggression. Within the boundaries of the circle, all members are High Priestesses in their own right, everyone is sovereign, and everyone has the right to speak and be heard. I do not say this to discount the respect deserved by those who have attained the High Priestess degree granted in many feminist spiritual traditions but, rather, to resist equating such organizational ascension with spiritual autonomy.

We do want to belong. In *The Spiral Dance*, Starhawk writes that "Goddess religion is lived in community. Its primary focus is not individual salvation or enlightenment or enrichment but the growth and transformation that comes through intimate interactions and common struggles." Handcraft your circle to be immune to the predatory behaviors unfortunately prevalent in numerous spiritual communities, those systems that feed on the devotion of the disempowered and voiceless student in order to maintain the power of an "infallible" few. Be endlessly wary of leading with an unfeeling hand, and, rather, stay keenly attuned to the energy of the circle as a whole.

Tuning to the Vibration, Part 1: Pouring the Foundation

Gather your Wild Ones, love. The early phases of the circle's life are akin to a newborn family of soft-bodied creatures; the members move around each other timidly, bonded by shared needs and a common origin, lovingly bumbling about their unfamiliar space and hoping for nourishment. The circle's space holder is long-armed and maternal during these early days, showing the members the proverbial ropes of communication and honoring the deep-running roots connecting each and every Priestess who has come to the space.

While the rules of each circle can and should vary depending on the circle's unique vision and intended mission, the guidelines offered in the "Water Rituals" chapter usually serve as a crucial baseline to minimize conflict and support an accessible agenda for each meeting. The overarching guideline is that every circle member retains her selfhood and is beholden the empathetic purity of the circle itself. If, as a circle member, you are questioning the value of a particular statement, do not ask yourself if it will serve you or another member to share it but, rather, ask if it serves the circle as a whole. This is never to condone the sacrifice of selfhood but instead to detach ourselves from normal communication in which unsolicited opinions and advice often wound, however unintentionally.

If the radiant heat of the circle's intention and values warms it from below, solid rules for communication form the foundation that is poured above that red-hot collective soul-born crucible of shared belief that will remind all members of why they are there, why they get in their cars, pay their hard-earned money for public transportation, or walk long distances in cold weather to arrive *there*, in that sacred space. The circle's foundation must be solid enough that it is a dependable ground on which each member can rely and stand.

Tuning to the Vibration, Part 2: Forging the Ring of Light

Once the foundation has been poured, the ring of light can be forged. While this may be a practice necessary at the beginning of each and every circle meeting, it is particularly valuable during the newborn stages of the circle's life. Have everyone stand or sit within a circle, left palm facing upward and right palm facing downward. Slowly, cue each member to move her hands, without turning her wrists, to hover above the circle member to her right and below the circle member to her left. The circle should now be connected by a palm-to-palm energetic link wherein no one is actually touching, but the palms and fingertips of everyone's hands are directly facing those of another circle member.

Have all Priestesses close their eyes and envision an emerald-green wellspring of light sourced from their hearts and flooding down their arms into their hands. As each circle member's light comes into contact with another's, a ring of intensely powerful energetic expression is formed. Most members will be able to physically experience this connection as a tingly sensation in the hands, a buzzing or slow pulsation in their ears, or another often-subtle change in their own frequency. Allow all circle members to verbalize what they are feeling, to describe the shared frequency of the circle, and to attune to and honor the collective vibration.

This is what binds the circle together. This is the power source that holds the potential not only to infuse the intentions of each member but to feed the shared vision for a juster humanity that undergirds this particular communion. If the circle is an entity, then this vibration is its electric pulse, its pranic flow, its very life force.

Tuning to the Vibration, Part 3: Simple Communal Spell Casting

As a Witch of Sacred Love, you will likely find there is some spellwork suited to the solitary path; that is, there are certain practices and rituals that just feel more authentic when performed in solitude. However, there are absolutely times for Priestesses to come together and work their magick. These may be times when a single circle member is in great need, when the wounds of the world have become particularly apparent, or when a ritualistic turn of the Wheel of the Year demands the circle's communion. The skeleton of any spell is formed from intention and energy raising, with its specific shape, the flesh laid over the bones, sculpted from the infusion of energy into the intention.

Remember, however, that the spell's beating heart is its connection to core values and shared vision. Draw from the energy that writhes beneath the circle's foundations, that nourishes the blood of every member, and the spell becomes a true conversation with the universe.

Know that I am describing only a shell for a communal spell here. There is much opportunity for adding, filling, and adapting, but the bare bones of communal spellcraft are the container, the intention, energy raising, infusion, grounding, and release. After you have attuned to the energy of the circle, after some openhearted sharing and

> *The skeleton of any spell is formed from intention and energy raising, with its specific shape, the flesh laid over the bones, sculpted from the infusion of energy into the intention.*

deep communion that aligns with the magick you will be working with, set an intention for the spell that all participants can feel. The intention must be one all participants resonate with and desire; it might be for manifestation, protection, banishing, or healing. It might be for the sake of only one person, or it might be for the good of the planet. Whatever the intention, streamline it as much as possible, and create the container.

Cast the circle strong and sure, calling to the directions and honoring the elements. Raise energy through dance, song, art, chanting, drums, or group visualization. Keep bringing the group back to the intention, gifting it with a burst of intention energy every time the minds of the participants stray and jump back to the present. Infuse the intention with the energy raised through sensory experience; see the outcome you desire. Hear it. Feel it. Believe it with all you are, and know that everyone else who is there with you holds that same commitment. *And so it is. So mote it be.* These are the heartfelt words of our Craft that state with certainty that our will shall be done. Open the circle when ready, ground the energy, and release the spell in perfect love and perfect trust, just as you entered the ritual. And so it is.

THIS IS HOW WE HEAL: BREWING OUR OWN MEDICINE

The Witch of Sacred Love is nourished by the energy of circle-craft, but it is not her only source of spiritual nutrition. She has worked enough with her own solitary magick to know what feels right and true, to know when she feels empowered and when she feels manipulated, and her participation in the circle is always wholly voluntary. She leaves circles that deplete her will and stays with those that sustain her. She is the red-hooded healer because she has learned how to heal herself. She knows what medicine works for her, and she shares this medicine with a great humility — knowing that her particular brew may not nourish all souls alike — but, for the sake of those who need her medicine, she will continue to offer it as part of her sacred work in this world.

I See You: A Blessing Prayer for the Lonely Babe

Oh, dearest innocent! I see you now, resting your damp forehead on your scarred and shaking knees. May you weep all you like, for no one can rob you of your right to feel, not tonight when the ghosts of lost souls have risen to encircle you with the truest, warmest spectral grace, not tonight when your tears are holy water blessing the fertile ground from which a better humanity will bloom. May you trust that, for all your brokenhearted loneliness, one day you will be cradled in the arms of someone who loves you unconditionally. For now, look to your bare toes curled in the cold soil, and hold steadfast to an in-the-bones faith in this planet's holy position; she will not forsake you, nor will I.

Chapter 12

Air Magick

The magick of the air element is that of connection, the alchemy of relationship, and the beauty of all our many intimacies. The required resources — the prerequisites, of sorts — for such transformational magick are vulnerability and courage, the traits of a strong heart and the hallmarks of the Witch of Sacred Love archetype. Consider the magick offered in this chapter, the practices and the pathworking, to be an ode to your unruined heart, and envision all the many unions of the past that have rippled through Grandmother Weaver's web in order to birth the body your soul is housed within at this moment. Consider the wealth of apparent coincidences and passing graces that made this moment, this moment in which you find yourself reading this book, possible.

The red-hooded Witch of Sacred Love knows she has been given this life for a reason: to leave her world a better place than she found it. Any voices that might speak to her and warn her against being seen, being too this or too that, are muffled by the voice of her inner Priestess, who tells her, *Yes. Yes, you have a right to be here, and you have a right to do this work.* This magick is for any woman who has felt a calling toward gifting others with the same feeling of homecoming she was blessed with when she first embraced the Mystery, when she first understood her Craft as a meeting place between what is and what must be.

THE CURRICULUM OF THE SOUL: BECOMING THE WILD TEACHER

Materials: *Journal and writing utensil*

Our task is to be as authentic as possible in every relationship; if each friendship, partnership, and familial bond is to shake us, to change us, and to do its part in stripping away our most outmoded layers of self-protection, then we must open ourselves fully to the potential for it to make us rethink who we are. We must consider the relationship an entity in and of itself rather than look to the other person to complete us, and we must be discerning in our choices. The Witch of Sacred Love does not enter any relationship lightly, and, for this reason, she may well be dismissed as coldhearted, unfeeling, or snobbish. She chooses, and chooses carefully, who will meet her where she stands on the Red Road of soul, and she leaves out those for whom she might perform by putting on an old, dusty mask that she had shed long ago.

For certain, it is not easy to show up as fully as possible at every moment of the day, to refuse to fall into childhood patterns of staying small and quiet or shielding oneself through aggression or escape. When the Witch of Sacred Love has mastered this skill despite all odds and all possibility for social rejection, she is then tasked with becoming a teacher. A permanent plateau in every Priestess's healing is reached when she has no choice but to become the woman she needed when she was younger, to hold others in the way she needed to be held, and to gift the very hard-won wisdom she wishes she had learned during her own torments and throughout every sacred wounding. In the teaching tale, the Witch of Sacred Love promises the ghost of her dead lover that she *will teach them the stories they will not read*. She will become the teacher she did not have, and she will speak the wisdom, a wisdom others might well call wicked, learned not only from her partner but from the relationship itself. The teacher continues to heal herself by speaking her truth to those who are open to receiving her words, and there is immense potential for greater global justice when the voices of women are heard, discussed, and respected.

We cannot know for sure what the Mystery has in store for us, what small part humanity plays in the grand intergalactic design, or what precise commitments we have made before this incarnation. There is merit, however, in asking ourselves why we might have lived, loved, suffered, and danced the way we have so far in these soft bodies of ours.

Choose a single relationship in this life to focus on now, be it romantic, blood-bound, or otherwise, and list as many key events and moments in it as you can. This can be the relationship you worked with in the previous chapter or another. You are not limited to relationships that have completely run their course and are now gone from your life. Just for now, try not to offer praise or assign blame, but otherwise feel free to describe it in whatever way you see fit. These moments can be positive, negative, or anywhere in between, and you may already see patterns emerging. Resist, however, the inclination to retell an old story. Look at this relationship with fresher eyes, and take an inventory of its most pivotal moments.

Once you have a list of at least five memories, number them as if they were lessons in a course your soul both designed and signed up for beyond the veil. Why would you have created that lesson for yourself, and, in looking at the entire list of lessons, what was the great course objective? Did you meet it?

Know that this exercise is absolutely not to excuse, forgive, or in any way condone the wrongdoings of others. Do not let yourself fall prey to the self-defeating assumption that you somehow signed up to be abused, trauma-tized, or otherwise ill-treated.

You are not a sacrifice, and you are not a teaching tool.

For this exercise choose only a relationship that you, in your bones, believe was, or continues to be, a true teacher, not one that seems so malicious that you have difficulty understanding your role. The Witch of Sacred Love is always seeking empowerment through relationship, continually asking herself how she can find more soulful freedom without giving up compassion, and, while she may well set herself up to be wounded, she also is well aware that not all pain is self-designed.

It will take some time, Witch, but feel free to apply the soul-curriculum steps to other relationships on your path. Look for the overall patterns, if you wish, but do not believe — not for one second — that you cannot rethread the design of your story, and do not feel that relationships alone are your soul's only teacher. Your roots, your desires, your art — all of these are just as indicative of purpose as your great loves and your wounds, if not more so. Sift through your memories, but know that this present moment — your breath and the beat of your pulse — is the only thing that is real. What will you do with the rest of this fragile life of yours, given all you have learned? What wisdom have you to share?

You have made it this far, Priestess, and you know enough to be a teacher. After our survival needs are addressed and we're given sufficient resources to care for our families, the greatest obstacle to sacred work is often a lack of self-efficacy. Do not believe you have no right to teach, and do not confine the word *teacher* to its traditional professorial definitions. Your voice matters, and your story is a change agent. If you were asked to write a five-lesson course in relationships today, what would the undergirding objective be? What are you here to say right now, in this moment? What do you wish every woman in the world knew for sure, and what do you want our children to be taught in schools not included in any present curriculum? If you were to teach them *the stories they will not read*, what would these stories be, and why are they important? Draw from your own experience, blessed one, for no one knows more than you about the journey you have taken.

MEETING THE MAGDALENE:
A PATHWORKING EXPERIENCE FOR THE SOVEREIGN WOMAN

In my most indulgent moments, I wonder this: What if, in every relationship that has ever presented its dysfunction to us, we were, at the root, wounded by searching for the absent sacred in another person? What if our mothers could never possibly have lived up to our expectations, could never have wholly been the warm light we needed, for we looked to them to fill the void left by the divine feminine's absence? What if those great loves of our lives could never possibly be everything we are telling ourselves they should be, for we are looking to them to reflect the virile Hunter, protective Father, and wise Sage as well as the sensual Maiden, generative Mother, and intuitive Crone? What if every human being we meaningfully encounter in this life, regardless of gender, is, in some small way, a mirror to our spiritual longing? The Witch of Sacred Love understands that we all look outward for salvation from time to time, but only when this search is turned inward do we truly find the wholeness we seek.

This is not to absolve those who wound of their sins, mind you. This is not to excuse the inexcusable or place blame on the victim. Not every relationship is a search for God, and not every plot twist in our stories is soul designed. There is, however, merit in looking at our own reflections from time to time to learn the lessons that are right there for us in the mirror, that have been right there for us all along.

Close your eyes, either lying on ground or seated, and imagine your pelvic bowl filling up with red light as if it was a primal feminine wellspring. Let this light pour over the edges of your sacrum and rise against your spine, pulsing gently in rhythm with your heart-drum and invigorating every bone, organ, and energetic center it touches. Fill yourself up with the vibration of feminine ferocity. Let it rise to your crown and spill over the edges of your skull, coursing through your aura now in vibrant scarlet spirals.

Protected and fueled by this energy, imagine yourself now walking along the sea slowly, with palms open and spine arched ever so slightly in a position of open reception. As you walk, you move with the frequency of the Priestess of Magdala, whom you know now as shunned woman and bride to Christ. She can feel you, and you can feel her. From out of the sea she walks, first treading on water, her red hood blowing in the wind against the graying sky, then diving into the waves headfirst. She is not removed from this element; she is tasting the salt and letting it sting her eyes. She does not transcend the lifeblood of the planet; she sinks into it with her whole heart and soul. With a purposed grace, she radiates an unbridled love so complete that you feel entirely fulfilled by her presence.

Just for now, you are aware that many of your expectations unmet by others were a result of your perpetual search for *this*, a true and holy love that feels much like swimming in the warmest, most nutrient-rich womb water. You want for nothing, for she is at once the whole of nature, the most unconditional mother-love, and the wisest grandmotherly presence. She is the sacred Hunter, dependable provider, and divine messenger. She is everything, and she is you.

You see that the face surrounded by this red hood is yours, and it is your feet that walked on water. You are the majestic Priestess who calls into her life exactly what she needs at every moment, and you are your own discerning lover. Where will your feet carry you now, my love? Ride a wave shoreward and notice where you are called to go. Find yourself there in that dream vision, imagining the next chapter of your life and yourself as Priestess. Who are you guiding? How are you the Priestess you needed when you were a lost wanderer of the heart? You are wide-hipped and thick-boned perfection, and you house all the lost relics of the feminine spirit inside your stalwart frame.

TO TEACH WITH GRACE:
AFFIRMATION MAGICK FOR SHE WHO IS WISE

To integrate the Witch of Sacred Love archetype into our feminine psyches, we must frame all this Witch stands for — her holy activism, sacred work, and sharp-tongued truth telling — as inextricably root bound. The ascent to reclaim a woman's spiritual integrity must be grounded in a certain security, a deeper selfhood than she often possesses if she has been recently wounded or is frozen by fear at the thought of rejection. She has lived through the garden escape, likely more than once, and has returned to her Red Road time and time again to reclaim pieces of her raw sensuality and righteous rage. She has burned her world down and risen from the ashes, and she has begun an authentic embodiment of the woman she needed when she was younger.

The Witch of Sacred Love is a space holder for herself and others. She teaches with grace because she holds a fundamental understanding that her truth is unique and there is no universality when it comes to wound-work, storytelling, spellcraft, and heartfelt communion. She honors others' will and respects the right of all beings to find and follow their own Red Roads, and she has learned to soften the shell around her hardened heart and dance to a more vulnerable rhythm than she did in those gradually brightening days that immediately followed her soul's darkest night. Nothing has been permanently fixed. Nothing has been skillfully stitched up so tightly that her betrayal scars do not ache, and there has been no white-robed savior who guided her home. She found her wild sanctuary herself, crawling on bloody knees and clawing at the mud below. She deserves every bit of joy that bubbles up from her belly, however fleeting it might be, and she has somehow managed to keep her most painful experiences from forcing her into spiritual rigidity.

At those moments when you are questioning your right to share your gifts and speak your wisdom, this affirmation is yours, my love:

> I am the Witch of Sacred Love, and I was born into this body to share what wisdom I can, to feel my feelings fully and own the majesty that is me. I am here and I am staying, and what I have learned from my many woundings and healings will drip from my lips like honey wine from the Magdalene's tongue, for these are the days of a new and

wild feminine fortitude that wears a red hood and walks forward with a brave heart.

RISE UP, JEZEBEL: THE MAGICK OF COMMUNITY

Materials: *Pieces of paper and writing utensils for each participant; drums or rattles (optional)*

Location: *A secret place*

You, my love, are the Witch who wonders why you were tasked with learning these long and cyclical lessons about struggle, agony, and loss. You have undergone the initiate's unraveling, untying the frayed knots that bind your truest beliefs with shaking hands, challenged to remember that specific childhood experience that bade you tangle and tame what you knew in your blood to be true about the cosmic mystery, magick, and your Goddess-hood. In cutting off the warm and running nourishment to your own divinity, quite subconsciously, you sought to starve away the part of you that would be too big, too loud, and too wild for others to accept.

You are the Witch who has become unbound. You are the robust Priestess who knows nothing for sure, who creates opportunities for liberated innocence every day, and who wants the children of the future to live in a world where individualistic dominance, stolen identities, and power hunger are mentalities that are scarcely remembered and never romanticized. You have examined your pain as separate from your privilege, your wounds as shapers of self, and your enduring passions as great beacons eternally lighting your way back to the Red Road should you get lost.

You, my love, are the Witch who is serving a holy mandate to rise up in this life and claim her right to craft her world as she wants it to be, to support others on their unique and soulful journeys, and to rally against the forces that impede her desired future for the next generation. Do not let the psychic scar tissue limit how far your spiritual crown can stretch, and do not discount the beauteous sanctity of the unburnt feminine as embodied by you, as only you can. You are at once Lilith, Salome, Mother of Babylon, and the Magdalene, and you are the resurrection of the divine feminine dark.

Summon all the Wild Ones you can, and bid them gather in a secret place. This is a simple ritual of spiritual affirmation where everyone has the right to proclaim their beliefs as they know them to be, standing against the notion that spiritual systems may not be questioned, dismantling the assumption that there are superior gurus who know best, and igniting the crowns atop the heads of all who attend. Everyone will be given a piece of paper and, in writing, respond to this prompt over and over again, for as long as time will allow: *In my bones, I believe…* The beliefs might be simple and universal truths about love and longing. They might be heavy statements that no one but the speaker understands. Whatever emerges from the prompt, however bizarre or mundane, is precisely what this ritual container is meant to hold. Trust the process as perfect, and it will be.

When ready, stand in a circle and begin chanting "Rise up!" Include drums, rattles, clapping, or stomping. Be as loud as possible, and shake the ground on which you stand. Moving clockwise from a starting point, have each person read her beliefs with conviction and through guttural howls. Once everyone has read, let the chant morph slowly into "I am Maiden, Mother, Crone. I am Hunter, Father, Sage. I am God, Goddess, Mystery, and I will not be caged!" Stay with this, honoring the natural ebbs and flows in group chanting rituals, then slow the rhythm and lower your voices to a whisper, concluding with several shared breaths and a long moment of sacred silence.

Honor the diversity of belief statements that emerge. Let this circle be a communal reflection of how spiritual communities can exist around even potentially conflicting belief systems as long as everyone has an open heart and wild mind, how even within a single psyche truths are constantly reorganized, dismantled, and reinforced. Ours is an ever-expanding practice that defies the inflexible nature of a system. Ours is the way of the unburnt feminine, the way of the Holy Wild.

AIR REFLECTION AND FINAL PRAYER: OUR HEART-TO-SPIRIT MARRIAGE

The air element speaks to us in whispers about our need to belong to the larger, louder conversation, to romance our world from the inside out. It is through our communion with others, through our intimate relationships with our partners, children, work, and communities, that we unite with the

Mystery, with the ether. The misty, mystical place where air meets ether is where our hearts meet spirit, where our relationships with those we love become microcosms of our relationships with divinity. Here, we find the answers to humanity's greatest questions, questions the Priestess still wants answered, wild and free as she may be.

In moving from air to ether, we become less tangible and less sure. We question what we know about the death-life-death cycle, divinity, and all the psychic mysteries that, for all our nature walks and communal sharing, remain unsolved. In the ether, we return to joy. We honor what we have learned through the wounding and the grief, but we exist in that liminal void between what was and what will be, and we exist there in a state of blissful acceptance. We become the red-hooded widow who watches the seabirds fly off together, catching a fleeting glimpse of radical hope again after great loss. In the ether, we have let go of a great something but have not yet embraced the next manifestation, and we find comfort in this fertile, dark grace.

Give Me a Death Ritual: At the Request of the Seer-Poetess

In lieu of flowers, please send joy and jazz. Forget the somber blubbering, sickening scent of overpriced wreaths, and white pearls on black dresses. Forget the eulogies and verses mumbled by someone I did not know to a God I didn't believe in. Forget brass handles on a wooden box, and, for the love of all things wild and holy, forget the halfhearted hymns sung by those attending only out of duty, checking their watches and busying themselves on their tiny screens while they hum on and on about amazing grace.

Give me a death ritual where only those who really knew me are invited. Give me a death ritual where the brightest colors are worn by the dreamers and the poets, for no one is a mourner at the memorial for the wildest life I have ever lived. If my body is tucked away in a tomb, may a bare-breasted Priestess come to rescue me and carry my stiff bones into the most haunted forest, where my soul is already dancing.

Give me a death ritual where my final freedom is honored, and I will watch it all happen from the shadows like a spectral and stealthy huntress. Let's forgo the heavy ceremony and talk of what I stood for while my heart was still beating, and my ghost will prance about like a thankful sprite blessing each and every guest with the lightest cobwebbed touch. Leave my stinking body right there, then, so the worms might overtake me, and I will wait for warmer days to be reborn into a softer shape.

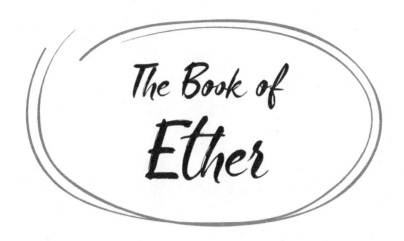

The Book of
Ether

Ether is the space between, the realm of spirit, and the void. Here, in
this fertile darkness that spans the liminality between death of the old and birth
of the new, we rest in perfect grace. We are neither creating nor releasing, neither
manifesting nor banishing, neither planting nor harvesting. In the ether, we are at
one with all that is, and we serve as our own wilderness guides who map out new
territories of belief, ancestral communion, and spiritual connection. We come
to know a new version of ourselves over and over again, relearning what divinity
means every time we find ourselves in this place of deep rest. In the ether, a
woman learns much about her spiritual autonomy and her right to believe what
she chooses, embodying the holy seeker as fully as possible, knowing nothing
for sure, and being so subtly nourished by the same whispers she has heard since
childhood assuring her that her soul is safe and well, forever and always.

> **Wild Feminine Archetype:** The Queen of the Ethereal Divine
> **Themes in Her-story:** The between places, the hunted Witch, autonomy
> in spiritual practice, communion with the Others, crown of belonging

We find ourselves in the mists once more, my sister, my friend.
I've learned to love it here, at long last, blissful in those quiet moments
when nothing is left but grace, when my magick has quieted and slowed to a still point.
My heartbeat and your company are all I have now, and I've never known such peace.

Chapter 13

Ether Verses

Pulsing with cosmic vibrations so subtle, so intangible that at many times in our lives we could dismiss the realm of spirit as an illusion or otherwise inconsequential, the ether is the writhing primordial soup that is at once unseen and the source of it all. Ether is where we begin and end, the very essence of the divine feminine dark. Here, we are everything and nothing all at once, an omniscient adventurer seeking the proof that God-Goddess-Mystery is real and palpable. If the air element teaches us to love and be loved, ether teaches us to grant that love the greater meaning it deserves.

The landscape of the ether is vast and unclaimed, thick with as many shadows as angels, and its diversity serves as evidence that no single system of spirituality could possibly serve us all. If earth and water are ruled by the Maiden and fire and air by the Mother, the ether is commanded by the Crone, that wise and knowing part of ourselves that considers all of time an unending dance of intermittent beginnings, fruitions, endings, and void. The Crone knows the enigmatic portal that is the ether, and she resists claiming any certainties about what is, in essence, the Great Mystery.

We face our most significant human challenge in this fertile void; we ask ourselves why we are here and how we came to be. We sift through our experiences, our stories, our wins and losses, hoping to gift our existence with a meaning beyond the roles we have played in our lives. Sometimes, we enter the void intentionally, carving out of our days a bit of stillness and silence to just be, to listen to the whispers coming from those indefinable edges between what is of this world and what seems otherworldly. More often, we are pushed into the void by some unexpected great loss, suddenly finding ourselves there in the dark and deep wondering what could possibly come next, pondering the nature of the sacred and questioning the existence of the afterlife. Regardless of how we enter the void, we always find ourselves closer to our ancestors there, holding hands with the dead and praying to whoever will listen.

In this chapter of verses, consider yourself an ethereal explorer. Recall those defining moments in your story when you truly touched the unreal, when you had a felt experience of otherworldliness that still haunts you, when you knew for sure that the Mystery was showing itself to you. We can use these moments, these experiences that often cause much trepidation, to scare us into adopting the beliefs espoused by the great philosophers and theologians, or we can allow them to teach us, to bolster our own spiritual autonomy, and to foster our own spiritual Craft. In the ether, we are both sovereign souls and interconnected spirits.

MEETING THE HOLY SEEKER: THE SPIRITUALITY OF THE HAG

In the space between, the rawest and most mysterious jewels in your psyche have been unearthed, and you are the hooded Crone who sees in the dark, who walks with wolves among the specters and the wildlings, and who may well be stalked but never be caged. We navigate the ether element using our intuition. Our greatest resources as we wander through the shadows are our intuitive night vision and our pathworking, and these are Crone gifts, the tools of the holy hag, traits that have been historically denigrated in society.

Ask yourself this: How have you, in the past, sought to reopen, bandage, or heal this soul-deep wound we all share? How have you remedied the undervaluation of our intuition, psychic powers, and embodied-oracle nature? What medicine have you brewed to build your immunity to the dismissal of the ethereal feminine divine, and how tightly have you pressed your lids to squint-see the myriad ways in which Goddess loss has affected your world?

Deeply embedded fears of the dark, death, and divination consume meaningful space within the Witch's psychic soil. There are those of us who are chosen to be Death Priestesses, feeling at home in the ethereal space between death and birth, finding comfort in ghostly communion, and living a little more in the shadows than those drawn to more brightly lit corners. Our Crone-selves think in cycles and deep, sustainable connections, wielding night vision like a weapon against shortsightedness and uncertainty. The Crone-Hag is the aspect of the Priestess's psyche that, while honoring the holiness of the body and acknowledging the merit of the Maiden, understands the ephemeral nature of the flesh all too well.

The kinship the Crone feels with the ether, the space after death and before birth, undergirds her power. Those who support the feminine within spiritual systems and various pathways to the divine do so, at least partially, through a commitment and connection to nature's elements and the subtle unseen vibrations that pervade and affect all. Paula Gunn Allen, in her essay entitled "Grandmother of the Sun," writes: "The concept of power among tribal people is related to their understanding of the relationships that occur between the human and nonhuman worlds. They believe that all are linked within one vast, living sphere, that the linkage is not material but spiritual, and that its essence is the power that enables magical things to happen." This sort of power is hag power, the ability to honor the unseen, to not only trust in your intuitive abilities but use them, and to befriend the very darkness that might terrify the Maiden.

Maiden spirituality is joyous and playful, and it needs to be so. We cannot take ourselves seriously every moment of every day, admonishing ourselves when we forget the moon was full or leave a spell uncast.

The Maiden's temple has no walls, and she prays with her body to the roots and the rivers, the oaks and the oceans. Mother spirituality is active, fierce, fiery, and loving. She creates, writes, reads, and is always banishing or manifesting something. The Mother is relational and communal, and she is not content to sit still and wait for guidance. Crone spirituality is quiet and unassuming. She is a holy seeker searching for proof that her magick is real but patiently waiting and carefully observing, being sure to not miss that moment when the Mystery shows itself to her.

> *We cannot take ourselves seriously every moment of every day, admonishing ourselves when we forget the moon was full or leave a spell uncast.*

THE QUEEN OF THE ETHEREAL DIVINE ARCHETYPE: THE WISE WOMAN SPEAKS

The Queen of the Ethereal Divine archetype is absolute feminine spiritual autonomy. She is the grief and rage transmuted, and she is the epitome of our untamed nature. The Queen of the Ethereal Divine is tethered to nothing aside from her own unruined spirit, and she speaks the language of the strong-backed ancestors who haunt. The Cailleach in Celtic culture, Hekate in Greek mythology, Baba Yaga in Slavic lore, and myriad other Dark Goddess deities all embody the so-feared, so-shunned Crone-self, the wild feminine archetype who is the one who sees and knows all.

Both the Cailleach and Hekate are hag Goddesses, ancient incarnations of feminine wisdom devoid of socially conventional outer beauty but immensely powerful. The Cailleach is the fearsome death Goddess who is also lustful, embodying the very essence of the fertile dark. She is both death and procreative potential, the final breath and the first. Hekate stands at the crossroads, an ominous keeper of secrets and underworld guide, a diviner of truth and lifter of the veil between worlds.

The hag is not a monster. The hag is the oracle, often a shape-shifter who moves fluidly between ages, appearing as the cunning, smooth-skinned Maiden as well as the stalwart, stone-faced Crone; all the while, she knows things her seekers do not. At the heart of Goddess tradition is the belief that women embody all faces of the divine feminine, including the fearsome and wise Priestess of Life-Death-Life who has lived long and knows all. With this understanding, with this inner conviction that the Crone lives inside the feminine psyche, a woman learns to not dismiss the subtle images from dreams and unexplained happenings in her home. She pays attention to what she can describe only as a "feeling" or sensation but what is really a resonant experience of the more-than-human, an experience she will embody and interpret in a way no one else will.

Priestess, know that we are all the hag, and your magick is yours and yours alone. There is no single authority over our wild collective that can show the one right way, for the paths forward are infinite in number. The challenge we face as the Queen is how to stop listening to our inner babble bidding us to find the right book, temple, or teacher where all the answers are housed. The Queen will not make herself known until there is a certain level of self-trust in our own enduring spirituality, in our own soul-mandated authority that chose this skin, these wounds, and these gifts.

The Biblical Jezebel was a Queen who worshipped a Pagan god in an age where such practice was deadly, even (or particularly) for a woman of her status. The death of Jezebel, executed for worshipping her God Baal, was supposedly intended to heal a kingdom suffering from a heathen religion's proliferation: "What peace, so long as the whoredoms of thy mother Jezebel and her witchcrafts are so many?" Her identity was distorted into that of a hypersexual rebel, and her name has become synonymous with the feckless and immoral temptress. She, a woman so devoted to her spiritual practice that she may have been willing to die for it, is a mirror for all of us as we psychically battle ourselves, wondering if the fight is worth it, choosing silence over conflict time and time again in order to preserve our energy.

The Queen of the Ethereal Divine, while certainly whole unto herself, does not discount the merit of circle, dialogue, sisterhood, and community. Conversely, she needs the Witch of Sacred Love archetype to support the manifestation of her beliefs within the collective. She needs the Prophetess of the Wildfire archetype to make space for her through the burning down of all that does not fit in the landscape of her soul, and she needs the Maiden of the Unbridled Sensual to fully embody the spiritual vows she has taken. The Priestess of the Wild Earth archetype fosters that initial break with all she was told to be true, the realization that this world is a place not just to explore with a light tread but to be tirelessly questioned and consistently exposed, two skills this Queen now possesses in spades.

Confessions of a Hunted Witch: Revisioning Jezebel

Sister, I must tell you, last night the moon went dark, the Crone's Moon, and I went for a wander through my haunted dreamscape. I was looking for an answer to those great questions you and I discuss over tea on those midwinter days, those lighthearted queries about our feeble human nature and the origins of the ascended masters. Believe me, I was not looking to find the disgraced Queen. Truth be told, I had not thought about her in years, but she was there all right, wearing a purple dress and dripping with jewels, hair mussed and eye paint smeared. I was not looking for her, Sister, but I'll be damned if she didn't have an answer to every question I have ever asked about spiritual sovereignty.

I happened upon the hunted Witch near an oak grove. Surrounded by bleating sheep like a wholesome shepherdess, she was, an eerie mist encircling the space and making me question how far I had come, how deep into my subconscious I had gone. The moonlight cast her dark curls in a silver light, sending streaks of brilliance from her crown to her well-fed hips. She was kneeling at the roots of an ancient oak, and I had interrupted her prayer.

"Why have you come, woman?" she snapped, and I stopped moving toward her, having no answer.

"Have they sent you to find me?" she asked, raising a single brow in suspicion — genuine or feigned, I could not tell — and standing. I could see now that her dress was torn, frayed at the hem and stretched loose around her neckline. Some of her jewels were missing from their settings, with even her crown tarnished in places with only a single ruby still in place. The dirt under her nails and leaves in her hair told me she had been living in the wild for some time, a wandering and lonely woman who, left to her own devices, had been lost in nature reverence and worship.

"Who-who were you praying to?" I stammered.

The Queen smirked. "If you know who I am, you know who I was praying to."

The sheep bleated on in sudden bursts, moving around the trees in slow and mystical spirals.

"You're Jezebel," I affirmed with certainty. "They pushed you from a window for worshipping a Pagan god."

The Queen inhaled sharply, tilted her head back, then conceded, "Yes. Yes, they did."

"I learned about you when I was a girl," I admitted.

She began to walk and I followed, intrigued by the fallen Queen and suddenly wanting to know everything I could about her, about her god, about her ways here in this ethereal place.

"You learned what they wanted you to learn," she mused. "Would you like to hear my real story? The one they did not tell you in Sunday school?"

"Tell me."

She turned sharply then and her crown went crooked with the movement. Every sheep in her sacred flock fell quiet and still, and she lowered her chin, her eyes staring up at me. "To understand, you must know what it is to be in love with divinity, to be ecstatic in prayer and full of faith that your enduring soul lives on long after this flesh has returned to dust. My god is the god of the wild, horned and heathen, as they said. I am his willing dedicant, but that part of my story is not important. Whom I pray to is none of your concern, nor is it anyone else's. What matters, child, is that I believe what I want to believe. I light altar fires for whom I choose, and I build my own temples.

"They pushed me from a high place, hoping I would die in the dirt, but I did not. My heart-drum still beat, and my body stayed warm. I was carried to a healing circle, where my Priestesses blessed me with their words, praying over me and bidding Baal to bring the life spark back into my body. Half-dead, I was, and I met my grand-mothers in the ether, in that place beyond the veil where spirits walk with a greater freedom than they ever knew in this life.

"They told me I had to return, that I would live the solitary life of a hunted Witch, wise and wild, my name living on long after my soul had come home to this place to join them again. I would be a shape-shifting symbol, they said, first a reflection of women's denigra-tion and then a beacon of braveheartedness and spiritual steadfast-ness. They told me I would serve my world best by sharing my story, by living on inside untamed feminine psyches like yours, and so I left the ethereal place and returned to my heavy body. I left my Priestesses when I was well enough, though they begged me to stay, and I became a wanderer."

The Queen laughed then. "You must think I look silly, filthy but still wearing my crown."

I clicked my tongue and lied, "No, not at all."

She took the heavy piece from her head and twirled it in her hands. "It's a reminder, you see. I keep it so I know that whatever graces these wild places have to offer me, whatever material blessings I might find or windfalls might come my way, my living royalty comes from my right to believe what I want, to know what I know, and to have my own intimate relationship with the sacred. This is my crown of belonging."

She gave it to me then, not placing it atop my head but handing it over with a casual curtsy, and the sheep started stirring again, bleating and moving about. She turned from me and stretched her arms high, singing in a language I did not speak, in heartfelt communion with her god. I suddenly felt as if I should not be there, as if I was witnessing something that was not mine to see, and I crushed my eyes shut, tracing the intricacies of the crown with my fingers and turning to find nothing but a blood-red road before me.

That's the last thing I remember, Sister, the feeling of the Queen's crown in my hands, and I couldn't wait to wake and tell you about her, our Jezebel. We have much to learn from her, I think, this wayward Queen, and I feel quite changed for having met such a woman.

No More, for the Hunt Has Ended: Spit Song of the Crone

No more does the flesh of my belly quiver in trepidation when a passerby lingers too long near my door, and no more will I mutter my prayers in secret for fear of being called a wild-eyed woman of the moon. Find me in the woods, if you will. I'm not hiding; I'm dancing.

No more will I bundle my bones together and crouch in the shadows to preserve your precious definitions of who I am. I'm stretched wide and long, spiraling these hearty hips in praise of wild feminine grace and whole-body passion. Find me in the streets, if you will. I'm not whispering; I'm howling.

No more do your threats of hellfire and damnation scare me. This little girl is all grown up, and I stopped following your dress code years ago. Find me here. Find me there. Find me everywhere you don't want me to be, if you will. I'm not running anymore. No more, for the hunt has ended.

Handwritten Verses: The Babe Meets the Crone

Dig through your memories now, my Crone-Queen. When did you first have a sense that divinity — or magick, if you prefer — had a larger shape than the one you were being shown? Begin your personal myth, your epic her-story of spiritual autonomy, *there*, in that moment when you truly felt her, the one they told you to reject, the one they split into the Jezebels and the Magdalenes, the one whose voice whispered to you while you slept and affirmed your wild worth. Use the prompts I offer here, or feel free to edit as you see fit.

> They had told her who God was, but she never understood the holy until that moment when...
>
> As she grew older, in her moments of desperation and dire need, she prayed to...
>
> The bond of spiritual shame from which she could not break free always tightened around her wrists when...
>
> In her quietest moments, when she could hear the voices of the dead, she believed...
>
> Now that she has unlearned many of the greatest lies, she knows...

Build your own humble temple in a wild place, my love, and share your words as if they were a benediction to the masses.

ENVISIONING A NEW AND WILD TRUTH: TO THE NEXT GENERATION OF WISDOM KEEPERS

You are a wisdom keeper, dear Priestess, a medicine woman who has a unique part to play in the here and now. When you feel unworthy and unready to join the great conversation, the cosmic dialogue about individual and collective purpose, you are really saying that all women are unworthy and unready to be the change agents and global architects of a more feminine future. Similarly, when you discount your right to engage in deep and meaningful rest, to check out of even your most sacred work for a time of restoration, you are urging every woman to press on and dismiss her energetic needs and precious boundaries.

How do we find soulfully meaningful and spiritually nourishing balance amid the chaos, and how do we find the motivation to care for our psychic development, spellcraft, and ritual? How do we find some small space in our lives to devote to our Craft in the absence of any societal support for doing so? How do we feed our inner Crones when our inner Mothers are busy feeding everyone else?

Like every other aspect of our lives, we need proof that our spirituality is serving us. We would not continue to invest our precious time and energy in a meal plan or exercise regimen that showed us nothing in return. We would not continue to pay for a class from which we have learned nothing. Where can we derive the required proof that our spiritual practice, a practice that does not necessarily yield fast and visible results, is providing us with what we need? In the absence of large socially validated communities, from where does the Witch draw continual inspiration?

We can begin with a mere feeling, but it is the bone-deep knowing that our actions have had an impact, not just on our world but on the world at large, that keeps us going. Every woman is a Jezebel, harboring a soul-deep rage against the atrocities committed against the female body, the feminine will, and the unique nature of a woman's spiritual path that is illustrated on no man's map, for how could it be? You may consider your individual spiritual autonomy to be inconsequential, and you may tell yourself that you have neither the time nor the education to decide who or what God/dess is. But, my beloved Wild One, what if the resurrection of the feminine divine begins with you? If we cast the bitterness and apathy aside, we must ask ourselves what the world might look like if human beings of all genders valued their feminine intuition and magick just a bit more, if the teachings of the Magdalenes not only were unearthed but spread like wildfire. Ask yourself to envision a social landscape in which oracles and mystics were again honored alongside the artists, scientists, engineers, bankers, and acceptable professions. Ask yourself:

What if erotic innocence were protected as fiercely as any other invaluable resource, and what would happen if the holistic and primal feminine were to be repowered with the voices and vibrations of every Witch, Wolf-Woman, wise elder, shaman, and world weaver?

What if the Liliths, Salomes, Mothers of Babylon, Magdalenes, and Jezebels of the world were truly vindicated not just in your own small piece of the world but everywhere, where the unburnt feminine goes by other names but walks with the same steady gait and confident grace?

When She Comes Home: A Bedtime Story

Cradle your babes close, ye saintly mothers! Let them hear the drumbeat of your sinners' shameless hearts. Whisper in their soft-skinned ears while they drift to sleep in the arms of whole-body and unconditional love, and gift them with these subtle truths so their dreams may be colored by the rich and fertile reds of the forgotten divine.

When she comes home, I will fear less and love more. I will keep my chin raised and heart open on my long walks when I have no one to protect me, for no more will I need someone with a larger frame to guard my body from those who would hold me down and carve their wounds onto my skin.

When she comes home, children will learn the ways of the land like they learn to count, and my words to you now are my heirloom seeds from which I hope a more compassionate future will sprout. Guard the blooms when they erupt, my love, and harvest the fruit in good time. Do not take for granted that one season of abundance guarantees another, for all new and fragile fields require sustained attendance.

When she comes home, we will cease to fear death as an abrupt end to our linear lives and will begin to relish the cycle of all things as the ancient skeleton key that unlocks every mystery. No more will we rush to fill the voids of our lives with all manner of vice, for we will know in our gut that our true and wild wealth is a buried treasure in the fertile dark of utter nothingness.

When she comes home, the Witches will rise to rage and the Priestesses will pray for peace, but all beings will understand that their interconnection with the universe does not disrupt or discount their selfhood. The ghosts of our past will make themselves visible once again not to terrify us but so we might better commune with our most haunted and healing experiences.

When she comes home, our work does not end; it begins.

Handwritten Verses: From a Witch to an Innocent

Consider this, Priestess. What is your legacy? What wisdom are you leaving behind? You may use the prompts I offer here or create your own, but ask yourself what you stand for now, in this moment, given all your great experiences and deep wounds. Pretend you are speaking to a five-year-old girl, innocently wearing a flower crown and, as yet, still full of hope.

I want you to live in a world where...
Always know that...
When someone you love hurts you, remember...
When you're ten years old, remember...
When you're twenty years old, remember...
When you're thirty years old, remember...
When you're forty years old, remember...
When you're fifty years old, remember...
When you're sixty years old, remember...
When you're seventy years old, remember...
When you're eighty years old, remember...
When you're a ghost, remember...
For now, look in the mirror and tell yourself...

Now, my love, envision that little girl as *you* at five years old, if you weren't already doing so, and reread your wisdom.

For Once, She Is Sure: To Build a Heathen Temple

Sit with me atop this mountain, Sister. For once, I am sure of one thing, and I have to share this epiphany lest I forget. You've never known me to be the adventurous sort, the backpack-wearing woman who reads the right maps and wears the proper shoes. I came here barefoot and without a sweater, as you can see. I was prepared for nothing, but I had to heed the call of the black-eyed angels who bade me understand, once and for all, why I was here.

I came here just as the sun was rising, following a white owl on its way to nest, just as an amber glow edged over the indigo horizon, and

I listened. I let my brain soften and sink down just enough to feel the violet crown arch beneath my skull, and, just as they told me, I sent my consciousness to rise and swim in that holy space so I could better hear the hushed hum of alien worlds and their star-children. I do not yet speak their language, Sister, but I'm learning. They are teaching me the nature of true nourishment and what lies under this of-the-soul connection for which our language has no better word than *divinity*.

This is my church now. Look for me here when my spellwork is done and the world remains wounded. Look for me here while I seek to transcend my human need to label and define mysteries that our fragile species is not yet ready to explore. Sister, we still harbor a desire to command and rule over that to which we fundamentally belong. Like a lone leaf at the end of summer trying to own the five-hundred-year-old oak and demand that it bow down, humanity is withering on the enduring earthly branches. We've made God a far-removed concept so that, in the absence of a well-honored divine presence, we ourselves might play the domineering ruler, and we made God so fearsome that to question his nature was to ensure eternal doom.

Sister, neither you nor I am ready to be gifted with all the knowledge of the ascended mistresses and masters and extraterrestrial records. We humans have much work to do to prove we can handle access to such great truths, truths that will surely humble us past the point of comfort and which extend far beyond what our technology can validate.

Even still, my dear Priestess, there is one thing I have learned here on this lonely mountaintop, on this mundane morning that somehow became my holiest day. For once, I am sure that spiritual nourishment such as this, sitting in my own sacred solitude and softening into surrender among the elements, is sufficient food for now. Nature knows the way, after all, and she works in perfect union and in perfect trust. I tell you this, Sister: It doesn't matter whether you call the lost attributes of humankind feminine or by another name, for what we are truly after is a more conscious participation in the dance we are already doing. The ills of this world are all born of a desire to dominate over rather than connect to — and, by Goddess, all the answers we need are visible in the turning of the wheel. For once, I know for sure that it is she who will bring us back into balance, and we need look not up but down to find the answers we seek.

Handwritten Verses: Hymn to the Holy Wild

Write your own harmonious blessing now, my love. Let it be a hymn your ancestors might have sung, a song you yourself once knew and howled to the moon when you were in another body. You may use the prompts I offer here or write your own, but let the essence of the message be heart born and soul true.

Here, on this Earth in spring, we find ourselves again among…
In summer, watch us swim within the…
Then, lighting fires of hope and rage, we will…
In autumn, we shall sing the songs of joy and…
At midwinter, we will remember the spirits who call to us from beneath…

An Incantation for the Vibrant Dead: To the Ghosts Who Haunt

Oh, sweet and sour ghost! Where have you been these last long years? I've been hoping you'd haunt me here, on the edges of my unconscious depths, in the misty fairy-tale landscape where all my secrets are buried. I've missed every part of you so much, your warmth and your chill, and there is nothing like loss to make you long for God.

I've been waiting for you without much hope, to be honest. Now here you are! Tell me what it's like to live without meat strapped to your bones, and I'll remind you what it's like to walk with heavy footsteps and swim in the sea. Thank you for visiting me right here on my holiest ground, for trusting me with your spectral shape, and for teaching me to hear the whispers beneath the whispers beneath the whispers.

For all you were and for all you are, blessed be you, and blessed be the Holy Wild.

Chapter 14

Ether Rituals

To engage with the liminal spaces in our psyches — to dare to peer into the seemingly empty places between the visible and the invisible, to reach out and touch those subtle vibrations and trust that we do, in fact, hold the ability to see past the heavy and tangible — is to enter into a world made more whole by the entirety of the life-death-life cycle. Our ether rituals grant us permission to walk between worlds, commune with our ancestors and guides, and stand at the fringes of what others will accept as real and valid. The heathen, the Witch, and the wild woman have always existed on those socially unacceptable edges, and, in the ether, we stand arm in arm with the freaks and the outcasts. We will ourselves forward in the name of what we know is true, and we expand the boundaries of what we once thought unreachable.

In this chapter of ether rituals, I offer ceremonies and practices for working with this most enigmatic element. Some of these tools will put you in touch with the space between you and the Others, those hearth holders of soul who have been walking with you throughout this life, and some will offer opportunities for dismantling any indoctrinated beliefs about your intuition and psychic ability that may be serving as obstacles to your Craft. Know that we all work with the ether in different ways, shifting and adapting our practices many times as we grow, so move through only the rituals that seem true to you in this moment.

ON THE EDGES OF JOY AND MEANING:
A RITUAL FOR THE SOVEREIGN PROPHETESS

Location: *A quiet place*

To forge connections between soul, that which separates us and renders us sovereign, and spirit, that which connects us to all things, is no easy task for a woman, for we have been told through various channels that we have no truly empowered place in the grand divine design. Your magick is a soulful expression, but its connection to spirit, to true universal outcomes, emerges when you examine its values with respect to the broader community. We can, of course, integrate all manner of plant medicine, herbal magick, ancestral deities, and multisensory flavors into our Craft to quite meaningful ends. These infusions are valuable expressions of the feminine that every practitioner will use differently, but *you* are the connected conduit, the center point of your work. At its heart, magick is the way we hold hands with the subtle vibration that is life force, that is God/dess, that is what spurs us forward on the Red Road. Permit your magick to mirror your shape-shifting nature, never digging a deep groove into your psyche or becoming a well-worn and mundane practice but always mirroring your vision for the world you will leave behind and then, yet again, reenter as a wiser yet somehow more innocent creature.

Our sovereignty and our joy come from the soul, and we integrate that which is uniquely us, granting greater meaning to our lives and our individuality, through the spirit. At that vital edge between joy and meaning, we find the ether and connect to the unseen. Guarding that misty space between what we know to be true about ourselves and what we believe about the Mystery and divinity are monstrous beasts who feed on fear and who hope we will not dare to venture beyond the safe and the seen.

As you descend into the depths of your psyche now, Priestess, consider the nature of your spiritual conviction alongside the indoctrination. What do you *know* to be true, and what were you only *told* was true with respect to divinity, the Mystery, the Goddess, the Witch, and the Priestess? If you have visceral reactions to these words, where do you feel those responses in your body, and how would you characterize them? Even the Priestess who has left the garden and released her binds long ago still must continually invite her inner Crone to surface, for none of us is shielded from the social assumptions that to be psychic is to be delusional, to hear voices is the mark of insanity, and to crave solitude over company is to risk irrevocable ostracism from our communities and inner circles.

The Queen of the Ethereal Divine resides in our upper chakras, our third eye and crown, and is the part of our subtle bodies that, despite all our caregivers' and teachers' best efforts to keep us from appearing too macabre, bizarre, or otherworldly, has remained keenly attuned to the world of spirit. The hag lives alone, for only in the silence can she hear the wisdom, warnings, and encouragement from her guides. Only in absolute psychic stillness can she rise above the mundane self-centered thoughts and truly commune with the divine, and only then does she know and trust the reality of our cosmic unity with the ultimate source. Once touched through felt sensory experience, the tangibility of the divine is undeniable, and the Queen will, like Jezebel, sacrifice her world to stand for what she knows to be true.

Sit in complete silence now, my love. Be in total and utter quiet, and feel into those upper energy centers. Imagine that the soft tissue of your brain softens just a bit, that the space between your skull and that powerful ethereal tissue that houses your power of consciousness expands, reaching out in all directions in violet-diamond light. Sense the edge between you, a sovereign and soulful Priestess, and the cosmic infinite. Affirm these words if they seem true:

I am both sovereign and at one with all that is. Hear my joyful heartbeat, Mystery; it's drumming out an ancient anthem just for you.

Listen to the silence now, and ask yourself what you hear. And so it is.

BINDING SIGHT TO SPIRIT: A RITUAL OF EMBODIED DIVINITY

Materials: *Several scarves or thin pieces of fabric; music (optional)*

We often learn the language of the ether during times of loss. If religions emerge out of *social* need, spiritual paths emerge out of *individual* need. What if we always ache for divine nourishment during those times of loss — those times of the immense and unchosen void when something has gone from our lives but nothing has yet rushed in to replace that relationship, that job, that thought pattern, or whatever has been pulled away from us and left us alone in the fertile dark? What if our God hunger during these seeming gaps between "this" and "that" is ultimately sourced from the potential to experience our own divinity in the fallows, a potential we are unable to name but do feel nudging at us from within during these voids?

For certain, the wild woman's path is not that of renunciation. However, when we have let go of the ties that bind us, renouncing parts of our material reality, we do find ourselves closer to that spirit-fertile void. The Queen of the Ethereal Divine has not turned away from the sensual needs of her body or the creative needs of her mind. The Crone cannot exist to any meaningful degree without the from-the-root support of the Maiden and the Mother; and yet, there is something about the material shallows that permits the psychic wealth of the world to shine forth. We cannot see the subtle vibrations of the Others, we cannot hear their voices, when we are packing all we can into our lives on a daily basis. The persistent pulse in our crowns is far too easily ignored when all is full and well with our worlds, and, just maybe, the stripping away of that which no longer serves, either by our own hands or without our decided approval, is precisely what is needed to understand our own Goddess nature.

To begin this solitary ritual, have at least three pieces of long, thin fabric that can serve as blindfolds. If you like, you might have a song of liberation playing or low, rhythmic drums. Cast a circle if that is in your practice, setting the intention to symbolically release any limitations on your clear vision, to "untie" any patterns that are blocking you from moving forward with grace, integrity, and courage. You do not need to name these limitations, but perhaps knowing the first three as fear of the unknown, fear of failure, and fear of success may serve you. If you have more pieces of fabric available, feel free to name any additional obstacles to your clear sight, your connection to spirit guides, or a felt intimacy with your ancestors. Make no affirmations while you tie the blindfolds on in layers. The intention is not to plant these obstacles, of course, but to release yourself from them.

Imagine there is a scene forming in your mind now, but, as yet, you can only see a dim and fuzzy version of this image. As you are ready, untie the first blindfold, feeling that it was covering not just your physical eyes but also your third eye, the center of intuition and the seat of spiritual reception and interconnection. Speak these words, if they seem true: *I release myself from the fear of the unknown, and I walk forward with integrity, grace, and an always-brave heart.* See that vision that was unclear become a bit more solidified now, with brighter colors and better-defined shapes. Untie the second blindfold and say: *I release myself from the fear of failure, and I walk forward with integrity, grace, and an always-brave heart.* See the scene become even clearer. What do you make out so far? Untie the third blindfold and affirm: *I release myself from the fear of success, and I walk forward with integrity, grace, and an always-brave heart.* Your imagined scene is crystal clear now, my love, sent just for you from the ether. What do you see? Notice all you can, and remember the gifts that have been given. And so it is.

FEMININE POWER LOST, FEMININE POWER REGAINED: A RITUAL DRAMA BETWEEN SISTERS

Soul necessarily separates us, while spirit fundamentally connects us. A felt experience of the Goddess feeds both soul and spirit, validating our individuality and affirming our connection to one another and the world at large. A glaring dysfunction in women's empowerment programs is their overemphasis on the individual souls of women who are largely privileged enough by their socioeconomic status, race, and able-bodiedness to afford costly self-improvement workshops. What results is a narrowing of experience, a recolonization of the Goddess landscape, this time at the hands of women themselves. A truly feminist spiritual path should act to dismantle what have been the Goddess's three greatest and interconnected foes — patriarchy, capitalism, and colonization — all of which arise from a place of individualized power hunger; emphasis on short-term gains over long-term sustainability; a tunnel-vision focus on the intellect as superior to both body and Earth; racism, sexism, and general targeting of all things "other"; and environmental degradation. As women, we must look for power in and through belonging to the larger conversation, letting our selfhood ground our spiritual crown without unwittingly using the same weapons that have been used on us.

A felt experience of the Goddess often requires letting go of not only what we have been told but what we have told *ourselves* about deity and divinity. For this ritual, perhaps call on a trusted friend to hold space for you while you read your part in this drama, changing any words that do not feel right or authentic and howling those that do so loudly that your bones rattle:

Oh! My prodigal sister! I hate that you're seeing me like this right now, with mussed locks and the ink of my lashes running in streaks down my overwet cheeks. Had you arrived just a bit later, I might have put myself together and better hidden the particular anguish that besets me now. Now that you're here, I suppose you're wondering why my walk has lost all its usual confidence and I've set a wildfire to burn in my backyard.

It happened last night while I slept, you see. A wide-winged creature came to me in a dream and bade me question what I know about this small life of mine. I woke with a terrible taste in my mouth and a deeper disdain for prepackaged spirituality, and I lit my many books and oracles ablaze in a mighty fury. None of them could satisfy my desire to see the feminine face of divinity, after all, and their apparent wisdom and gold-embossed glory suddenly seemed so trite and trivial after a demoness had simply asked me to look inward.

Please, Sister, lower your brows. I promise this purification ritual has been absolutely necessary, and, while you worry for my sanity, I am planning a revolution. The creature of my dreams did not ask me to fetch weapons or gather the masses, nor did she urge me to write a manifesto.

"The truest feminine power," the winged thing began, "the grit between the fangs and the marrow in the bones of the She-Gods, comes from your belief, your prayer, and every energetic infusion you give her every day with your thoughts, words, and actions. She does not exist to serve you or anyone else. She is you. You are she, and without a felt understanding of how closely you're bonded to the universal sacred — not the palatable and fluff-filled sacred but the primal, enduring sacred — your spiritual Craft is groundless and sorely superficial."

I defended myself then, babbling on to the creature about my endless knowledge of the lunar cycles and the Wheel of the Year, and she let me lecture her on the Goddess archetypes and wax poetic about the path of the Priestess.

"Go deeper," she said, after I had spouted all I knew. "Have you ever really known yourself as her? Have you ever really let your body buzz with primal feminine power and seen your prayers to her puff into the air and form a full-figured, vibrating, deified fog that became more and more palpable with every word you spoke? And then a Witch who lived nearby cast a spell in her name, and you could see the feminine flesh of God? And then a little girl who sat lonely on her bed staring at the moon in a far-off place prayed to a mother she never had, and the heft of this Goddess became irrefutably clear? Have you witnessed as she stomps her feet and shakes her breasts and asks why more women aren't feeding her with their micro-rituals and their body prayer, wondering aloud why there are so many who speak of Goddess without ever meeting her?"

I was silent then, consumed by an immense emptiness that my thinking mind struggled to fill with excuses. I tried to will myself to wake, but I was trapped in this dream state with this harsh spectral teacher.

"Well, have you?" the demoness pressed.

My frame was hunched, as my ego had taken a blow, but I still stood upright on my shaking legs, sifting through memory after memory. Yes, there had been times I had felt the presence of the Goddess. There had been times I had seen the mysterious, ethereal mist emanate from my hands and heart. There had even been times of bone-cutting grief when I had felt held by the ancient maternal, but had I ever sensed her ecstatic expression inside me? Had I ever witnessed her words coming from my mouth, her body taking shape out of my own gifted energy?

"No," I muttered, and my admission of feminine power lost, of Goddess absence, took the wind from my lungs. She was my life force, and my lifeline, and this bitter beast was telling me I had never really known her.

The compassionless creature spread her wings, grinning like the gruesome monster from horror films who preys on the innocent and the unsuspecting.

"Then you are ready to begin," she said, and those were her last words to me.

I woke in a cold sweat and rushed to my altar, lighting every candle I had and praying to every Goddess from every culture I could think of, recounting their names mechanically and referencing my library when one escaped my fragile mind. I summoned ghosts, played with pendulums, and arranged all my crystals just so. But, all the while, I found myself unsettled by a deeper desire to learn a language I did not yet speak. I set the fire not out of malice but out of a need to move beyond the beauteous tools, these things I know so well, and into the dark unknown.

Looking in your eyes now, my sister, I must wonder if every woman must lose that first felt sense of the Goddess, the urge to own her, stripping away all she knows for certain, in order to really come to know her. Perhaps we must lose all knowledge of divine feminine power in order to regain a more vital, vibrant understanding of who she is. I can almost see her right now in the blue-gray mist framing your familiar face, and I think I will forever be changed since last night. It's no coincidence that you're here, though, I know, and I'm glad to have a woman by my side this melancholic morning.

Help me douse these flames, my love. Let's spread the ashes of my spiritual quest all over our naked bodies and chant incantations to our own wild worth. Let's find the plant elementals, those devas that walk about this heathen landscape, and write them a poem. Let's nourish the Goddess by ridding her of her pink color and soft, diluted shape, and let's look for her in everything we see from this day until our souls soar into the blessed ether and pulse once again in the rhythm of all things. Let's forget what we were told about her, for the glow of her face falls on every woman differently, and she never casts the same reflection twice.

And so it is.

THE FIVE ACTIONS OF THE SHE-GODS:
RITUAL VOWS FOR THE HEATHEN SPIRAL

The Queen of the Ethereal Divine does not separate herself from any and all aspects of universal truth. The light and the shadow are part of her, and she will not run screaming into the sunlight for fear of the night. In Tantric philosophy, there are five Actions of the Divine; these are essentially *manifest-ing, concealing, sustaining, releasing,* and *resting in grace.* When a woman chooses to create anything, she is also choosing to conceal all other possibilities for what that thing might have been had she used the raw materials, her own energetic resources, and her time to another end. There is a hard-core bravery required to birth something into being. And through these actions of bringing some-thing about, obscuring all other possibilities, sitting in the fruition, and then releasing it before resting in the serene and fertile void, the cyclical wild self is fundamentally divine.

Consider times in your life when you moved through these five acts with respect to your art, your relationships, or any other life area. Akin to the phases of the moon — with manifestation and concealment reflecting the energies of the waxing phase, sustained fruition embodying the full moon phase, releasing relating to the waning moon, and resting in grace relative to the dark moon — these five actions are the processes of enacted divinity. Nothing separates these small evolutions from the spiral dance of the universe.

If you alone and by your hand were able to shape the entire world as you want it to be, the global community you hope the children of the future will live in, what would it look like? Ask yourself this: *What have I, as an omniscient Goddess with an enduring spirit and experienced soul, learned about the world that, if I were able, I would use to inform, uphold, and continually support the greater good of all?*

In order to effect real change in her world, it is not sufficient for a woman to tell herself she is a Goddess, for she has been told her entire life, either through her household religion or broader social indoctrination, that she is only loosely connected to an external representation of the divine. Even in religions where the divine feminine is apparent, the divine masculine is usu-ally framed as superior through later and more prevalent mythologies, written after the demise of Goddess cultures but often using her same holy names. A woman must often reconcile a rejection of organized religion with her per-sistent ache for Goddess when the world is telling her she cannot have both; she cannot release religion but embrace the Mystery, shun systemic and one-size-fits-all belief but honor her unique understanding of spirituality, or balk at the notion of ancient deity but relish the forgotten and misunderstood Goddess. These are the issues a wild woman ponders while walking the Red Road, while entering her liminal psychic spaces.

Indulge yourself now, and imagine that you are enacting these five events in a single breath. First, with your wide-open third eye, envision a new, thin moon. In the northern hemisphere, the right edge of the moon is illuminated as a sliverlike crescent. In the southern hemisphere, the new moon's light runs along the left side of that celestial shape-shifter. Inhale slowly now, and imagine the moon waxing toward fullness as you breathe, swelling to complete fruition at the peak of your inhalation then waning from full toward dark on your exhalation. In the northern hemisphere, the moon will wane from right to left, and vice versa in the southern hemisphere. The dark moon comes just at the bottom of your exhalation.

Stay with this vision, coming to know the waxing inhale as the moments of manifestation and concealment. On the in-breath, you are birthing worlds into being. At the peak of the inhalation when you are full of breath, you are sustaining all you have created, and as you exhale, you are releasing attachment and letting go of what once was. Breathless at the dark moon, you are sitting in pure grace, in pure void. This is the ethereal place, the Great Between. Stay with this breath, expanding the void space at the end of the exhale just a bit longer than feels natural.

Know yourself as ever-changing and all-powerful, holy and heathen. Stay with the breath and the visualization, thinking these affirmations silently to yourself. As you inhale, affirm: *I am the Maiden-Creatrix, willing the world to bloom.* At the peak of the inhale, affirm: *I am the wild Mother, full, balanced, and whole.* On the exhale, affirm: *I am the wise Crone, letting go of all that was and entering pure grace.* At the bottom of the exhale, be at peace in the void, in the silence. Stay with this for as long as you are able. And so it is.

A WITCH'S WEATHER: A SIMPLE RITUAL FOR THE HUMBLE PRIESTESS

Location: *A wild place*

To fear a Witch's power is to fear the Earth's power, the autonomy of the body, the inevitable death that will claim us all, and all that is better known in the dark and less visible by the light of day. I believe many women, regardless of their religious affiliations or where they are on their spiritual journeys, practice Witchcraft, for all intents and purposes, if only by another name. They have their own rituals and their own symbolic actions, they stare just a little too long at Mother Moon, and they have an intuitive understanding of their own unique psychic and physical cycles. To be a Witch is more than the practice of the Craft, however. It is an embrace of the name *Witch*, a claiming it for one's own, and a commitment to a beginning rather than an end.

The Witch is no master but an eternal student. She looks to the elements to teach her, and she has begun to fear for humanity's future on this blessed planet far more than she fears her own power. Every woman has a bit of the Witch in her when she wanders alone in nature, softly gazes at a candle flame for hours on end, or hears the growled promise of a storm in a distant rumble of thunder.

Here, in these moments, she is at once the center of the entire universe and the strongest bridge line in the great cosmic web. Here, she can feel the static buzz of electric life force stretching out of and well beyond her fingertips and heart, and,

> *Every woman has a bit of the Witch in her when she wanders alone in nature, softly gazes at a candle flame for hours on end, or hears the growled promise of a storm in a distant rumble of thunder.*

here, she no longer fears her uniquely held power, for she can see quite clearly that it is no different from the natural forces shaping the world as it was long before she was born into this body and long after her ephemeral flesh sinks back into the holy source of it all.

Consider the power of nature a larger mirror of the sovereignty of the feminine soul. The convergence of wind and water during a hurricane or earth and fire during a volcanic eruption are organic, elemental relationships that embody true cocreation and cyclical fem-force. No so-called natural disasters continue forever, for they are fleeting expressions of the planet bringing itself back into balance. The Queen of the Ethereal Divine understands that all parts of her — her feeling body, her creative mind, and her wondrous spirit — are always seeking balanced integration. She may feel all-powerful one day, erupting into a frenzied wildfire of will and action, and settle into smoldering-ash surrender and misty melancholy the next. These cycles are holy expressions of how she seeks balance in her world, and no woman will enact her natural spiral dance the same way.

This is not, of course, to discount the effects of disease, illness, or injury but, rather, to encourage an examination of the Priestess's ebbs and flows as often born from within out of a whole-being effort to stay sustainable in her world. While a Witch must regularly affirm her right to effect change, be it through spellcraft or another form of her sacred work, she must do so with a certain humility, a certain and particular understanding that her selfhood is a vital but ultimately infinitesimal part of the greater whole. Her magick is unique to her only because it emanates *from* her, but the resonating ripple she sends out into the ether is destined to rejoin the same collective pulse that has been drumming along for billions of years.

Go into nature now, whatever the weather. Stand near a persistent blade of grass growing through concrete framed overhead by steel and glass under a gray-blue sky, or stand ankle-deep in the waves of an angry ocean before a storm. She is all around us all the time. Despite our best efforts to contain, dominate, and own her, nature remains *virgin* in the original sense of the word; she is whole unto herself.

Turn your palms away from your body slightly and notice which direction you are facing. If your logical mind does not know, ask inward for an answer. Let your gaze go soft and tune in first to your heartbeat then to the pulse of the energy that emanates from the back of your heart. It may be the same rhythm or slightly different, but see if you can hear, with your soul's power of deep listening, the pulse of your unique vibration. Begin to feel the same beat ascending from below the ground, rattling your foot bones just a bit and showing you where you belong. Here, in this place, you are a living altar to her, a soft-skinned creature praying for her protection with every breath.

Here, you are sensing the heartbeat of the ancient Earth, for it has remained unchanged. Here, you stand in synchronicity with the elements you are born of, and here you are the epicenter of all things and yet the dominatrix of none. Raise your arms high, humble Witch, and envision the Earth's small place in the beauteous interplanetary waltz around the stars. Envision the orbits as a swirling cosmic prayer to the sun as it performs the great rite of stellar fusion, the feminine helium in constant union and reunion with masculine hydrogen. See other star systems around us moving through the same circular benediction. Then see the whole of our spiral-shaped galaxy body-praying to every other galaxy as they endlessly house countless births and deaths, moving slowly but surely toward the fertile dark void anchoring it all by the promise of inevitable, eventual collision and compaction, with all of it — every invisible particle — destined to sink back into the source of everything, just like you, so, yet again, it can be poised for the eruption of birth.

See it all in this moment, my love. Sense the Mystery. Feel the painful humility of wanting so badly to know every answer and yet, in essence, embodying every answer in the cosmic pulse beating from within and below. You are a living expression of an ancient heathen memory. And so it is.

Psalm of the Warrior Crone: Ritual Poetry for the Wanderer

Sing unto my heart a new song, for I've grown weary of all that is tried-and-true. I so long to hear your sultry and somber dirge, and nothing makes me rethink God like the holy voice of a Jezebel.

Speak for me, for your voice is my voice, but do not waste your wails on those who fail to speak the language of the wild, who never learned creaturespeak or the lessons of the night. Those who are gutlessly sure of their sinlessness may never pray the way a Priestess prays, with all the red-hooded grace of a Magdalene.

Fight for me, but leave the weapons that bloody the body locked behind closed doors. Use your wit and your wild, my love, and I will stand with you until my legs grow tired, steadfast as a Witch Warrior and humming in the same primitive low note of a woman in the middle stages of labor, birthing the new world into being like the Mothers of Babylon we are.

Dance for me, but forget the steps midtwirl and let your bone memory take over the stage. You have the thick hips, rough nipples, and full belly of a wanton Witch, and your worth could never be contained within carved-out marble of a hard body or the repetitive dance steps of the royal. Go ahead and alchemize the dust around your feet into gold, you perfect and peculiar princess, you saintly Salome.

Run with me, for we are indeed in exile from a crumbling world. Let us call out the differences between privilege and pain, colonization and exploration. Let us demand our Maidens be free of oversexualization and body shame. Let us gift our Mothers with rest, and our Crones with reverence. Let us call out every injustice when we see it with our wild words, for there is a part of every woman that is the dark-winged and fast-flying Lilith.

And so it is.

Chapter 15

Ether Magick

In truth, we might consider all magick to be ether magick. Only within the between places, those sacred edges marking where we end and the infinite begins, does the magick manifest. Only in the ether do we feel the subtle vibrations that gift us with the evidence we need to keep going, to keep praying, to keep alchemizing.

The Witch, the wild woman, wants proof. She wants an in-the-body experience of magick, a felt and tangible divinity that others may question but she never will, because she knows what her senses were telling her, *showing* her, in those moments when the veil between the heavy material and subtle ethereal lifted. When we are young girls searching for the one right way, when we still believe that one right way exists, we heed our caregivers when they admonish us to deny what our senses are telling us: that our dead grandmother was speaking to us in a dream, that we wished for something so hard that it came to fruition, or that we have memories that do not seem to be ours from this life.

The Mystery winks at us time and time again, offering us the evidence we seek with an open but unaggressive hand. Our training has taught us to not believe in something, despite all our sensory input proving its truth, unless it thunders into the room and grabs our face in both hands; only this will pull our attention away from the brightly lit screens and noise pollution, after all.

There comes a time in a woman's life where the workaday distractions not only cease to amuse her but begin to starve her spirit, and she has no choice but to drink the medicine of solitude, stillness, and quiet, no choice but to see what the Others have been showing her all along.

In this final chapter, I invite you to demand the proof you seek, to be witnessed in your Craft by your heathen ancestors and, wherever you might be on your Red Road journey, to honor your position in the greater web of life and death. Take to the wilds, Priestess, and let others join you there. Know yourself as a pan-elemental being of light and dark, the sovereign Prophetess who is Maiden, Hunter, Mother, Father, Crone, Sage, and the genderless Goddex all at once. By the hand of the divine, you will neither be caged nor tamed, for you are the sacred embodied in the soft skin of a woman.

BEGINNING A CONVERSATION WITH THE OTHERS: DEVELOPING A PRACTICE OF PATHWORKING

All of us are able to commune with the Others, with those beyond the veil, and all of us have those in spirit who walk with us, who hold us, who send us dreams when our hearts are broken into tiny jagged, thumping pieces. Pathworking is deep meditation, a Craft of descending body and mind in order to permit the barriers between the conscious and subconscious to crumble into dust. Pathworking is a tool of the Crone-Shaman, a method of connecting to those who vibrate with a subtler energy than that to which we are accustomed. During those still, silent moments when your physicality softens just enough to let the Mystery bubble up from the depths, ask the Others to come forth. Ask the ancestors, the guides, the angels, or whatever you prefer to call those certain ethereal presences you feel during the fallow times to send you signs, whispers, and dream visions of the yet-to-come.

To be sure, there are born-gifted psychics and mediums who have always been able to commune with the ethereal. These beings usually have a high degree of feminine energy, and their intuition was so much a part of who they were that dimming it, wishing it away, or pretending it did not exist was never an option. For the rest of us, hearing spirit in a way that grants us the proof we crave takes practice. It is a skill that must be honed as any other, and the nature of our modern lives is not conducive to such communion.

To begin a conversation with the Others, we require silence, solitude, and, often, stillness. For some, physical stillness produces a sort of anxiety as they crush their brows together and try to actively produce something that, in fact, already exists and only wishes to be received. If a Maiden's practice is wandering in the forest, brushing fingertips on bark and inhaling the scent of leaf rot, pine, or whatever earthen grace is there for her that day, then the Mother's practice may be painting, writing, heartfelt communication with friends or family, or an otherwise generative practice. The Maiden's senses are gateways, and she permits herself to become blissfully attached to the input she receives, to forge connections between this experience and that experience, and to truly feel and emote with her entire soft-skinned body. The Mother is a doer, and our overvaluation of the Mother as the ultimate feminine archetype has created an enormous block to the Crone-selves inside our psyche.

The Crone does not act upon the world; she witnesses it in all its beauteous and grotesque glory. She knows all because she sees all, and her domain is the darkening moon, the space between death and birth, and the holy void. Turn off the screens and the sounds, and let the world wait for just an hour in the morning or evening. Move about your house if you find yourself trying to perform or *do*, but let the movement be more of a moving meditation than purposeful action that requires thought or strategy. Be open to receiving images or voices that seem more like subtle but sudden bursts than your normal thought patterns, and consider this: If you can hear the thoughts in your head or perhaps see the images you are being shown, then *you* are not these thoughts. You are something quieter, something greater. You are the witness, the one who sees and hears. In these moments of realization, you are the Mystery.

If you are able, move through this practice once a day for twenty-one days, even if it is only for a few short moments in your morning or evening. Grant yourself the chance to walk in the liminal places at will, dancing with the Others and letting them speak. There is much freedom to be found in the ether, my love, but be careful not to become lost there in the mists. The Queen knows how to strike a balance between soul and spirit, between soft-bodied joy and diamond-light spiritual liberation. Know that you do not have to choose between one or the other, and the ether will wait for you when the material world begs for you to revel in all its hedonistic delights.

MEETING THE ONE WHO WAITS:
SIMPLE PATHWORKING FOR THE WAKEFUL DREAMER

The Crone relishes the fertile space between awake and asleep. On an evening when you are not too tired, when you will not fall off the edge of wakefulness too abruptly, shield yourself and let the body go still and soft. Imagine yourself in a familiar, natural place where you feel safe and held by the Earth. Be there with all that you are, wandering about these grounds you know so well, walking as the Witch Warrior walks. Set the intention to meet an ancestral guide, someone who has been with you for many lifetimes. Look for them here, within your psychic landscape.

Who steps out from the shadows to meet you? You may know their face well or not at all. Notice all you can about them, and do not pull yourself out of the meditation by deciding you are concocting this vision. Let it feel as a lucid dream feels, like a subtle surrender. You have control, and yet you do not. You are speaking, and yet you are not. This is liminal space and in-between time. The rules of the waking, light-of-day world do not apply here, and this being may choose to commune in images, via vibrations, or through your own memories rather than through voice. This spirit speaks the Mother Tongue of the ether, and, dear Queen, so do you.

Ask this being what you need to know most right now, and ask if they have a gift to give you. Importantly, ask how you will know when they are nearby. Is there a sign or a sound they can give you during your waking life to show they are close? Offer this being the gratitude they deserve for showing themselves to you, for walking with you without recognition, and for choosing their role as one of your hearth holders of soul. And so it is.

SHIELDING THE PSYCHIC WARRIOR:
PRACTICAL MAGICK FOR THE EMPATH

Psychic shielding is another Crone tool, one she often uses out of a necessary self-preservation. There are a number of ways to psychically shield, but in the absence of an existing method that feels true to you, begin here: Envision your aura, your unique vibration and electric pulse. Just at the edge of that energy field, build a hard, semipermeable crystalline shell through which you can push any emotion, memory, or communication out but which can't be entered without your permission. This is your psychic house, and nothing comes in unless your invitation is given. Fill this shield with colored light, gifting it a hue that symbolizes protection to you, and you are ready. And so it is.

CROWNING THE FEMININE FACE OF GOD: A SPELL TO CLAIM OUR HEATHEN BIRTHRIGHT

Materials: *Crown-making supplies (see suggestions below)*

Here, in these moments when the house is empty and the hum of appliances, traffic, and nature have dulled to a low and easily ignored drone, the Crone is home. The material comes into alignment with the ethereal, and the Witch gets the proof she needs. Few human wounds are greater than the spiritual oppression of the feminine, and few resources are available to women looking to honor their inner Crone; dismantle fairy-tale notions of the Witch and the Sorceress; and reintegrate discussions of death, divination, shadows, and darkness into the spiritual landscape. Very often, women find a home in the pink-glitter-filled fantasy of the Priestess, feeling fed just enough to keep from seeking out anything heartier than soft and sweet sisterhood. If they stay too long here, however, they begin to sense a familiar pang in their gut, a hint that such sisterhood may have become just another garden, and a drool-dripping, whole-body craving for something more.

The true nature of the feminine divine is neither fragile nor passive, aspects of the feminine that have not been suppressed in our society but, rather, valued for their ineffectual and nonthreatening attributes. The true nature of Goddess is much deeper than what we have been spoon-fed as modern Priestesses. It is fearsome and destructive. Very likely, the feminine face of God we find easily is not the one we need most. Yes, the Goddess is light, but she is also the death ritual and the breakdown. In our modern society, death is exiled into sterile buildings, and our end-of-life ceremonies are overly mechanical, their heart and soul bleached away by the need to hurry past the pain. Our grief is something to be rushed through and transcended, and, very much connected to our practice of turning away from death, the word *Goddess* is used as a tool, a product, and a commodity.

How do we begin to repower the Goddess and shatter notions of her precious, porcelain nature? We pull her power from the shadows and show her to the world. We look our own fears dead in the eye, and we question the connections between our wounds, shadows, and death. We become Jezebel, unapologetic in her spiritual practice and unwilling to stay quiet. We speak out against all that does not belong in our world, in her world — racism, institutionalized prejudice, misogyny, environmental degradation, and the old world order. We empower her by becoming her.

To begin, cast your circle strong, with your crown-making materials inside the space; these can be strong-stemmed wildflowers or grasses, ribbons, wire, or anything else you would like to use. Feel free to create the crown of your dreams or a more metaphorical representation. Given the right intention, a circle of interconnected pipe cleaners could work, so do not feel pressured to invest an inordinate amount of resources.

Stand and face the north; call out to your ancestors who lived off the land and spent long winter nights sharing ghost stories around the fire. Face the east; call out to those of your bloodline who gathered herbs in spring to better season their brews. To the south, ask those wild heathens who celebrated summer solstice with much celebration and joyous dance to join you in your circle; then face the west and howl to your grandmothers, those wise elder women who knew the arts of healing and divination and knew them well. Ask these holy beings to protect your space, and declare the circle closed.

At circle center, feel the palpable energies rising from below now, warming your feet and climbing your leg bones. Open yourself to the swirling vibrations above your head, and begin to fashion your crown now, repeating these words while you work: "The Goddess is both dark and light. The heathen claims her true birthright." When your crown is finished, place it atop your head and stand, holding arms wide and letting your voice grow louder, sourcing the power of your words from a low place in your body. Envision your ancestors around you, holding space for your coronation and welcoming you home. Stay here for as long as you like, opening your circle only when ready and offering gratitude to those who witnessed this magick. Keep your crown on your altar, adding to it and wearing it when you feel called. And so it is.

CRONE SPELLS: HANDCRAFTED MAGICK FOR THE SOLITARY WITCH

If any spell can be broken down into its core elements of containment, intention, energy raising, infusion, and release, then what renders it an authentic expression of the Witch's magick? Why are spells an integral part of a feminist and feminine spiritual path? Why should we not simply copy the spells written by those who have done the work, who are presumably better versed in metaphysics and the science of magick? These are the questions a woman asks herself once she has walked the Red Road long enough — once she has experienced abandonment, betrayal, and loss — and after she has come to the hard-won realization that she has the right to ask such questions, though no two seekers are likely to give the same answer.

Spellcraft is a practice of molding our world, and magick is our conversation with the universal energies about what we want that world to look like. When a woman casts a spell, she is reclaiming her right as a human being to act upon and shape her reality by making the energetic landscape look otherwise than had her will not been implemented. From the belly, she is howling that she has the right to effect change in her world, operating within the realm of subtle energy that is alternately dismissed as utterly unreal and feared as completely unnatural. All things that vibrate in the ethereal, less visible world have been discounted as false because they are less tangible and therefore less controllable. Magick, divination, ghosts, angels, faeries, auras, premonitions, psychic predictions, and all manner of spellcraft have been necessarily rejected by the patriarchy in order to rob the feminine of its power. Consequently, a spell cast is a stone hurled at the spiritual glass ceiling, and it holds far more power than a wand, crystal, or tool.

Consider, just for a moment, that while our wands, herbs, and crystals can certainly be gateways to magick for the new practitioner, it is very possible to become stuck here, in the material nature of the Craft. While moon circles, sharing circles, and other forms of softer coven-craft absolutely serve both new practitioners and seasoned Witches entering or leaving the spiritual fallows, many of these groups will continue to dance around the hearty majesty of spellwork. In effect, they are denying their right to use their energetic resources in the name of activism and global justice when, for all intents and purposes, they are the change agents embodied in a small circle of openhearted, strong-willed women.

Part 1. An Elemental Inventory

Materials: *Journal and writing utensil*

Go back one more time, Priestess, into the moments throughout your life when you felt your body, mind, and spirit had been yoked together. If your body was dancing, so was every part of your being. If your hands were digging in dirt, every thought you were having was a micro-prayer to Gaia as you became every tiny mineral particle, every minuscule nutrient and droplet of moisture. Begin in childhood; carry on through young adulthood and all the life stages and shifts along the way. Let it take some time. Split your life into multiple chapters if that makes the practice easier for you, but do not feel the need to be linear with this. How many of these moments, these fleeting moments when your ancestors were winking at you from beyond the veil, can you recall? When was the last time you felt truly whole, as if you were right where you belonged, as if there was a key section of your soul's contract that specifically described that point in time?

Now, my love, look for the patterns of action. Is there a common theme of creative work? Visual or performance art? Gardening? Cooking? Writing? What is showing up for you now, knowing that these memories are shaped entirely by the woman who sits with her journal right now, reading the words of another woman she has never met and trusting herself with a radical faith in her own self as oracle, as omniscient, and as soulful scholar. Look for the patterns of elements if you can. Is there a predominance of earth, in trees, mud, and grass? Alternatively, are you commonly near water in these moments? Or is fire evident in sunrise epiphanies and communal bonfires? Does the air element show up for you in windswept walks when the grasses were bending in such a way that you just knew you belonged there? Are there moments when the ether element challenged you and changed you with a sense of spaciousness as you gazed upward at the pinpricks of starlight through the vast indigo fabric of nighttime?

> *When was the last time you felt truly whole, as if you were right where you belonged, as if there was a key section of your soul's contract that specifically described that point in time?*

Search in these moments now for patterns of solitude and relationship. When are you alone, and when are you with others? Is there any relationship between the specific actions, the elemental patterns, and whether you are by yourself or in the company of one or more people? Can you ascertain the difference between your whole-being moments spent alone and those spent with another? Did the nature of the feeling differ, and how so?

Finally, my love, look for the moments when you had a felt sense of divinity. When did you know there was a mysterious connection between you and all things? When did you know for sure that the Mystery was holding you during and beyond the so-curious, so-perplexing childhood years?

Synthesize all this now within the context of the Wheel of the Year. What are your particular patterns of action, elements, solitude and relationship, and divine connection with respect to autumn, winter, spring, and summer? Take nothing for granted and dismiss nothing as universally true for everyone. These moments are not only clues to your soul's purpose but the very foundation of your authentic, unique spiritual practice.

Part 2. Cocreation of Spells in Partnership with the Soul

Materials: *Objects or a sacred totem representing your elemental inventory (see suggestions below)*

Spellwork can fall under any number of categorical umbrellas; for now, though, design a full-moon manifestation spell during which you call in more of something the exercise in part 1 showed you as authentically yours, something you long for and deserve, something that feels so truly your own that it is as if you are remembering the future when you picture yourself living with what you have manifested. Do not choose a vision you have worked with already in a magickal way. What's done is done. Choose a new vision to anchor you, a key scene in which your spell has come to fruition; see yourself in that moment; feel it in ultimate pan-sensory detail. This is your intention.

From your action categories emerging from the elemental inventory, how do you feel at home in movement? Do you often raise energy through singing, dancing, writing, painting, or another avenue of generative expression? What is the language your soul speaks when it creates, when it chooses to make something new out of the fertile raw? This is how you will raise and infuse energy into the intention.

Prepare your space in your home or in nature as close to the full moon peak as possible. If you are able, represent the elements the way they were represented within your inventory, setting a bowl of mud to the north if you always made mud pies as a child, a feather to the east if you love watching the blackbirds soar or vultures encircle their meal, an oil lamp to the south if you collect them, or a chalice of water from your favorite river to the west. Let yourself be visible in this circle, this perfect ecological representation of who you are right now in this moment.

Cast your circle by calling out to the north, recalling a moment of earth connection, then east, bringing to mind a connection to air from your lived experience, to the south and honoring fire, then to the west and harvesting a water memory. Your circle is closed, and your canvas is ready. Call to mind your intention, your anchor a vision of the spell's fruition, and begin raising energy through your authentic action. Let your movement be a channel for the energy that will feed this spell, and take as long as you need, resting if you must but holding on to the intention all the while. If you are raising energy in such a way that a physical representation of it will not be produced — for example, through dancing, singing, or chanting — then consider having a sacred totem at circle center to feed and nourish with your less tangible art.

When the spell feels done, after only minutes or long hours, sit in the energy for a time, no longer active but holding on to the intention. Speak now, letting whatever comes through come through, trusting that the circle is protecting you and rooting into you your right to be here, in this moment, witching your world from the inside out. Let whatever object is with you — a plant you have nested, some clay you have fashioned, or a crystal that has been charged to the brim with your wild voice — embody your vision now and open the circle. Move from west to north, revisiting the same memories or different ones for each element and releasing your attachment now both to the object and the spell, placing it within or around the element to which you feel most drawn and trusting that the spell has been cast well and strong. Declare it a reflection of your Crone-self's authenticity, your most genuine magick, and know that all is coming.

THE RIGHT TO REST:
COMFORT MAGICK FOR THE MODERN WITCH

The first part of the threefold task of the modern Witch is to know herself well enough to understand when it is time to surrender, to withdraw, to engage in deep rest. For those with seemingly endless familial and workaday obligations, this often means stripping away all that is perceived as nonessential. If stepping away from her art and her spiritual journey is what is required of her, she knows. If self-preservation demands she write that poem, the one for which she will never be paid and which will take an hour away from her income-generating work, she knows. If she must bring the babies to the park in order to feel the grass under her feet and touch the cosmic truth of all things if only for one breath, she knows.

However the Witch claims rest, she knows when it's time, and she allows those small moments to restore her; to reinvigorate her sense of purpose, to cocoon the fire of her will long enough so she can feel it burn red-hot again. Her will then becomes the great transformer, the crucible that boils the raw rage at social injustices down into diamond-bright liquid so that it might be poured into a shape with meaning, a shape that might be wielded to drive lasting change in her communities.

The bridge between soul and spirit is built from relationship and generative action, be it spellcraft, protest, or simply a word spoken in support of the bullied or belittled. Our individuality and our selfhood render our spiritual practice an authentically felt experience in the body, an experience that provides evidential proof that the ethereal is just as real as our bones and our blood. Our spirituality, our understood universal connection, renders our souls' uniqueness all the more valuable, charging us to rest, rage, and repeat, to cycle between the spiritual ascent and the soulful descent, and to uphold our birthright in the twenty-first century to change the trajectory of humankind. There may be long years spent in the rest phase and as many spent angry, and a woman begins to intuitively sense her next steps in the spiral dance of time, hearing the whispered call to bed when it comes and the howl moonward as a battle cry, listening for them both in the quiet moments when she is fully present, fully home, fully here within the Holy Wild.

When you feel called to rest, my love, these words are yours:

Now I lay me down to rest,
Snuggled soft within my nest.
Trust me, love, I'll rage again.
For now, just grace within my skin.

HEAR ME, HEATHEN:
MAGICK WORDS FOR THE UNTAMED WOMAN

Any woman's journey on the Red Road is yet another tale of ultimate home-coming, a story of injustices witnessed and battled, woundings survived, sacred work enacted, love gifted and received, and a spiritual quest fulfilled. The Red Road journey is not spawned by romantic wanderlust or a desire to achieve enlightenment. It is the autobiography of a woman's search for wholeness, and we are all writing the epic bible of our lives breath by wondrous breath.

Priestess, you are a bride to the ephemeral, and, one day, you will rejoin your ancestral congregation of souls. What if the part you are playing in the feminine awakening is written in your soul's contract? What if what we call feminine is only that which has been lost and forgotten these last long years, this short space between the exhale and inhale in the massive life cycle of our venerable planet? Whether or not we label intuition, magick, and death mysteries; our felt connection to the elements; or our lived relationship with our soulful, physical, emotional, and spiritual cycles as *feminine* matters little. What matters is that we acknowledge that these are the traits socially suppressed by the dominant powers that be. These are the traits of the Holy Wild that we, as women, are tasked in this life with resurrecting and fully, shamelessly embodying.

We are the medicine. The world we live in now was built with minimal input from the Holy Wild. If we are to regain the balance, if we are to truly uphold our vision for pan-human equality, then, at some point along the journey, each privileged Priestess must come to the realization that every instinct she has about reacting to accusations of colonization, appropriation, and prejudice, every urge to defend and boast of her understanding, is wrong, for it exists within the confines of a culture that, while it may not have saved her from trauma, has saved her from experiencing those wounds as a woman more affected by compounded oppressions. While this is a difficult realization, a true in-the-belly blow to who the evolving Priestess knows herself to be, we must collectively acknowledge that giving that initial nod to our indoctrination is a change agent in itself.

The untamed woman is feared because she is constantly examining the extent to which her beliefs are not her own so she might better be an agent for change. A woman who will not swallow what she's been spoon-fed is dangerous indeed.

To a certain extent, she is never satisfied enough to be passive, never content to stay comfortable. Her knowledge of her cyclical nature allows her to sit still in a certain level of understanding about divinity only for a time before she questions its validity and must, yet again, go to her own hand-built church on the mountaintop and unlearn it all. In those mountaintop moments, Priestess, these magick words are yours:

> *A woman who will not swallow what she's been spoon-fed is dangerous indeed.*

On this night and every night, I am stripping away the day's layers of beliefs that are not mine, vows I did not take, and any accumulated dust from others' sympathies or disdain. I put myself to sleep a woman untamed and unclaimed, the truest version of myself I know, and I will wake in the morning an even more genuine soul for having spent the night walking my heathen dreamscape and communing with those who know me best.

ETHER REFLECTION AND FINAL PRAYER: THE SPIRIT WAKES WILD

The ethereal is where the Mystery lives, the subtle, dark vibration where the Crone meets the Maiden, where death gives way to life. Here, we are the beauty and the hag. Here, we come full circle, having risen up from our rootless garden liberation; swum in our depths; set our worlds to burn; loved, lost, and loved again; and found a kinship with spirit. Now, we return to the earth, to these uncultivated lands that surround us, to that small piece of green we can call ours or the sliver of a mountaintop we can see from our window. A wild woman can only live so long in her head, and the crown of spirit does indeed become heavy. She returns then to the earth, to the element she knows for sure will catch her no matter how high she flies. From the ether, we descend. We descend to begin again, to rise a more potent and full version of ourselves.

Know that in-the-bones, felt divinity is cyclical. We do not wake every morning adhering to a rigid regimen of prayer and contemplation, for our pleasure-seeking psyches will not allow sustained renunciation of time spent wild, body satiated, and creative impulses unfulfilled. A woman coming to Witchcraft, Priestess ways, Goddess worship, and other divine feminine traditions will eventually become irrevocably disenchanted with her new path if she believes it should be a source of constant inspiration and an enduring sense of spiritual belonging. To remain authentic in her practice is to continually explore the relationship between soul and spirit, between her individuality and her collective place in the cosmos; to do this, she must truly know that she did not wake in the morning the same woman who went to sleep.

My love, we are ever changing, and so our spiritual practice must ebb and flow with us. If we track the times in our lives when we knew ourselves to be complete and whole, when we sift through the muck of have-tos and obligations and find the gems of our long-held passions, talents, and even in-the-gut woundings, we come to know the true nature of our blessed, soul-selected place within the Holy Wild. This is not a practice that is completed once and is forever static, for the examination of experiences and memories is filtered through the lens of who we are today. What we remember as so profoundly valuable from our past today may not be what we value about that very same time in our lives when we explore it tomorrow, and, if we permit the memory of our lived experience to inform our spiritual path, then we must surrender to the shape-shifting nature of *both* our memory and our spiritual practices.

Trust that every time you undergo those radical shifts in perspective, those sudden and often unexpected leaps from being so sure of everything to knowing absolutely nothing, you are integrating yet another piece of your wild nature. We come home to the wilds when we feel into our cyclical experience without needing to define it, when we welcome the death of the old without rushing to the birth of the new. In these ethereal moments, we truly find ourselves on heathen land, and we find the deepest grace the Holy Wild has to offer.

At Home in All the Spaces Between

Blessed be this mist-filled morning, for the spirit wakes wild. I am choosing to hand-brew this day out of sweet gratitude and pure joy, spiced to perfection and served still steaming. I am welcoming what comes and staying steadfast in my sovereignty. I am a child of the earth and water, well versed in the languages of fire and air, and I am at home in all the spaces between.

And so it is.

Conclusion

Her Revelation

A woman houses the unburnt feminine within her ever-resilient and forever-untamed heart. Her felt kinship with the elements, with nature, is the living antidote to the social dis-ease of separation — separation of body from spirit, of nature from humanity. She is the holy weaver, the Crone spider, who can spin sticky webbing around and through the broken pieces of our spiritual landscape, making whole again what has been fragmented and binding us to the greater cosmic design.

A woman certainly can bring about the End of Days — the end of the world as we know it, the world of normalized war and innumerable other ills to which our present generations are accustomed. Casting outmoded assumptions about violence and vengeful gods into the lake of fire with her words, her magick, her will, her work, and her love, she can birth into being what is at once ancient and futuristic, simultaneously a clear memory of the past and a fiery desire for the yet-to-come.

> *She is the holy weaver, the Crone spider, who can spin sticky webbing around and through the broken pieces of our spiritual landscape, making whole again what has been fragmented and binding us to the greater cosmic design.*

The depth and breadth of women's experience is undeniable, but connecting us all are our bone-deep wild feminine tattoos, ink-on-ivory reminders written in whatever tongue we speak that we are, for all our technological advancements and high art, first and foremost of the Earth. It does not matter which Goddess whispers to us while we sleep. It does not matter how skilled we are at spellcraft or how committed we are to our rituals. What matters are our unique on-the-Earth experiences, the patterns in our lives that show us clearly our gifts and our wounds, and how we, with all of our feminine long-sightedness, can best embody our immense self-knowledge in this particular incarnation to leave the world a better place than the one into which we were born.

Needless to say, nature-based practices are not new, nor are Goddess traditions or feminist spiritualties. What is unique about our present generations coexisting on our planet now is the urgency with which we need to call our Mother home. The sustainability of our species is in real and imminent danger, but for the first time, our technology and our media have the ability to connect us all, the one to the other, the *I* to the *thou*. We have created weapons that could potentially destroy our collective ecosystem and life as we know it. So, too, for the first time, we have the means to truly come together, to make globally apparent the wounds most in need of healing, and to unite what is ancient and ancestral to what is far-reaching and fast moving.

While one could certainly argue that the intimacy of our relationships is waning as the scope of our connections is waxing, social media is promoting an unprecedented interconnectivity within the human community. The Crone spider is busy spinning her web, and that web is made from the ethereal, energetic cords linking and binding us all, repeatedly piercing the backs of our hearts as we scroll through our updates, our "feeds" that, for all their distractive nonsense, do in their own way nourish our collective need to *see* one another; to make visible what is otherwise hidden; and to widen our views beyond what has been disproportionately narrowed by colonization, capitalism, and patriarchy. Not once in the thousands of years since the demise of Goddess culture have we been better positioned to come together and bring Her back, claiming the primal feminine's right to regroup and resurge right now when she is needed most.

A POTENT MOURNING: TO BRING HER HOME

The heathen Priestess grieves for the spiritual subjugation not only of herself but of her many brothers and sisters. Human beings of all genders share the same mother-wound. We are all spiritual orphans who, however unconsciously, both yearn for the soft-breasted comfort of the divine feminine as well as understand it is her far more feared, long-tongued visage that needs to first be welcomed home. Finding Her here, in our industrialized and high-tech world, means acknowledging our collective loss. To bring Her back means to first admit we have been without Her, not just verbally or through superficial nods but, rather, through a courageous examination of how the entire global community might be different had the sacred feminine not been surgically removed in many cultures.

Write yourself a permission slip, with no expiration date, to both mourn for what our wounded world might look like had the primal feminine divine not been lost and rage against the spirit-damaging concepts that have kept Her away. Bless it with the weeping wet of your tears as well as hot spit and moon blood. Many Wild Ones move through several grief stages before they accept the innumerable ways the global community has suffered from Her oppression, and we do not all experience Her loss in the same way. In *Weaving the Visions*, Judith Plaskow and Carol Christ write: "Western religion is not simply sexist but racist, imperialist, ethnocentric, and heterosexist as well. These distinct forms of oppression are not separate from or incidental to sexism, but are thoroughly interstructured with it as different aspects of a dualistic and hierarchical religious worldview." While women, in particular, have a deeply seated, socially indoctrinated resistance to knowing themselves as pure, concentrated divinity, as true change agents and magick makers, in a world where male deities have long reigned supreme, we must acknowledge that the notable absence of Her within our current, collective spiritual landscape will not be remedied by boasting the sameness of women's experiences. We do not feel the pain of Goddess-loss in the same way, nor will we call Her home in the same language.

INTEGRATING THE HUMAN SHADOW: NAMING ALL PARTS HOLY

The majesty of the Holy Wild does not exist to blind us into submission or dazzle us into ecstasy. She is a muse for integration, a howl to come home, and a gut-born urge to transmute the rage we feel when our collective feminine soul-wound reopens into meaningful action that moves us all just a bit closer toward a more lasting equanimity. This is not a call for anarchy and the end of civilization; this is a call for a sustainable balance. It is not enough to wish for a better world when you are a living part of that world. A cell in an ailing body does not surrender to the illness and hope for the best. It knows its purpose well enough to wield its unique abilities to work toward healing the whole. You identify as a woman in the twenty-first century for a reason, at a time when the pendulum has swung in a dangerous direction. Women live closer to the feminine, to those lost traits that are the forgotten medicine to all manner of global dis-ease, and we are tasked to descend into our depths, dig out those parts of ourselves that have been shamed, and integrate them into our light-of-day personalities so that they can be seen within, and eventually shape, the world at large.

The act of dismantling the symbols of the shamed woman within Western religion is far less important than that of harvesting and integrating the traits these women represent at their root. In Jungian psychology, the shadow embodies what we have suppressed about ourselves during childhood with such fervency that these otherwise benign personality traits and psychic attributes are now perceived as malicious and vile. Vulnerability within the parentified child who needs to mature quickly in order to care for herself or younger siblings may become the shadow of weakness or laziness. A quite natural craving for independence in an overbearing parent-to-child relationship may become the shadow of social rebellion or the outlaw. Neither vulnerability nor a desire for more freedom are inherently negative; it is only in their perpetuated suppression they became twisted, darker incarnations of what is quite normal within the childhood psyche. The shadow is not, at its root, negative or dangerous; it is our training that makes it so.

The shamed woman is the current human shadow, and the unburnt feminine is what has remained within the collective unconscious despite all social, economic, political, religious, and legal attempts to bind and burn her. Like our individual shadows, She is not an inherent threat to our goodness, but she has been in exile so long that even women may perceive her as the enemy. What we are after is not the embodiment of her shadow traits, those qualities often evident in women's lived experiences that may weaken feminine power rather than embolden her. Rather, we are after those root traits, the living and holistic Maiden, Mother, and Crone qualities that we suppressed in our younger years not out of spiritual need but out of social conditioning.

The shadow is not an enemy to be defeated but an only seemingly sinister reflection of who we truly are and the nourishment we need most. The shadow is the medicine, and humankind's most sorely needed remedy for the infection plaguing us all since the wild was ripped from our spiritual skin is She.

The shadow is the hunted Witch, and every untamed woman is a living and breathing inoculation to the virus of nature-human separation. We are the cure for what ails us, Priestess, so consider this your call to action.

> *The shadow is the medicine, and humankind's most sorely needed remedy for the infection plaguing us all since the wild was ripped from our spiritual skin is She.*

CHARGE OF THE HEATHEN PRIESTESS: THESE ARE THE BLADES WE WERE BORN WITH

Here, in this book, I offered you no religion. To be heathen is to predate the spiritual systems that have bound us. To my mind, our modern religions have too often, though certainly not always, been a largely male-led dimension of systemized spirituality that is easily spoon-fed to the masses when seasoned with a good deal of fear. This is not to say that the feminine spiritual landscape has no room for religion, and I have certainly seen many religions be compatible with the wild feminine ways, Witchcraft, and the Goddess path. Religions where women are in positions of leadership as often as or more so than their male counterparts could benefit the world tremendously, proving that feminine power can coexist with systemized religious practices and hierarchical order.

Ultimately, it is not religion itself but the connection between male-dominated religions and fear that has done the most damage to the wild feminine heart. Throughout history, groups whose survival was perceived to be threatened by natural disasters, dropping fertility rates, forced migration, conflict, or other legitimate terrors that held the potential to disrupt the existing structures of authority gave rise to power-hungry, individualistic religions along with countless other social structures problematic for the feminine. The parallels between the environment's rape and the same fear of scarcity that has driven both capitalism and colonization are undeniable, and the collective mother-wound has been bleeding all over the holy books of religions born long before the sustainability of our planet was truly precarious.

Our survival will accept nothing less than a fearless commitment to Her, to all the elements of the primal feminine that have been cast into the shadows out of pure and senseless panic; these are the very essence of our wholeness, our ecological consciousness, our holistic connection to the entirety of the life cycle rather than a mere and narrow emphasis on short-term existence and creation. What is required is a level of feminine spiritual activism that extends far beyond the attendance of an occasional moon circle or in-the-woods ritual. We must be the agents of change we long for. We must rally against racism, sexism, classism, heterocentrism, and environmental destruction. For some of us, we must strip our spiritual landscape right down to the bare bones of the elements themselves, for therein is our widest and rawest human experience. We must continually and willingly descend into our depths in order to retrieve the buried treasures of authentic belief, these deep knowings that are truly ours rather than those gleaming just on the surface, planted there by others in an effort to distract us from the downward, soul-bound journey where we just might harvest a necessary and destructive fearlessness. We are of the Earth, a living heathen memory, and the path of wild spirituality requires a brave heart and the will of a Warrioress.

Let those who identify as women understand that, yes, men too need their Mother to come home. Let those who identify as men not mistake spiritual equality for subjugation after thousands of years of patriarchal dominion. Let white women not discount the impact of their particular privilege on every aspect of their lived experience nor mistake their woundings for a lack of privilege. Let us not ignore the pervasive impact of colonization, appropriation, and capitalism on our spirituality or discount the unique impact of these patriarchal ills on the lived experiences of women of color, trans women, those with nonbinary gender identities, and other groups whose stories have been far less apparent in his-story than those of white, cisgender, young, middle-class, neurotypical, and able-bodied women.

To bring about change, we must be willing to be uncomfortable, and we must know that we, as fully sovereign Priestesses, can both be intensely self-compassionate and yet still engage in the self-inquiry necessary to drive the global changes we seek. At the core of the dark feminine shadow is the acceptance of nature's great wheel, the ever-turning cycle of birth-death-birth that permits our heavy bodies to be born, fatten and swell, and then thin out and sink back into the source of it all. To hold hands with this shadow is to befriend the primordial Mystery that is the fertile void between death and birth. We can claim to know with great certainty what awaits us after this incarnation's final breath, but, ultimately, we are only speculating, whether we long for a golden heaven or a misty Summerland, whether we adamantly assert the finality of death or believe fervently in reincarnation. We do not know, yet the great lesson of the Holy Wild is to sit in grace with that not knowing, to trust in the spiral dance of time, and to do what we can with the time we have been given.

In looking to nature, in learning from the wild, we see reflections of sustainability and balance over and over again. We see entire ecosystems, blessed landscapes of earth, water, fire, air, and ether, perfectly sustained by intermittent and inevitable waxing and waning of multiple forces. A herd thins out so another might regain strength, a plant strangles its competitor for sunlight so it might flourish to feed the hungriest creatures, or rains flood out an overpolluted river. In the absence of willful human intervention fueled by voracious and unmitigated consumption of her resources, nature is positively flawless.

What we, in our individualistic worlds, have forgotten is not how to live with Her but how to live in and of Her. In order to remember our earthly nature, to integrate the wildest parts of ourselves, we must make better friends with death, the dark, the void, and all-things-Mystery. We must confront our own fears of the unknown. The scariest face of the feminine shadow is that of the destructive Goddess, the long-tongued warrior and snake-skinned sorceress, for she is the great equalizer. The inevitable breakdown of all things humble us, drive us to make the most of our time here, and support an undercurrent of joy despite the aches and pains of being human, for we are, after all, on a planet of limitless pleasure. Remember, heathen Priestess, what it is like to live on uncultivated spiritual land.

Remember with your mind what your soul has never forgotten: You are both diamond-bright spirit light and sultry-red selfhood. The ephemeral

Remember, heathen Priestess, what it is like to live on uncultivated spiritual land.

nature of your flesh makes your body no less sovereign than your enduring connection to the divine source, for your body and spirit are, after all, one and the same. Your story matters. The places where your fears, wounds, and passions intersect the fears, wounds, and passions of historically shamed women matter, for it is here at those wild psychic crossroads where we must choose to stand and stand firm, resisting the urge to shrink back out of trepidation, apathy, or a feigned conviction that we have little to do with social change.

Wherever you are on the Red Road journey, whether you resonate with the labels of "feminine," "Goddess," "Witch" or "wild woman," whether you saw parts of yourself in all five elemental archetypes or none of them, look to your lived story for the lessons. Reflect on all aspects of your identity — as you know it to be, not as they told you it was — and seek *healing* not through fixing, not through one-size-fits-all spiritual elixirs, but through continual and cyclical descent; *awareness* through the retrieval of tiny soulful treasures long buried; and *integration* of those recovered bits not just into your lived-out-loud life but also into your larger community. Be who you needed when you were younger. If you are one electric-pulsing cell in the great global heart, then your medicine, even in its uniqueness, is likely sorely needed by others, who, in turn, may have their own brew to gift you.

The task of the modern Priestess is to be the living antithesis to short-sighted individualism; this also means being an antidote to oppression as it is enacted through our economic markets, social structures, spiritual systems, and government institutions. You were born into your body, your skin, at this time for a reason. Whatever enrages you, whatever curls your hands into fists and sets your jaw firm, however seemingly small or immense, is a sharp and divine nod straight from her to you. Look for the ways you have uniquely suppressed your own wildness, awaken those heathen parts of your psyche, then take your show on the road. Rest, rage, and repeat. Do not let the healing end with you, for you will one day be reborn into much the same world you left behind and the little ones of today are inheriting the lands pillaged by those who still claim ownership of Her.

These are the blades we were born with: the capacity to both share and change our stories and a bone-deep, blood-true kinship with nature, with the Mother that bore us. Given all you have been through, given your stories of cages busted and passions fulfilled, wild feminine lost and wild feminine regained, given all that makes your story the holiest book ever written — an integral text in the million-volume anthology that documents Her slow but certain return — surely you are poised for an epic and timely eruption, a permanent and fiery reclamation of your crown of belonging. I will be there at your coronation, Sister, as will the Liliths wearing their serpentine adornments and serving up forbidden fruit, the Salomes unveiled and temple dancing, the Mothers of Babylon reciting blessed prophecies, the red-hooded Mary Magdalenes praying with their whole unruined hearts, and the Jezebels performing the Crone rituals of rest and reflection. They will be there. Your many proud grandmothers will be there, those stalwart, flame-tending and joyous souls who want nothing more than for you to live the life you long for in your quietest moments.

Blessed be the unburnt feminine in them all, blessed be your heathen spirit, and blessed be the Holy Wild.

Sonnet of the Shape-Shifter

Walk with me, Sister, along the Red Road.
I'm lonely at dusk, and I'm missing your words.
Let's speak of the dark, when brighter moons glowed,
When Witches wore hoods and gathered like birds.

Run with me, Sister, and spread your wings wide.
Shape-shifters we are. In shadow, we'll fly.
We'll land in the churchyard where sinners may hide,
Blessing the ground then back to the sky.

Change with me, Sister, once more on the road,
As She-Wolves lamenting all spells left uncast.
Howl with me where the great river once flowed.
Claw deep with your paws, and unleash the past.

Lie with me now on my grandmother's grave.
It's near sunrise, no more visions have I.
Such a journey we've made, and you, so brave
Here with a heathen who taught you to fly.

Sing me to sleep like a Crone soothes a child,
Grant me the grace of your still-Holy Wild.

Appendix

Further Study for Women's Groups, Covens, and Other Wild Circles

THE BOOK OF EARTH

Wild Feminine Archetype: The Priestess of the Wild Earth
Related Triple Goddess Archetype: Maiden
Themes: Rightful rebellion, tasting the forbidden, spiritual initiation, sacred solitude in nature, coming home to the wilds
Chakral Connection: Muladhara (root) to Sahasrara (crown)
Study and Open Discussion Prompts for Women's Circles, Covens, and Wild Gatherings:

1. When in your life have you been Lilith escaping a garden, choosing the fertile unknown over what is certain and predictable?
2. If the "wild home" is an inner altar we carry with us that houses our truest values and deepest convictions, what are the "house rules" for the wild home? Who is permitted entry?
3. What aspects of Lilith, of the Priestess of the Wild Earth archetype, are most fearsome for you? Why? What aspects of Lilith do you love, and why?
4. When and where do you feel truly connected to nature, most at home in the wild?
5. How would you define the "Dark Goddess" archetype as she exists in your life right now?

THE BOOK OF WATER

Wild Feminine Archetype: The Maiden of the Unbridled Sensual
Related Triple Goddess Archetype: Maiden
Themes: Calling joy home, reclamation of embodied feeling, honoring desire, awakening our wild art, hope and longing
Chakral Connection: Svadhisthana (sacral) to Sahasrara (crown)
Study and Open Discussion Prompts for Women's Circles, Covens, and Wild Gatherings:

1.   How have you experienced the sensuality-spirituality connection? Can you describe the feelings emergent from this union?

2.   When have you created out of pure joy in your life? What was your medium?

3.   Have you ever experienced art as worship? How did this differ from art making with a specific outcome in mind?

4.   When does your body feel truly yours, and when does it feel like it belongs either to something greater than you, as if you are part of an essential whole, or to another person or multiple people?

5.   What do you wish you'd been told as a young girl about your body, sex, gender, birth control, or blood mysteries?

THE BOOK OF FIRE

Wild Feminine Archetype: The Prophetess of the Wildfire
Related Triple Goddess Archetype: Mother
Themes: Radical hope, righteous rage, transmutation, feminine will, magick as activism
Chakral Connection: Manipura (solar plexus) to Sahasrara (crown)
Study and Open Discussion Prompts for Women's Circles, Covens, and Wild Gatherings:

1.   Where in your body do you feel rage? Where do you feel the duty to act? Where do you feel compassion?

2.   What causes and social justice issues do you care about most? What ignites a fire in your belly?

3. Have you ever experienced communal energy raising for the purpose of creating change? Was it at a protest? During a spell to heal the environment? How did you feel as a powerful part of that powerful whole?

4. If you were able to gather one hundred Wild Ones who would stand with you to raise energy right now and direct it toward a single intention, what would that intention be?

5. What can you predict about the next year of your life, the lives of those in your inner circle, the lives of those in your local community, and the world at large?

THE BOOK OF AIR

Wild Feminine Archetype: The Witch of Sacred Love
Related Triple Goddess Archetype: Mother
Themes: Divine union, the healer-teacher, the cauldron of relationship, the cosmic web
Chakral Connections: Anahata (heart) to Sahasrara (crown), Vishuddha (throat) to Sahasrara (crown)
Study and Open Discussion Prompts for Women's Circles, Covens, and Wild Gatherings:

1. What is the greatest love story you've ever heard?
2. How, in your life, does the divine feminine balance the divine masculine?
3. What feelings do you have around the divine masculine, either the attributes of the Hunter, Father, and Sage; a male deity; or another manifestation of him?
4. How would you define the word *healer*?
5. What kind of world do you hope the children of the future will live in?

THE BOOK OF ETHER

Wild Feminine Archetype: The Queen of the Ethereal Divine
Related Triple Goddess Archetype: Crone
Themes: The between places, the hunted Witch, autonomy in spiritual practice, communion with the Others, crown of belonging

Chakra Connection: Ajna (third eye) to Sahasrara (crown)

Study and Open Discussion Prompts for Women's Circles, Covens, and Wild Gatherings:

1. What initial reactions do you have to the name Jezebel?

2. What initial reactions do you have to the words *Witch, wild woman, Priestess,* and *Goddess*?

3. If you had to synthesize your spiritual upbringing in five words, what would they be?

4. What do you know to be true about the divine feminine? What do you hope is true but don't know for sure?

5. As you walk the Red Road, continuing your spiral journey of spiritual growth, what do you want to remember no matter what, no matter how dark the night becomes or how blindingly bright the day?

Acknowledgments

To all the uncultivated lands this heathen has called her church, I will forever sing your hymns and dance your prayers. To my family's cabin in the Pocono Mountains, where I spent countless summers among the elements, to my grandparents' garden and spiderwebbed backyard, to my parents' untended apple tree and wild forsythias, to the rocky beaches of western Ireland and the misty stone circles of southern England, and to the magickal medicinal herb garden left for me at my Moon House, you have all been the greatest source of this Witch's wisdom, and I thank you.

Importantly, this book would not have been possible without the support of three wise women. To my editor, Georgia Hughes, and literary agent, Sheree Bykofsky, I owe you my endless, open-armed gratitude. To Tristy Taylor, publicist extraordinaire and hardworking Witch, thank you for investing so much time and energy in spreading the wild word, keeping me organized, and encouraging my next steps on this bizarre and wild path.

To my sons, Bodhi and Sage, and partner, Ryan, you are the loves of my life. Thank you, Bodhi, for teaching me to not take myself too seriously. Sage, thank you for reminding me that nature is everyone's reset button, even yours. To Ryan, thank you for feeding my coven and me, loving me, and listening to me even when I am not speaking out loud. You three wild men have my whole heart and soul.

To the *Rebelle Society*, *House of Twigs*, *Urban Howl*, School of Witchery, and *WITCH* publications that have allowed me to have regular columns and reach a wide, wise audience, thank you for supporting my work, correcting my typos, and offering heathens like me a chance to speak and be heard.

Finally, to all the majestic souls I have worked with over the years in councils, teaching covens, yoga teacher training, and numerous other circles that have entered my life just when I needed them, you are the spiritual warriors, the Dark Goddess embodied, and the reason I write in the first place. Thank you. I love you. Thank you. I love you. Let's keep descending, retrieving, and integrating together. You are my wildest inspiration. All blessings be.

Notes

INTRODUCTION: HER GENESIS

Page 3, *The spiritual wisdom of the feminine*: See Carol Christ and Judith Plaskow, eds., *Womanspirit Rising: A Feminist Reader in Religion* (San Francisco: HarperCollins, 1992), for essays written by women about the role of feminine experience in women's spirituality and religion.

Page 4, *"one inhabiting uncultivated land"*: *Online Etymology Dictionary*, https://www.etymonline.com/word/heathen.

CHAPTER 1. EARTH VERSES

Page 15, *In later Hebrew texts*: Demetra George, *Mysteries of the Dark Moon: The Healing Power of the Dark Goddess* (San Francisco: HarperCollins, 1992), 180.

Page 15, *In Mysteries of the Dark Moon*: George, *Mysteries of the Dark Moon*, 181.

Page 16, *The holy feminine longs for liberation*: See George, *Mysteries of the Dark Moon*, for greater discussion of Dark Goddess mythology.

Page 16, *Just as Lilith's story*: See Jalaja Bonheim, *Aphrodite's Daughters: Women's Sexual Stories and the Journey of the Soul* (New York: Touchstone, 1997), for connections between the mythologies of Inanna and Persephone-Kore and women's sexual stories.

Page 16, *In Aphrodite's Daughters*: Bonheim, *Aphrodite's Daughters*, 236.

Page 24, *In Womanspirit Rising*: Carol Christ and Judith Plaskow, eds., *Womanspirit Rising: A Feminist Reader in Religion* (San Francisco: HarperCollins, 1992), 7.

Page 25, *Our right to spread our spiritual roots*: Rosemary Radford Ruether, "Motherearth and the Megamachine," in Christ and Plaskow, *Womanspirit Rising*, 43–52.

CHAPTER 2. EARTH RITUALS

Page 38, *In Witches, Sluts, and Feminists*: Kristen Sollée, *Witches, Sluts, and Feminists: Conjuring the Sex Positive* (Berkeley, CA: ThreeL Media, 2017), 150.

Page 42, *Lilith is a too-much woman*: See Demetra George, *Mysteries of the Dark Moon: The Healing Power of the Dark Goddess* (San Francisco: HarperCollins, 1992), for more information on Lilith's myths.

CHAPTER 3. EARTH MAGICK

Page 48, *Go back into the lived chapters now*: See Shiva Rea, *Tending the Heart Fire: Living in Flow with the Pulse of Life* (Boulder, CO: Sounds True, 2014), for discussion of *bhava* and *bhavana*.

Page 49, *The root chakra is unique to every wild woman*: See Anodea Judith, *Eastern Body, Western Mind: Psychology and the Chakra System as a Path to the Self* (Berkeley, CA: Celestial Arts, 1996), for an in-depth examination of the chakral system.

CHAPTER 4. WATER VERSES

Page 65, *Her seven-veiled dance*: Oscar Wilde, *Salomé* (1893; repr. London: Methuen & Co. Ltd., 1917; Project Gutenberg, 2015), http://www.gutenberg.org/files/1339/1339-h/1339-h.htm.

Page 65, *"he did not want to refuse her"*: Mark 6:26 (NIV).

Page 65, *Freya is an incarnation of the feminine divine*: See Sophia Sheree Martinez, "Consent within Heathenry," in *Pagan Consent Culture: Building Communities of Empathy and Autonomy*, ed. Christine Hoff Kraemer and Yvonne Aburrow (Hubbardston, MA: Asphodel Press, 2015), 21–30, for more information on Freya's story and the appropriation of her name.

Page 65, *the archetypes of the wild feminine*: See Demetra George, *Mysteries of the Dark Moon: The Healing Power of the Dark Goddess* (San Francisco: HarperCollins, 1992), for research on the suppression of feminine sexual power.

Page 66, *Lalita reflects embodied, sensuously expressed love*: See Sally Kempton, *Awakening Shakti: The Transformative Power of the Goddesses of Yoga* (Boulder, CO: Sounds True, 2013), for discussion of Lalita, Kali, and other Tantric Goddesses.

Page 71, *"Thespian at the Oasis"*: Bill Plotkin, *Nature and the Human Soul: Cultivating Wholeness and Community in a Fragmented World* (Novato, CA: New World Library, 2008), 167.

Page 76, *Personal myths are meaning makers*: See Bill Plotkin, *Soulcraft: Crossing into the Mysteries of Nature and Psyche* (Novato, CA: New World Library, 2003), for more information on personal mythwork and similar practices.

CHAPTER 5. WATER RITUALS

Page 83, *When we speak of passion and pleasure*: See Anodea Judith, *Eastern Body, Western Mind: Psychology and the Chakra System as a Path to the Self* (Berkeley, CA: Celestial Arts, 1996), for more information on the wounds of the root and sacral chakras.

Page 84, *Audre Lorde writes in her essay*: Audre Lorde, "Uses of the Erotic: The Erotic as Power," in *Weaving the Visions: New Patterns in Feminist Spirituality*, ed. Judith Plaskow and Carol Christ (San Francisco: HarperCollins, 1989), 211.

Page 89, *The energetic womb lives within us all*: See Padma and Anaiya Aon Prakasha, *Womb Wisdom: Awakening the Creative and Forgotten Powers of the Feminine* (Destiny Books, 2011), for meditations and philosophies on the energetic womb.

Page 99, *all that is required for art making*: See David Bayles and Ted Orland, *Art & Fear: Observations on the Perils (and Rewards) of Artmaking* (St. Paul, MN: Consortium, 1993), for a discussion of the complex interplay between passion and fear in the artist's mind.

Page 99, *In* What We Ache For: Oriah Mountain Dreamer, *What We Ache For: Creativity and the Unfolding of Your Soul* (San Francisco: HarperOne, 2005), 181.

CHAPTER 6. WATER MAGICK

Page 105, *The* Prana Shakti *force*: See Christopher Wallis, *Tantra Illuminated: The Philosophy, History, and Practice of a Timeless Tradition* (Petaluma, CA: Mattamayūra Press, 2013), for a comprehensive review of Tantric philosophy.

Page 107, *women artists working in most media*: See *Miss Representation*, dir. Jennifer Siebel Newsom (New York: Virgil Films & Entertainment, 2012), for information about the under- and misrepresentation of women in the media and the arts.

Page 107, *Audre Lorde writes*: Audre Lorde, "Uses of the Erotic: The Erotic as Power," in *Weaving the Visions: New Patterns in Feminist Spirituality*, ed. Judith Plaskow and Carol Christ (San Francisco: HarperCollins, 1989), 212.

CHAPTER 7. FIRE VERSES

Page 116, *feminine traits most feared and most subjugated*: See Demetra George, *Mysteries of the Dark Moon: The Healing Power of the Dark Goddess* (San Francisco: HarperCollins, 1992), and Marija Gimbutas, "Women and Culture in Goddess-Oriented Old Europe," in *Weaving the Visions: New Patterns in Feminist Spirituality*, ed. Judith Plaskow and Carol Christ (San Francisco: HarperCollins, 1989), 63–71, for discussions of Goddess cultures and their demise.

Page 117, *They were medicine women and midwives*: See Anne Llewellyn Barstow, *Witchcraze: A New History of the European Witch Hunts* (San Francisco: HarperCollins, 1994).

Page 117, *Modern-day Witch-hunts*: Kent Russell, "They Burn Witches Here," *HuffPost Highline*, October 29, 2015, https://www.huffingtonpost.com/entry/highline-papua-new-guinea-witches_us_56325Id0e4b0c66bae5b6dbf.

Page 118, *the wheelhouse of the primal feminine*: See George, *Mysteries of the Dark Moon*, for greater discussion of Dark Goddess mythology.

Page 118, *Tattooed on her forehead*: Revelation 17:5 (KJV).

Page 118, *She was the downfall of man*: Revelation 17:4 (KJV).

Page 118, *Her primal feminine power*: See George, *Mysteries of the Dark Moon*, for discussions of Medusa's mythology.

Page 119, *She is a nature Goddess*: See Judith Gleason, *Oya: In Praise of an African Goddess* (San Francisco: HarperCollins, 1992).

Page 119, *Kali is the shaken foundations*: See Sally Kempton, *Awakening Shakti: The Transformative Power of the Goddesses of Yoga* (Boulder, CO: Sounds True, 2013), for discussion of Kali.

Page 124, *It is the epicenter of our egos*: See Anodea Judith, *Eastern Body, Western Mind: Psychology and the Chakra System as a Path to the Self* (Berkeley, CA: Celestial Arts, 1996), for a discussion of the solar plexus during and beyond childhood.

Page 124, *In* Women Who Run with the Wolves: Clarissa Pinkola Estés, *Women Who Run with the Wolves: Myths and Stories of the Wild Woman Archetype* (Ballantine, 1995), 390–91.

Page 129, *Know the feminine will*: See Kempton, *Awakening Shakti*, for discussion of *Iccha Shakti*.

CHAPTER 8. FIRE RITUALS

Page 134, *In the absence of models drawn from nature*: See Bill Plotkin, *Nature and the Human Soul: Cultivating Wholeness and Community in a Fragmented World* (Novato, CA: New World Library, 2008), for more information on the importance of connecting to nature during childhood.

Page 136, *Starhawk writes in* The Spiral Dance: Starhawk, *The Spiral Dance: A Rebirth of the Ancient Religion of the Great Goddess* (San Francisco: HarperCollins, 1999), 155.

Page 142, *This is practical magick*: Tracey Damron, in discussion with the author, June 17, 2017.

CHAPTER 10. AIR VERSES

Page 164, *one of Christ's most favored disciples*: See Caitlín Matthews, *Sophia: Goddess of Wisdom, Bride of God* (Wheaton, IL: Quest Books, 2001), for scholarly discussion of Mary Magdalene as a disciple of Christ.

Page 164, *In* The Once and Future Goddess: Elinor Gadon, *The Once and Future Goddess: A Symbol for Our Time* (San Francisco: Harper & Row, 1989), 208.

Page 164, *In Goddess traditions*: See Matthews, *Sophia*.

Page 164, *Oshun is a protectress*: See Diedre Badejo, *Osun Seegesi: The Elegant Deity of Wealth, Power, and Femininity* (Trenton, NJ: Africa World Press, 1995).

Page 164, *Parvati is the fierce consort of Shiva*: See Sally Kempton, *Awakening Shakti: The Transformative Power of the Goddesses of Yoga* (Boulder, CO: Sounds True, 2013), for a discussion of Parvati's mythology.

Page 164, *Aphrodite is the change agent*: See Jean Shinoda Bolen, *Goddesses in Everywoman: Powerful Archetypes in Women's Lives* (New York: HarperCollins, 2014), for a discussion of Aphrodite as the alchemical Goddess.

Page 171, *the more "armored" qualities of the love Goddess*: See Bolen, *Goddesses in Everywoman*, for a discussion of shadow Aphrodite.

CHAPTER 11. AIR RITUALS

Page 188, *if our spiritual journeys were rooted in nature's lessons*: See Bill Plotkin, *Nature and the Human Soul: Cultivating Wholeness and Community in a Fragmented World* (Novato, CA: New World Library, 2008), for discussion of soul purpose in relation to nature.

Page 191, *In* The Spiral Dance: Starhawk, *The Spiral Dance: A Rebirth of the Ancient Religion of the Great Goddess* (San Francisco: HarperCollins, 1999), 22.

CHAPTER 13. ETHER VERSES

Page 211, *Paula Gunn Allen, in her essay:* Paula Gunn Allen, "Grandmother of the Sun," in *Weaving the Visions: New Patterns in Feminist Spirituality,* ed. Judith Plaskow and Carol Christ (San Francisco: HarperCollins, 1989), 26.

Page 212, *She is both death and procreative potential:* See Patricia Monaghan, *The Red-Haired Girl from the Bog: The Landscape of Celtic Myth and Spirit* (Novato, CA: New World Library, 2003), for a discussion of the Cailleach's mythology.

Page 212, *Hekate stands at the crossroads:* See Demetra George, *Mysteries of the Dark Moon: The Healing Power of the Dark Goddess* (San Francisco: HarperCollins, 1992), for a discussion of Hekate's complicated mythology.

Page 213, *a heathen religion's proliferation:* 2 Kings 9:22 (KJV).

CHAPTER 14. ETHER RITUALS

Page 224, *To forge connections:* See Bill Plotkin, *Soulcraft: Crossing into the Mysteries of Nature and Psyche* (Novato, CA: New World Library, 2010), for discussion of the distinction between soul and spirit.

Page 225, *The Queen of the Ethereal Divine:* See Anodea Judith, *Eastern Body, Western Mind: Psychology and the Chakra System as a Path to the Self* (Berkeley, CA: Celestial Arts, 1996), for in-depth discussion of the third-eye and crown chakras.

Page 230, *In Tantric philosophy:* See Christopher Wallis, *Tantra Illuminated: The Philosophy, History, and Practice of a Timeless Tradition* (Petaluma, CA: Mattamayūra Press, 2013), for discussion of the five Acts of God or the Divine.

Page 231, *often using her same holy names:* See Demetra George, *Mysteries of the Dark Moon: The Healing Power of the Dark Goddess* (San Francisco: HarperCollins, 1992), and Sally Kempton, *Awakening Shakti: The Transformative Power of the Goddesses of Yoga* (Boulder, CO: Sounds True, 2013), for discussion of the divine feminine's denigration under patriarchal religion.

CHAPTER 15. ETHER MAGICK

Page 239, *If you can hear the thoughts in your head:* See Michael Singer, *The Untethered Soul: The Journey beyond Yourself* (Oakland, CA: New Harbinger, 2007), for philosophical discussion of the ego voice and the witness.

Page 243, *All things that vibrate*: See Serena Roney-Dougal, *Where Science and Magic Meet* (Somerset, UK: Green Magic, 2010).

CONCLUSION: HER REVELATION

Page 255, *In* Weaving the Visions: Judith Plaskow and Carol Christ, eds., *Weaving the Visions: New Patterns in Feminist Spirituality* (San Francisco: HarperCollins, 1989), 2.

Page 256, *In Jungian psychology*: See Bill Plotkin, *Wild Mind: A Field Guide to the Human Psyche* (Novato, CA: New World Library, 2013), for a discussion of the shadow.

Page 257, *Religions where women are in positions of leadership*: See Karen McCarthy Brown, "Women's Leadership in Haitian Vodou," in *Weaving the Visions*, ed. Plaskow and Christ, 226–34, for research on female leadership in the Vodou religion.

Page 257, *power-hungry, individualistic religions*: See Demetra George, *Mysteries of the Dark Moon: The Healing Power of the Dark Goddess* (San Francisco: HarperCollins, 1992), for historical accounts of the connection between natural disasters and the demise of Goddess cultures.

Additional Resources

These are books written by women of color about the Goddesses Kali, Lalita, Oshun, and Oya, mentioned in the Books of Water, Fire, and Air.

KALI AND LALITA

Shoma Chatterji, *The Goddess Kali of Kolkata* (New Delhi, India: UBS Publishers, 2005).

Kavitha M. Chinnaiyan, *Shakti Rising: Embracing Shadow and Light on the Goddess Path to Wholeness* (Oakland, CA: New Harbinger, 2017).

Swamini Sri Lalitambika Devi, *Mantra and the Goddess: A Poetic Interpretation of the Sri Lalita Sahasranama* (Hampshire, UK: John Hunt Publishing, 2010).

OSHUN AND OYA

Diedre L. Badejo, *Osun Seegesi: The Elegant Deity of Wealth, Power, and Femininity* (Trenton, NJ: Africa World Press, 1995).

Joseph Murphy and Mei-Mei Sanford, *Osun across the Waters: A Yoruba Goddess in Africa and the Americas* (Bloomington: Indiana University Press, 2001).

Monique Joiner Siedlak, *Seven African Powers: The Orishas* (n.p.: Oshun Publications, 2017).

Index

About the Author

Danielle Dulsky's work is rooted in the wild feminine, or humanity's deep and embodied connection to the natural world. While translating the wild feminine into writing, multimedia art, motherhood, Witchcraft, yoga teaching, and energy-healing, she aims to have her core message constant in all of her work: It is the birthright of every woman to resurrect an in-the-skin spirituality, a unique holiness that is lived out and experienced in the body and on this Earth.

Website: DanielleDulsky.com
Book website: TheHolyWild.com
Facebook page: Danielle Dulsky (@WolfWomanCircle)
Instagram: WolfWomanWitch